The Folktales of Palestine

SOAS PALESTINE STUDIES

This book series aims at promoting innovative research in the study of Palestine, Palestinians and the Israel-Palestine conflict as a crucial component of Middle Eastern and world politics. The first ever Western academic series entirely dedicated to this topic, *SOAS Palestine Studies* draws from a variety of disciplinary fields, including history, politics, media, visual arts, social anthropology, and development studies. The series is published under the academic direction of the Centre for Palestine Studies (CPS) at the London Middle East Institute (LMEI) of SOAS, University of London.

Series Editor:
Gilbert Achcar, Professor of Development Studies and International Relations at SOAS, Chair of the Centre for Palestine Studies

Board Advisor:
Hassan Hakimian, Director of the London Middle East Institute at SOAS

Current and Forthcoming Titles:
Palestine Ltd.: Neoliberalism and Nationalism in the Occupied Territory, Toufic Haddad
Palestinian Literature in Exile: Gender, Aesthetics and Resistance in the Short Story, Joseph R. Farag
Palestinian Citizens of Israel: Power, Resistance and the Struggle for Space, Sharri Plonski
Folktales of Palestine: Cultural Identity, Memory and the Politics of Storytelling, Farah Aboubakr
Representing Palestine Media and Journalism in Australia Since World War I, Peter Manning
Palestinian Youth Activism in the Internet Age: Social Media and Networks after the Arab Spring, Albana Dwonch

The Folktales of Palestine

Cultural Identity, Memory and the Politics of Storytelling

Farah Aboubakr

I.B. TAURIS
LONDON • NEW YORK • OXFORD • NEW DELHI • SYDNEY

Centre for Palestine Studies

Published in association with the Centre for Palestine Studies,
London Middle East Institute

I.B. TAURIS
Bloomsbury Publishing Plc
50 Bedford Square, London, WC1B 3DP, UK
1385 Broadway, New York, NY 10018, USA
29 Earlsfort Terrace, Dublin 2, Ireland

BLOOMSBURY, I.B. TAURIS and the I.B. Tauris logo are trademarks of
Bloomsbury Publishing Plc

First published in Great Britain 2019
This paperback edition published 2023

Copyright © Farah Aboubakr, 2019

Farah Aboubakr has asserted her right under the Copyright,
Designs and Patents Act, 1988, to be identified as Author of this work.

For legal purposes the Acknowledgements on p. xi constitute an extension of this
copyright page.

Cover design: Adriana Brioso
Cover image © The Palestinian village of Aqabat Jaber in Israel in November, 1986.
(© Eric BOUVET/Gamma-Rapho via Getty Images)

All rights reserved. No part of this publication may be reproduced or transmitted in
any form or by any means, electronic or mechanical, including photocopying, recording,
or any information storage or retrieval system, without prior permission in writing
from the publishers.

Bloomsbury Publishing Plc does not have any control over, or responsibility for,
any third-party websites referred to or in this book. All internet addresses given in this
book were correct at the time of going to press. The author and publisher regret any
inconvenience caused if addresses have changed or sites have ceased to exist, but can
accept no responsibility for any such changes.

A catalogue record for this book is available from the British Library.

A catalog record is available from the Library of Congress.

ISBN: HB: 978-1-78831-426-8
PB: 978-0-7556-5099-6
ePDF: 978-1-78673-579-9
eBook: 978-1-78672-579-0

Series: SOAS Palestine Studies

Typeset by Deanta Global Publishing Services, Chennai, India

To my mother, Majda: The roots ... the past ... the first generation

To my daughter, Majda: The flower ... the present ... the third generation

Contents

Series Foreword	ix
Acknowledgements	xi
Note on Transliteration	xiii
Introduction: *Speak Bird, Speak Memory*	1
1 Collective Memory in Palestine	**7**
Palestinian oral history	8
The 1948 *Nakba*, trauma and nostalgia	14
Storytelling and language	21
2 Palestinian Folktales: *Speak, Bird, Speak Again* (1989) and *Qul Ya Tayer* (2001)	**27**
Folktales: Reality versus imagination	27
Palestinian folk narratives	31
The society of storytellers in Palestine	35
The functions of folktales in Palestinian society	39
The psychological function	40
The social function	41
The belief function	46
Paratextual material in *Speak, Bird, Speak Again* and *Qul Ya Tayer*	47
Pre-introduction paratextual materials	49
Paratextual materials within the tales	59
Post-tales paratextual materials	65
The tales	66
3 Palestinian Women and the Preservation of Memory in Palestinian Folktales	**69**
Mother–daughter narrative	71
Mother–son narrative	77
Sibling narrative	87
Sexual awakening	95
Marriage	101

4	Cultural Identity and Sites of Memory in Palestinian Folktales	115
	Peasantry as a site of memory and identity	116
	Recreating the homeland	117
	Peasantry and collective identity	121
	Language and folk religion in society, environment and universe groups of folktales	127
	Food and memory	140
	Prospective memory	141
	Sensuous memory	149
	Food and women: Agents of memory	153

Final Reflections	163
Appendix 1: Interview with Dr Sharif Kanaana	167
Appendix 2: List of the Tales	178
Appendix 3: Summaries of Tales in Chapter 3	180
Appendix 4: 'The Old Woman and Her Cat' (Al-ʿjūz w al-bis) and 'Dunglet' (Baʿīrūn)	187
Appendix 5: Summaries of Tales in Chapter 4	195
Notes	198
Bibliography	213
Index	233

Series Foreword

The question of Palestine – with its corollaries, the Israel–Palestine and Arab–Israeli conflicts – has been a key issue of world politics and a major source of world tension since the 1917 Balfour Declaration. Few global issues have attracted so much attention over such a long period of time. As a result, despite its small territorial size, Palestine has become a key component of Middle East studies in the academic community and a field of study in its own right, in the same way that France or Germany are each the subject of individual study while being part of European Studies. This 'disproportionate' status of the Palestine topic is due to several factors.

First is the strategic location of Palestine at the Mediterranean door of the Middle East and the 'East of Suez' world. This strategic position – the source of British interest in Palestine at the beginning of the twentieth century – has been enhanced by the greater importance of the broader Middle East in global affairs as manifested by the high frequency of wars and conflicts in the region since the Second World War, and even more since the end of the Cold War.

Second is the very particular fact of what has been described as a 'settler-colonial' project in Palestine that was boosted by the huge human tragedy of the Nazi genocide of European Jews in 1941–5. The result has been a complex mingling of the Holocaust, which the Zionist movement claims as legitimizing its actions, with what Palestinians call the *Nakba*, or 'catastrophe', which describes the 'ethnic cleansing' of Arab Palestinians from great swathes of Palestine in 1948 by the Zionist drive towards the creation of Israel.

Third is the sheer complexity of the Palestine question engendered by the *Nakba* and the subsequent occupation by the state of Israel of the West Bank and Gaza following the Six-Day War in 1967. As a result of these, the Palestinian people today are living under very different conditions and legal regimes: they encompass those who remained in Israel after the state's establishment in 1948, those, including refugees, under direct Israeli occupation or indirect Israeli control in the West Bank and Gaza; those displaced by the wars of 1948 and 1967 to the eastern bank of the Jordan River, some of them still living in camps, and most of whom became Jordanian citizens; those living in the refugee camps of Lebanon and Syria; those of the diaspora living in other Arab countries and those of the global diaspora.

Finally, the question of Palestine plays such a major role in Arab politics in general and represents such a major trauma in collective Arab memory that it has been the focus of prolific artistic and literary energy, a drive that goes beyond Palestinians to include creative minds and talents from all Arabic-speaking countries.

This complexity and the unparalleled diversity of contemporary Palestinian locations and situations help to explain Palestine's 'disproportionate' status and account for the abundance of publications on Palestine and its people. And yet, surprisingly, there has until now been no university-based English-language book series specifically dedicated to Palestine Studies. The SOAS Palestine Studies series, published by I. B. Tauris in collaboration with the SOAS Centre for Palestine Studies (CPS) at the London Middle East Institute (LMEI), seeks to fill this gap. This series is dedicated to the contemporary history, politics, economy, society and culture of Palestine and the historiographic quarrels associated with its past.

The subject of Palestine has aroused intense passions over several decades. On such a topic it is very difficult to exclude passion, and the pretension to be 'neutral' is often disqualified by both sides. But we will make sure that none of our books stray beyond the realms of intellectual integrity and scholarly rigour. With the Palestine Studies series we hope to make an important contribution towards a better understanding of this most complex topic.

Professor Gilbert Achcar, Editor
Chair of the Centre of Palestine Studies,
SOAS, University of London

Acknowledgements

This book is based on my PhD dissertation, which I completed at the University of Manchester in the United Kingdom. I faced many academic, personal and health problems during this journey, making me consider many times quitting my writing battle. The undefined source of strength and passion for my homeland energized me in my dark moments. The search for an identity and belonging in the diaspora, the complex relation between past, present and future in my life pushed me to seek refuge in my writing in the hope of finding some answers for my pending questions.

There have been some exceptional people along the way, who have brightened my life during that period, whether through their advice, support and/or love. I am greatly indebted to my supervisors at the University of Manchester, Dr Ursula Tidd and Dr Dalia Mostafa, for their academic guidance and wisdom. They never ceased to support me, particularly during my difficult times. I am very thankful to Ms Amanda Mathews, the Graduate School Manager at the University of Manchester, for her unforgettable kindness. Her caring presence and belief in me encouraged me a lot. I am very thankful to my external examiners, Professor Zahia Smail Salhi and Dr Dina Matar, for providing me with constructive feedback and for encouraging me towards publishing my monograph.

I would like to convey special thanks to Dr Sharif Kanaana, whom I had the privilege to interview in 2012. Dr Kanaana's efforts as a Palestinian thinker and folklorist are exemplary and inspirational. I would also like to thank PARC (Palestinian Association Research Centre) for supporting me financially in the early stages of my research. A big thank you goes to my colleague and friend Dr Sarah Irving for her editorial advice and comments on the text at the end of my PhD.

I am indebted to the love and care my friends have offered me throughout my happy and sad days. I am extremely thankful to my friends in Morocco, Spain, Manchester and Edinburgh. Special thanks to Radia El Badrawi, the friend I have had for longest, for her continuous support, love and patience with academic moodiness and absence.

For his patriotism and passion, I will never be able to thank my father, Atef Aboubakr, enough. He is an exceptional man, and I hope I can do him pride. I am also exceptionally grateful and thankful to my beloved stepmother, Saeda Alkhammash, who to me is a mother, friend and sister. Her love, care and endless support will forever brighten my days. Last but not least, my heartfelt thanks and gratitude to my soulmate and husband, Ali Kazerooni, whose extreme care, love and support make me every day stronger and happier. He has never ceased to believe in me and has always been a good listener to my long boring talks.

Note on Transliteration

For the transcription of Arabic, this study follows the style used by *ALA–LC* (American Library Association – Library of Congress). However, for Arab authors with publications in a language other than Arabic, their names are kept in the form under which they were published, and Arabic words or titles found in quotations are kept in the form in which they were transcribed by the authors of those quotations. The symbols used to transcribe Arabic sounds are as follows:

Transliteration

ء	ʾ	س	s	ل	l
ب	B	ش	sh	م	m
ت	T	ص	ṣ	ن	n
ث	Th	ض	ḍ	ه	h
ج	J	ط	ṭ	و	W
ح	ḥ	ظ	ẓ	ي	Y
خ	Kh	ع	ʿ	ال	al-
د	D	غ	gh	ة	-a
ذ	Dh	ف	f	ا	Ā
ر	R	ق	q	ي	Ī
ز	Z	ك	k	و	Ū
´	A	---	i	´	u

Introduction: *Speak Bird, Speak Memory*

As a child who has never lived in Palestine, I grew up learning about my roots and origins through storytelling. The moment of sitting and listening to my mother telling folktales in Palestinian Arabic was very special to me. It was a unique encounter between the world of imagination and the quest for identity. Even though it may have been constructed, my 'Palestinianhood' was nourished while learning more about the destiny of Tunjur or about what happened to Khunfse.[1] The fact that childhood memories have always been associated with my mother and her stories about Palestine has helped me to overcome the amnesia of diaspora. My life was always on the move from one place to another, leaving me completely dependent and seeking with nostalgia to protect my childhood memories, as to me they represented the only comforting and stable source of identification. This book as a result draws on two key concepts that affected me, namely, memory and folktales. I analyse forty-five of the most popular and best narrated pre-*Nakba*/1948 Palestinian folktales, compiled, annotated and translated by Ibrahim Muhawi and Sharif Kanaana in *Speak, Bird, Speak Again* (1989, hereafter known for convenience as *SBSA*) and its corresponding Arabic collection *Qul Ya Tayer* (2001). Unlike most Palestinian folktale compilations, Muhawi and Kanaana's work is not just a disinterested record of Palestinian culture, society and folklore but rather an active scholarly – and potentially subversive – attempt to document, safeguard and give voice to Palestinian oral culture for Western, Arab and Palestinian readers. In analysing the forty-five folktales, Muhawi and Kanaana's book is the first to consider closely the significance of Palestinian oral narratives in framing Palestinian identity and memory.

Apart from being a means of entertainment and a source of education, folktales are instrumental in strengthening communal bonds and in ensuring the survival of a people's oral traditions. Both the stories and the actual process of storytelling help to define a community's social, cultural and political identity. For Palestinians, the constant threat of denial, falsification and forgetfulness which overshadows their heritage under Israeli occupation has engendered a sense of urgency among both storytellers and Palestinian folklorists. This book can be considered as a timely step towards analysing the renewal and prevalence of oral artistic forms of expression in the Palestinian context, which, as I will show, presents an alternative way of advocating the Palestinians' voice and aspirations. The latter has lacked academic scrutiny and analysis within cultural and memory studies in particular. As with other world literatures, Palestinian literature, particularly oral, should be considered worthy of academic and critical evaluation. This is particularly important when forms of orality, such as narratives of oral history, are under constant threat.[2] Hence *The Folktales of Palestine: Cultural Identity, Memory and the Politics of Storytelling* aims at addressing the following questions:

How can Palestinian folktales safeguard the nation's cultural identity? What do folktales achieve for a people who have experienced national trauma that other forms of literature cannot achieve? Why is it all the more urgent to collect, document and conduct academic research on Palestinian oral narrative, particularly folktales? How does the work of some Palestinian compilers and folklorists, such as Ibrahim Muhawi and Sharif Kanaana contribute to framing Palestinian identity and memory? What is the agency of the compilers and storytellers? How do storytellers, mostly Palestinian women, characterize this genre of folk narratives? How can peasantry, food and religion narratives in folktales activate Palestinian memory?

I invite the reader to think about the Palestinian folktale in relation to generational memory transmission and as a form of cultural resistance, as well as situating the agency of the Palestinian folklorist and storyteller within memory, cultural and social movement studies, where it has been rarely examined. The analysis of the Palestinian folktale in this book illuminates the specificity of the sociocultural and familial environment in the construction of Palestinian cultural identity, highlighting the interwoven historical and national narratives and their impact on cultural and collective memory. Given the contemporary political situation in the Middle East and following the Arab Spring, there has been a rise in various forms of popular culture, using art to express revival, resistance and longevity. To understand how oral narratives, mainly folktales, contribute to framing Palestinian memory and identity, the argument of this book will concentrate on three main aspects: the folktales and the storytellers, the role of the compilers in both the Arabic and English volumes and the conceptualization of these two aspects within the theoretical framework of memory and Palestine Studies.

The compilers

As Palestinian compilers, folklorists, translators and scholars, Muhawi and Kanaana did not present the folktales initially to an Arab audience. Instead, they first published the English translation, *SBSA* (1989), which has become a reference for teaching anthropology of the Middle East – its folklore, society and literature – in both the Arab world and English-speaking countries. Soon after Muhawi and Kanaana sought to extend the national dimension of their project through the publication of an Arabic version, *Qul Ya Tayer* in 2001, targeting Arab audiences in general and Arab students, scholars and universities in particular. Both collections provide readers with extensive social, cultural and anthropological annotation: substantial introductions, cultural footnotes, analytical endnotes, indexes to tale-types and motifs and a bibliography of Palestinian folk narrative. Earning comparison with the Grimm Brothers' collection of fairy tales, *SBSA* (1989) and *Qul Ya Tayer* (2001) have gained recognition and academic weight within the study of Middle Eastern folklore at both Arab and Western universities.

Taking memory and social movement studies as the core of my analysis, I examine the contribution of the Palestinian folklorist in creating a discourse of cultural resistance. The role of the folklorist deserves not to be ignored, particularly in the Palestinian case, where knowing and sharing knowledge helps to put forward a more accurate image of Palestinian cultural identity. Hence understanding the national and scholarly contexts, together with the compilers' creation of an extensive folkloric, anthropological, historical and literary apparatus around and within the folktales, is important in helping us appreciate the necessity of documenting folktales, uncovering as they do Palestinians' rooted culture across time. The fact that the compilers of these collections chose the Palestinian folktale rather than the novel or short story is also significant in understanding their strategy.

The folktales

In spite of the proliferation of Palestinian folktale collections in Arabic since the 1980s, there has been remarkably little attention paid to the scholarly and academic study, contextualization and understanding of the Palestinian folktale and its relation to the narrative of memory, and many aspects of identity and language. In order to understand how folktales frame Palestinian memory and identity, the discussion throughout this book relates memory, mainly post-, cultural and communicative memory, to cultural identity. In so doing, I look closely at the narrative of language and folk religion, peasantry and food.

The storytellers

The study of Palestinian oral history in general and oral literature in particular suffers from a lack of organized archives and scientific methodology. Within the field of oral history, for instance, Palestinian historians were only 'preoccupied with political issues and the history of political elites' (Zu'bi, 2014: 3) from the *Nakba* until the 1990s. This not only neglected the role of Palestinian popular culture but also disregarded women as witnesses of history within the social and cultural spheres. For decades, women's historical narratives or history have been associated with politics and nationalism (Kassem, 2011). In the case of Palestinian oral literature, Palestinian women have suffered even more from a lack of representation, with barely any mention of their roles as storytellers. Unlike the majority of Palestinian folktale compilations, where very little attention was given to the identity of storytellers, let alone their roles, in *SBSA* and *Qul Ya Tayer* we are not only informed about the storytellers' age, names and place of residence, but most importantly we know that out of seventeen storytellers only three were men.

To the best of my knowledge, there is no study on the role of Palestinian women storytellers within oral literature and memory studies. It is hence my aim in this book to show how the Palestinian folktale genre is attributed to Palestinian women within their domestic spheres, among their neighbours and family, explaining how 'Palestinian women are largely responsible for developing this style and they carry on the tradition' (Muhawi and Kanaana, 1989: 3). Men's storytelling, meanwhile, features epic stories and happens in a more public sphere known as *Al-dīwān*.[3] The fact that Palestinian women dominate this genre is important to highlight, since their narrative, whether as storytellers or protagonists, transforms the political discourse of Palestinian collective memory into a social one. Palestinian collective memory is usually interpreted through the lens of oral history; the latter has always been framed within the discourse of resistance, taking up arms and an explicit fight for justice and land. However, in this book I argue that fighting for the Palestinian cause or reaffirming the nation's identity can take different forms and does not have to be channelled through nationalistic political activism or through public representations and participations. Moreover, given the severe lack of representation and silence that shroud the subject of Palestinian women in almost all historical and political (not to mention literary) writing, it is important to highlight their role beyond the usual issues of honour, fashion, embroidery or clothing, as Rema Hammami (2004) and Fatma Kassem (2011) pointed out, where Palestinian women appear as 'objects (and not subjects) of cultural norms' (Kassem, 2011: 4). Palestinian women, through storytelling whether in domestic or public spheres, I argue, extend pre-*Nakba* cultural memory and identity to younger generations, bridging past, present and future. Palestinian women's credibility as reliable observers of society is also projected in their roles as female protagonists in the folktales, establishing immediate connections with their own lives, the patriarchal world and the overall social structure. Analysing and contextualizing their roles as daughters, mothers, sisters and wives throughout folktales, as I will show, enables us to understand the process of memory transmission, in which women are seen as active agents of cultural resistance and preservation.

Nakba and memory

In theoretical terms, Palestinian oral literature still suffers from a lack of academic scrutiny and contextualization within memory and cultural studies. In an attempt to situate the Palestinian case within the map of memory and cultural studies, I examine the main markers of Palestinian memory and identity in order to better understand the folktales within their political, cultural and historical contexts. Unlike the Holocaust, which has international recognition and is the focus of many studies, the traumatic phase of the *Nakba* (Catastrophe) in 1948 and its repercussions for Palestinian folk narratives and orality has received very little attention within memory and trauma studies. One of the aims of the present book is also to situate the *Nakba* within memory studies, in order to understand its manifestation in literature in general and folk narratives in particular. I also argue that the *Nakba* narrative should not be compared to other traumatic historical events since Palestinians have not yet reached a closure. Instead of romanticizing the pre-*Nakba* narrative, I attempt in this book to reveal how the folk narrative genre, specifically in *SBSA* and *Qul Ya Tayer*, creates a narrative of cultural resistance and identity affirmation across time. The desire for life and regeneration never ceased for Palestinians before or after the *Nakba* nor can long-established heritage be altered. The aftermath of the *Nakba*, in spite of its sentimental weight, encourages ordinary people and folklorists (in this case) to reinforce cultural continuity, collectivity, transmission and preservation across generations. My discussion of post-memory, prosthetic memory and communicative/cultural memory helps to explain how a narrative of continuity is established, particularly among generations which do not have first-hand experience of pre-1948 Palestine or have never lived there.

1

Collective Memory in Palestine

Go back where you started, or as far back as you can, examine all of it, travel your road again and tell the truth about it. Sing it or shout or testify or keep it to yourself: but know whence you came.

James Baldwin (1985: xix)

Subject to our past experiences and lives, memory is an active factor in moulding and shaping our daily existence, visions and expectations. Remembering an event can be a source of enjoyment and a longing for a beautiful past, or it can be an unforgettable scar of trauma, anxiety and loss. Expressing memory, especially collective memory, can take multiple forms, depending on our position in the present and our relation to the past. Memory in modernity has been a crucial element in the formation of nations and states; it has the capacity to regenerate or destroy the flow of individual narratives in the sphere of history and identity. There has, however, been much debate over the relationship of history and memory[1] and their binary opposition.[2] It is, in my opinion, very difficult, if not impossible, to treat memory and history as separate entities. Memory, in fact, works within the mechanism of a society: 'It is in society that people normally acquire their memories. It is also in society that they recall, recognize, and localize their memories' (Halbwachs, 1992: 43).[3] Because of the multiplicity of the social structure, it is hard to say that memory is monolithic. Collective remembering is a highly complex process, involving different people, practices, materials and themes. Every society has many social groups, thus many collective memories to relate to, but the ways of remembering and representing its components can be different and/ or contested. In this regard, Jeffrey K. Olick describes collective memory within two kinds of models. The first is what he refers to as the 'Traditionalist' model, which 'assimilate[s] collective memory to heritage, patrimony, national character, and the like, and view[s] collective memory as a bedrock for the continuity of identities' (Olick, 2008: 24). The second model, 'Presentist', he argues, 'assimilate[s] collective memory to manipulation and deception, a mere tool of the arsenal of power' (Olick, 2008). The latter model discusses the intervention of contemporary interests in shaping the past, making the use of memory highly variable. Combining Olick's models, I will explain what I see as the essential elements in the construction of Palestinian collective memory and identity, namely, oral history and language. I will also situate the *Nakba* as a contested narrative in shaping Palestinian collective memory within memory and trauma studies. Such a discussion is needed, prior to discussing the folktales themselves, in order to understand the agenda of the compilers of *SBSA* and *Qul Ya Tayer*, as well as the context of storytelling in Palestine.

Palestinian oral history

Collective memory has so far been understood as a social construct aimed at preserving and shaping a group's cultural, social and political identity. Collective memory, as many writers and scholars consider it, is a living mobile account of a specific historical event which transcends time and place. The mobility of collective memory is based mainly on 'everyday communication', or what can be also referred to as 'communicative memory' (Assmann, 1995), which can flourish by relying on oral history. The latter is divided into two types, as stated by Jan Vansina in 'Adil Yaḥya's *Al-laji' ūn al-Falasṭīniūn 1948–1998 ta' rīkh shafawī* (Palestinian Refugees: 1948–1998 Oral Historisation):

> Oral history is a research methodology. It is the study of the past through a spoken language transmitted orally. There are two kinds of oral history: The first is oral heritage which is the study of a remote past through widespread oral stories in a particular society. These stories are transmitted orally over generations or within one generation at least. The second kind is the history of life which focuses on studying the near past through the accounts of eyewitnesses; it is about people's oral stories, about their lives and experiences. (Vansina in Yaḥya, 1998: 45)

The role of oral transmission is important for the survival of memory as people interact communicatively in exchanging their accounts, jokes and experiences.

Formlessness, wilfulness and disorganization, according to Assmann (1995), control the nature of oral communication among people. Via this form of communication, each individual creates a memory which, as Halbwachs has shown, is socially mediated and connected to a group. Through the practice of oral history, people gain more insight into and a better understanding of a particular collective memory. In this sense, memory is communicative since it transmits the experiences, stories and lives of individuals belonging to a specific group to other individuals belonging to the same or other groups. In other words, each individual memory exists through communication with others. These individuals consolidate their sense of belonging in a unified group by promoting a shared past over time. The sharing can be within families, neighbourhood and professional groups, political parties, up to whole nations or indeed even further (Assmann, 1995). Every individual belongs to numerous groups and therefore entertains numerous collective self-images and memories.

Oral history research is not merely about information gathering. Since the late 1970s, oral historians have established 'the significance of storytelling and the idea that all memories are selective social constructions' (Field, 2006: 34). Storytelling in all its forms enlightens insiders as well as outsiders; it is a vivid depiction and transitional phase between the past, the present and the future of a group's joys, endeavours, pains, nostalgia and hope. Māhir Al-Sharīf, a Palestinian thinker and writer, considers collective memory to be 'oral memory'. According to him, oral memory is 'an oral discourse adopted by a group of people. ... It reflects the changes that occurred in the life of the group; it expresses the need for redefining the original identity which can be at stake' (Al-Sharīf, 2004: 128). Oral history is, in fact, perceived as vital for the preservation and continuation of a whole culture and society, especially if the latter is witnessing multiple threats and risks of disappearance. Alessandro Portelli (1991) argues that memory has more to do with the 'creation of meanings' than with what exactly happened in the past. The creation of sense and consensus can take different shapes and is told by different people, most of the time orally.

Much research on collective memory and orality has drawn attention to the point that nations suffering from severe political or social instability feel the urge to protect and strengthen their cultural and/or national identities.

In other words, collective memory tends to play a more substantial role in shaping the self-perception and culture of peoples who have suffered historical defeats (such as the Serbs, the Jews and the Palestinians, among others). In the words of Ernest Renan (cited in Lowenthal, 1994: 50), 'suffering in common unifies more than joy does. Where national memories are concerned griefs are of more value than triumphs, for they impose duties, and require a common effort'. Miller and Miller (1991), for example, conducted a study on diaspora Armenians who were expelled by Turkey in 1915–18. The Millers' research aimed at measuring and analysing the degree of transmission of Armenian collective memory over three generations (grandparents – parents – children in diaspora). The results show that Armenian collective memory is strong and vivid, since Armenians ensured it was preserved by not mixing with other communities and by consolidating cultural identity through oral literature and folklore. By doing so, Miller and Miller indicated the detail with which Armenian history, cultural identity and social strata are being preserved and strengthened from one generation to the next.

Another prominent example in memory studies, showing people and institutions' efforts in preserving and highlighting a nation's identity, is Holocaust memory. Having been threatened with eradication, Jews witnessing the aftermath of the Nazi massacre attempted to strengthen a sense of communal destiny and identity. In so doing, the preservation of memory has been manifested in art, literature and historical archives. In addition, memorial sites are safeguarded through continuing events and commemorations, which represent a source of constant remembrance. In a study undertaken by Howard Schuman, 'Keeping the Past Alive: Memories of Israeli Jews at the Turn of the Millennium' (2003), Schuman conducted his research on 2,800 Israelis of different ages. The study shows that the most important and memorable two events for Israelis are first, the Holocaust and second, the establishment of Israel. With regard to the Holocaust, the study shows that there are no differences in describing the Holocaust among most Israelis across age, sex, level of education, knowledge or degree of remembrance. Schuman attributes this to the fact that the Holocaust, as a central concept in Israeli-Jewish history, receives much interest and attention especially from academic institutions and religious schools among others. The latter play a major role in helping preserve Holocaust memory through lectures, visits to sites such as Auschwitz, visits to geographical sites such as Yad Vashem and through annual commemorations of the event (Schuman, 2003).

Another key example is that of the Palestinian case, which is the focus of my analysis. Like Armenians and Jews, Palestinians have witnessed important ruptures in their history which have greatly affected their collective memory. Over the course of the twentieth century the task of safeguarding Palestinian cultural collective memory and oral history, seen in folksongs, folktales, clothing and traditional social practices, has become an urgent one, given the level of political instability and threat of disappearance. There are two main historical events that have changed Palestinians' lives and nationhood: the *Nakba* and the defeat in the 1967 war. Initially, Palestinian national identity emerged during the Ottoman period, throughout the nineteenth century, but became more prominent 'in the wake of World War I as a result of several interlinked processes and political upheavals' (Litvak, 2009).[4] Since 1914 Palestinians have striven to build a national identity. However, with the rise of the Zionist movement, and the expulsion of half of the Palestinian population in 1948, Palestinians marked the *Nakba* as one of the most tragic turning points in their memory.

Being exiled and under occupation, many Palestinians found themselves either as outsiders struggling to create new homes as refugees in different parts of the world, or as insiders living under occupation. Palestinians found themselves threatened with the loss of their identity and collective integrity since there was no official written or documented history. According to Sonia El-Nimr (1993: 55),

> What has been written of Palestinians' history (mainly by their colonizers and occupiers), ignores their culture, aspirations and point of view, and in many cases falsifies this history. As stateless people, the Palestinians have compensated for the lack of official institutions which document and preserve their history by sustaining collective memories.

Promoting collective memory under unstable social and political circumstances has become a vital element in developing Palestinian identity. For example, Palestinians in refugee camps in the Middle East regrouped themselves into similar social structures to their village society in Palestine prior to 1948. They were and are making continuous efforts to preserve their habits, costumes, customs, folk stories and sayings, songs, dances and food.

Most of all they sustained intra-village marriages to secure the continuity of village communities from one generation to the next (El-Nimr, 1993). In her research on Palestinian costume, Shelagh Weir interviewed refugees from the village of Bayt Dajān who were living in Jordan, Gaza and the West Bank in the 1980s and observed the following:

> Village identity and pride remain strong among refugees. Much intermarriage still takes place between fellow villagers, the older women still wear costumes which proclaim their village origins. (Weir, 1989: 52)

Along the same lines, Rosemary Sayigh noticed the same phenomenon during her research in the 1970s among the Palestinian refugees in Lebanon:

> So even today a camp Palestinian's speech gives away his/her village of origin. Other cultural methods – embroidery styles, songs, folk sayings dishes – are further evidence of village particularism, reinforced by inter-village [sic] marriage, a custom so strong it is still that marriage that camp people prefer. (Sayigh, 1998: 22)

During El-Nimr's research into pre-1948 revolutions in Palestine, she found that in Galilee and other areas under Israeli rule, village traditions, habits, intra-village marriage and ritual occasions have been kept almost completely intact from the pre-1948 period. One of her interviewees told her,

> Peasants in general are passive people, they don't accept new things easily, especially if they are imposed on them. We kept our traditions, and we took a strong hold on them as a way of expressing our refusal of the new life and culture the Israelis are imposing on us. (El-Nimr, 1993: 54)

This is a key point in my discussion of peasant identity within the folktales in the compilation under study, being a form of protecting Palestinian cultural memory and identity, which I will elaborate in more depth in the Chapter 4.

The defeat in the 1967 war also increased the need to consolidate and revive Palestinian collective memory and identity. The hope of regaining the homeland was shattered by the defeat of Arab troops by Israel. As a result, an immediate and urgent sense of the need for securing and transmitting Palestinian heritage, culture and identity to younger generations emerged. After coming to terms with defeat, the 1970s and 1980s saw 'the proliferation of folk songs, traditional dance, interest in and use of traditional costume, publications of collections of folktales and research about folklore' (El-Nimr, 1993: 54). Thus, more recently, there has been an increasing interest and intense awareness of the significance of oral history in the Palestinian situation, particularly with the passing away of the older generation.

Because there is little research and documentation in the Palestinian case, in comparison to other countries affected by traumatic events, some Palestinian thinkers, anthropologists and intellectuals are making efforts to contribute to the documentation of Palestinian oral history and the revival of Palestinian cultural identity. Two leading researchers, among many, are Rosemary Sayigh and Sharif Kanaana. Sayigh began her oral research among Palestinians in the refugee camps in Lebanon, carrying out an important study in 1979, entitled *Al-falāḥūn al-Falasṭīnīūn: min al-iqtilā 'ilā al-thawra* (Palestinian Peasants: From Uprooting to Revolutionaries). Sayigh then looked at women in some Palestinian camps in Lebanon in a work entitled *Nisa'al-mukhayamāt al-falastīnīa: ruwāt al-tārīhk* (Palestinian Camp Women as Tellers of History) in 1998. At the end of her study, Sayigh concludes by saying,

> We can consider writing the history of a village, a city and a camp in recent years as an attempt to regain, at least partially, those places which did disappear because of destruction or forgetfulness. ... Women played a major role in narrating history since they represent a crucial element in the national history, without whose role our history would be missing and incapable of explaining the continuity of Palestinian resistance. (Sayigh, 1998: 58)

Palestinian women have, as I will elaborate in the next chapters, played a major role in narrating, promoting and preserving Palestinian collective memory. They are reliable eyewitnesses of life and history and very good narrators and storytellers.

In the 1980s, Sharif Kanaana (co-compiler of *SBSA*) published a series of booklets entitled *Tawthīq al-qurā al-Falasṭīnīa al-mudamara* (Documenting the Destroyed Palestinian Villages). In this series of twenty-four booklets, Kanaana's principal objective was to document social, political and economic life in some Palestinian villages before they were destroyed by the Israelis, as well as documenting the traumatic memories of Palestinians expelled in 1948. His study focuses on the importance of Palestinian oral history in safeguarding Palestinian heritage, culture and identity. As Kanaana and Sayigh's research shows, refugees have developed 'communities of memory' (Magat, 2000: 22), in which people take part in activities that reflect a commitment to both the memory of the past and the dreams of return to an independent Palestine in the future. In Litvak's words,

> On the one hand, Palestinians have experienced major historical changes and dislocations in the past century, culminating in the 1948 *Nakba*, which has largely eliminated an old way of life. On the other hand, the living memories of 1948 are still alive – even though those who have actually experienced these events are gradually passing away. It is because of the current political status and living conditions of many individuals in the refugee camps and the proximity to the lost villages in what is now Israel that these memories are kept alive. (Litvak, 2009: 14)

The 1948 *Nakba*, trauma and nostalgia

Scholars of collective memory and historians argue that someone who undergoes a traumatic experience develops belated memory and performs what Kammen (1995) refers to as 'memory work'. With the passing of time, the individual comes to terms with his/her traumatic experience, folding it into a past that has a closure and thus is able to distance him/herself through the telling of memories. In fact, narrating the past lies in having a detached perspective in the present. But to what extent are Palestinians detached or distanced from their trauma? To answer this question, we need to position the Palestinian trauma, marked by the 1948 *Nakba*, within the discourse of memory. Although my analysis of the folktales does not touch on trauma per se, I do however deem it essential at this stage to highlight the historical and physiological contexts in order to understand the impact of folktales as well as motives behind maintaining storytelling traditions.

The *Nakba* and its aftermath provide a central element in Palestinian collective memory, and it has been extremely influential for Palestinian concepts of nationalism, identity and survival. Nonetheless, the discourse of *Nakba* suffers from a lack of research and representation within memory studies. The 1948 war that led to the creation of the state of Israel resulted in severe fragmentation of Palestinian society. 'At least 80 per cent of Palestinians who lived in the major part of Palestine upon which Israel was established – more than 77 per cent of Palestine's territory – became refugees' (Sa'di and Abu-Lughod, 2007: 3). For these reasons the *Nakba* has become a demarcation line between two distinct periods; it has come to represent a sanctified symbol of identity – a unique and unprecedented historical experience. For Palestinians, the 1948 war led to a 'catastrophe' on a par with events that are remembered as world atrocities such as the World Wars and Holocaust, among others; it has come to mark the onset of a humanitarian disaster which disintegrated and dispersed its society, destroying the communal and social life. The rupture within Palestinian collective life also produced four distinct populations: Palestinians in diaspora, the refugees, the Palestinians inside Israel and those in the West Bank and Gaza. These four groups have a unified collective sense of responsibility to remember and to revive Palestinian collective and communal past and memory (Doumani, 1992; Khalidi, 1997; Sa'di, 2002).

To read the *Nakba* according to theories of trauma, it is necessary to highlight some relevant points in the field of trauma studies. The interest in trauma studies started following the First World War, the impact of industrialization and the atrocity of the Holocaust (Rossington and Whitehead, 2007). The clinical definition of trauma, from a psychiatric approach, is when 'a person has experienced an event that is outside the range of ordinary human experience' (American Psychiatric Association, cited in Caruth, 1995: 3). Loss, death, rape and violent acts among others can be diagnosed as traumatic events. The problem with traumatic experiences lies in the fact that human beings can carry post-traumatic symptoms, or what is clinically referred to as Post-Traumatic Stress Disorder, which can be difficult to diagnose and treat. The main problem with traumatic symptoms, according to Freud (1921), is that 'memory became an effect of the impact of the outside world on the unconscious and the preconscious where censorship takes place' (Freud in Whitehead, 2007: 187). The struggle between the conscious and unconscious in controlling an individual's memory negatively affects the patient's reaction to the external world, present and future. From those basic understandings of trauma in psychology, scholars including Caruth and LaCapra have expanded this work to analyse trauma at the social rather than the individual level, looking at mass and historical traumatic experiences. Caruth (1995) has reflected on the dreams and flashbacks that shell-shocked soldiers suffered after the First World War. Other scholars such as Langer (1995) have looked at the significance of testimony among Holocaust victims. Looking at work such as Caruth's and LaCapra's, among others, can help us to approach the *Nakba* in a similar way to such traumatic experiences.

Traumatic events in individual and collective cases can be unforgettable, causing deep scars. Trauma can also be lived twice through the medium of narration and/or testimony. Caruth (1995, 1996) raises the question of how 'the crisis at the core of many traumatic narratives often emerges as an urgent question: Is the trauma encounter with death, or the ongoing experience of having survived it?' (Caruth, 1996: 7). By reliving traumatic experiences, the line between past and present can become blurred, bringing the past into the present via flashbacks or nightmares. The verbalization of trauma into narrative, however, can involve a loss of the past's precision, a loss of 'the force of its affront to understanding' (Caruth, 1995: 153). This could be true to some extent in cases where forgetting details is subconsciously helping the traumatized person to overcome the pain of remembering. However, the opposite is true in the Palestinian case. Palestinians, who either remained or were deported following the *Nakba*, have vivid memories and testimonies of their tragic experience.

In order to better understand this, it is useful to refer to Dominick LaCapra's distinction between 'historical trauma' and 'structural trauma' (LaCapra, 2001). Historical trauma usually refers 'to historical human made occurrences' such as the Holocaust, slavery, apartheid, child sexual abuse or rape. Structural trauma involves, in LaCapra's view, 'transhistorical losses', such as the entry into language, separation from the mother or the inability to partake fully in a community (LaCapra, 2001: 70–98). Both categories involve trauma; the difference between the two lies in the fact that historical trauma can be worked on or healed with time; structural trauma cannot be changed or healed. The function and interconnection of both kinds is useful to analyse in cases where the division between the two traumas is clear. In the Palestinian case, it is possible to argue that the structural trauma is the result of the historical one. This is because following the *Nakba* (which in LaCapra's definition can be considered as historical trauma) many victims not only suffered directly from the catastrophe but have also found that subsequent generations are paying the price of displacement, uprooting and reconstruction: a situation of chaos which cannot be changed in the near future. The painful memories of ordinary Palestinian individuals place their personal traumatic experiences into the larger historical significance of the *Nakba*. In Palestinian literature, for example, individual memories were narrated and adjusted so as to create a collective shared vision of memory and endurance. Palestinians are still paying a high price, because their historical trauma has resulted in structural traumas. 'Unlike many historical experiences, such as the bombing of Hamburg, World War II, the Holocaust to the World Trade Centre attack, which all lasted a specific period of time, the *Nakba* is not over yet' (Sa'di and Abu-Lughod, 2007: 10). As a result, it is hard to say that one category can be healed easily whereas the other cannot. Both structural and historical traumas in the Palestinian case cannot be easily healed because the historical trauma is pertinent and is still part of the present.

LaCapra views traumatic narrative as helping one to change the past not through a 'dubious rewriting of history but to work through post-traumatic symptoms in the present in a manner that opens possible futures' (LaCapra, 2001: 128). LaCapra's idea alludes to some kind of reconciliation with past trauma through efforts of recovery in the present. However, the traumatic experience of Palestinians is different from other historical traumatic experiences. In the case of most historical traumas, such as the destruction that accompanied the two World Wars, civil wars in Latin America or the Holocaust, time has tended to act as a healer of pain and an agent of forgetting. The inability of Palestinians to deal with *Nakba* as part of the past, the impossibility of storing it safe in their minds and turning the page from that era is simply because Palestinians' current situation is distorted by the past. Usually, a trauma can be healed when victims are given a safe space and a platform to express their suffering. This is the foundation for post-traumatic recovery and dialogue. Since the present Palestinian case lacks such possibility, there can be no resolution. In revolutionary France and in the United States, the need to commemorate arose out of a desire to heal and break with the past. For the Palestinians, the opposite is true: collective memory and commemoration have assumed particular importance in order to attempt to overcome the break with the past that was caused by the 1948 *Nakba*. In other words, efforts to remember in the Palestinian context are meant to reconnect dispersed and dispossessed Palestinian voices and reiterate the urge to revive Palestinian collective identity and memory.

If we look at Palestinians following the *Nakba* we find that the tragedy has formed a constitutive element of Palestinian identity, a site of Palestinian collective memory that 'connects all Palestinians to a specific point in time that has become for them an "eternal present"' (Sa'di, 2002: 177). In his article on 'The Continuity of Trauma and Struggle', Haim Bresheeth sees the prevalence of *Nakba* themes in recent Palestinian films. The latter are 'always connected to the second *Intifada*, suggesting that the *Nakba* is not mere memory or a trauma of the past; instead, these films seem to point to both a *continuity of pain and trauma*, reaching from the past into the heart of the present, as well as a *continuity of struggle*' (Bresheeth, 2007: 161; italics in original). Violent clashes in the present and recent past, such as the Al-Aqsa Intifada in 2000, or the war on Gaza in 2008/9, awakened memories such as the massacre of Dayr Yasīn in 1948.

There is no state of normality between Israelis and Palestinians, rendering as a result the neutral distancing hard, if not impossible, to realize. One can argue that the subjectivity of Palestinian narrative traumas is governed by the political situation that perpetuates displacement and exile, a life dominated by nostalgia and will to change, which is always obstructed by present political pressures. The history of trauma in the Palestinian case shows that 'the trauma remains a vivid event, extant and unchanged, as if it is fully present and not represented in memory' (Gertz and Khleifi, 2006: 8). This is why history cannot be told as a chronology of events, or a rational sequence of cause and effect. The traumatic events of Palestinian history have, however, acted as a unifying national factor. In an attempt to overcome differences and fragmentation and controversies, the *Nakba* has formed one history around one shared memory. 'The trauma of Al-*Nakba* is imprinted on the psyche of every Palestinian, on those that witnessed it as well as those that did not' (*Al-Ahrām Weekly*, 22 September 2005).

Likewise, if we look at the *Nakba* and its aftermath within the concept of nostalgia in memory studies, we get a better understanding of the intertwined relationship between identity, collectivity and continuity. As the field of nostalgia is broad and interdisciplinary, in my current analysis I will focus on some aspects of nostalgia which are relevant to my discussion. Nostalgia in the broad sense of the word is defined as 'suffering due to relentless yearning for the homeland' (Sedikides et al., 2008a: 304). Nostalgia had been associated with homesickness up until late twentieth century, when people started to 'regard nostalgia as different from homesickness' (Sedikides et al., 2008a). Gradually the meaning of nostalgia developed into a sentimental longing for one's past (Wildschut et al., 2006). Longing for one's past is usually triggered by lack and/or disruption in people's lives, a feeling explained by Melinda Milligan (2003) as caused by ruptures 'to place attachment or the bonding of people to place' (Milligan, 2003: 382). In other words, the disruption to the 'built environment' (Goffman, 1959) – physical surroundings manifested through social interaction – can cause identity discontinuity. Having discussed at the beginning of this chapter how memory, being social or collective, revolves predominantly around the individual's identity (Goffman, 1963), 'felt identity' is an individual's 'subjective sense of his own situation and his own continuity and character that an individual comes to obtain as a result of his various social experiences' (Goffman, 1963: 105). Felt identity is mainly characterized by its urge towards continuity, in case of complete change, or aims at preserving aspects of its former image; 'In most situations of loss, individuals look for a mean to preserve their former identities or to establish new ones in order to regain a sense of continuity' (Charmaz, 1994; Davis, 1979 quoted in Milligan, 2003: 383).

Understanding the mechanism of identity development enables us to understand its connectedness with society and culture and its resistance to change or disruption. One of the main triggers of nostalgia is the inability of self-identity to establish a form of continuity within a new setting or circumstances. As Davis (1979: 107) argues, 'The sources of nostalgic sentiment are to be found in felt threats to continuity of identity.' In spite of how sentimental or undesirable it might sound, nostalgia can be seen as a proactive element in identity development and construction; it is 'one of the means we employ in the never ending work of constructing, maintaining and reconstructing our identities' (Davis, 1979: 31). Another important feature of nostalgia is the fact that it creates a sense of collectivity among people, all of whom take part in a common past, possibly linked to a shared sense of loss, and who all share the fight against identity discontinuity. Davis (1979: 115) argues that

> nostalgic sentiment dwells at the very heart of a generation's identity; that without it, it is unlikely that a generation could come to conceive of itself as

such or that generations in advance or in arrears of it would accede to the distinctive historical identity it claims for itself.

For Palestinians the loss of land, instability of life and constant displacement have all nurtured the sense of longing for pre-*Nakba* Palestine. On the one hand, nostalgia can be seen as a mechanism or tool for reconstructing new identities or safeguarding a former one, collectively employed due to the shared experience. In this regard, and as I will elaborate more in the next chapters, nostalgia psychologically generates a positive feeling or 'positive affectivity' (Sedikides et al., 2008a: 306) as the individual recalls the experience with a positive perception. For Palestinians, this feature might not be very obvious due to the persistence of a volatile political situation, yet in forms of popular culture and oral literature, nostalgia reinforces people's hope in the existence of long-established heritage or cultural identity. The latter is at the heart of Palestinian discourses of survival, recognition and regeneration. A second important feature of nostalgia is the fact that it 'fosters affiliation or stronger social bonds' (Sedikides et al., 2008b: 231). Because Palestinians suffered from a shared experience of loss and identity discontinuity, nostalgia can be in this case a vehicle for unifying people's memories and experiences as well as hopes and dreams. Nostalgia thus fosters the sense of collectivity among Palestinians all over the world via different forms of popular culture, specifically storytelling and folktales, and can work towards fighting oblivion. Nostalgia, on the other hand, can also evoke sentimental feelings, which would limit people to a fixed past, making them romanticize a lost paradise by constantly mourning their present. The *Nakba* can be seen as 'the creator of an unsettled inner time. It deflects Palestinians from the flow of social time into their own specific history and often into a melancholic existence' (Sa'di and Abu-Lughod, 2007: 5). For Palestinians, in particular, nostalgia is quite complex and ambivalent. The fear of melancholia and being trapped in an idealist belief of the past is unavoidable sometimes, particularly if the trauma of the past is not over yet. Finally, nostalgia 'carries existential meaning, serving as a reservoir of memories and experiences that is helpful for coping with existential threat' (Sedikides et al., 2008b: 231). This particular feature is very important in the sense of safeguarding Palestinian cultural memory across time and space, especially if both present and future are unpredictable. Once more the fear of losing the foundation of Palestinian cultural identity and memory triggers the collective and shared desire to establish a continuum between past and present, between older and younger generations. To ensure identity continuum and cultural regeneration, concepts such as 'post-memory' and 'prosthetic memory' will enrich as well as complete my discussion when I discuss Palestinian women's narrative as storytellers in Chapter 3.

Storytelling and language

In every society, collective memory is transmitted from one generation to another and so requires a reliable medium of expression. In this regard, language is an important element in the process of remembering, recollecting and narrating. By language, I mean written, readable and spoken words, imagery and symbols, all of which are considered crucial for the construction of memory: 'Language is the place where collective memory is stored'. The role of a language in transforming or strengthening collective memory lies in transmitting oral and written texts, in particular literary ones such as poetry, short stories or novels.[5] Reviving memory requires giving importance to language, which can represent a group's national language, in order to preserve its cultural heritage. And by reviving the language heritage in literary, religious and historical texts, memory is strengthened – hence transmitted – from one generation to the next. In such ways, both memory and language are key elements in the construction and maintenance of national identity, and it is useful to consider this 'triangle' of memory, identity and nationalism when dealing with the Palestinian context.

The use of language in reviving and strengthening Palestinian memory is seen vividly in Palestinian literature, both oral and written. Themes of nostalgia, trauma and displacement are present in most Palestinian literary works. Nostalgia and trauma feature in Palestinian writing as sources of power, regeneration and continuation. For Palestinians, the places of the pre-*Nakba* past and the land of Palestine itself have an extraordinary charge. They are not simply sites of memory but symbols of all that has been lost and sites of longing to which return is barred. Language in this case becomes the witness, the voice of resistance and endurance as well as the hope of change and return. The strength of the language used by Palestinian novelists and poets increases when subjected to the threat of erasure or silencing. One of the main characteristics of Palestinian writing is the use of the collective first-person voice, a communal collective voice. This collectivity is represented in the choice of words, style and themes which are shared among the whole Palestinian society. Lena Jayyusi (2007) believes that the repetition of collective first-person voice, 'ours', in stories articulates the speaking of different stories as shared. This stylistic choice, in her opinion, has a 'generalized impact on the coherence of collective subjectivity and on the integrity of communal fabric' (Jayyusi 2007: 111).

When we look at Palestine, the role of language in the narration of collective memory appears particularly significant. Writing for Palestinians is more than just a means of expression or description; it is their weapon to write back against imposed political and historical narratives supplied by Israel or the West. Most importantly, writing acts as a modifier and activator of communal tragedy, resistance and hope. 'Writing is a political act that not only represents the past, but also, within the Palestinian-Israeli context, molds the past. Words determine what is remembered and what is forgotten' (Slyomovics, 2007: 1). Such written language, particularly when it takes a sophisticated literary form, tends to be accessible to and shared only by a specific social category, mainly educated urban Palestinians: to understand the style of Ghassan Kanafani and Mahmud Darwish, among many others, Palestinians would have to be familiar with the styles and complexities of language, connotations and metaphor.[6] This category of readers would enjoy the linguistic and stylistic sophistication that is embedded between the lines; however, it can be difficult for other readers to do so. Peasants or Palestinians from rural areas may have no literary background and hence face difficulties in understanding or reading this kind of literature. This is where the importance of orality or oral literature, mainly storytelling, comes into the picture.

There are two kinds of storytelling: the first is personal accounts or individual testimonies shared by people of the same group. This type of storytelling usually refers to lived past experiences, oral testimonies of the occurrence of an important event or the witnessing of a tragic incident. Oral accounts in the form of storytelling about past events are used in the Palestinian context to 'reclaim' and 'revive', mainly to strengthen the communal shared voice of endurance, nostalgia and remembering. Oral stories are like the Palestinian history: a source of knowledge (Sayigh, 1998). It is via storytelling, the medium and form of communication, that narrative identities are made and maintained in an interactive space. The individual's life story interacts with other life stories, creating a unified medium of representation and expression (Gergen and Gergen, 1983: 270; Mancuso and Sarbin, 1983: 236; Carr, 1986: 111; Ricoeur, 1990: 190; Cavarero, 1997: 82).

The second type of storytelling is part and parcel of Palestinian popular culture and folklore; it is the narration of folktales which combine real and imaginary elements. This type of storytelling, which this book discusses in depth, has historically tended to be most common among peasants in rural communities but is less widespread today. The setting of this type of storytelling is relaxed and harmonious. According to Muhawi and Kanaana, 'The folktale tradition we have been describing falls within the context of the extended family and forms part of the social life of a settled and flourishing peasant community' (Muhawi and Kanaana, 1989: 8). It is through the narrative mediation between personal and social existence that identities are framed, and as I will explain in my analysis of the folktale collection, the framing of Palestinian folktales emphasizes the idea that the integrity of our narrative identities depends on their concordance with the versions others offer of ourselves (e.g. Rosenwald and Ochberg, 1992: 9; Bruner, 2001: 34). For example, Muhawi and Kanaana, unlike other Palestinian compilers, grouped the folktales in both collections thematically. They divided the folktales into five groups which reflect the individual's life cycle from childhood to old age. The folktales in their thematic order reflect the individual's interaction within wider social layers, which 'ground the tales in the culture from which they arise' (Muhawi and Kanaanaand, 1989: 11).

The tradition of storytelling was very common before 1948 but decreased after the *Nakba*. When both compilers, Muhawi and Kanaana, recorded the tales between 1978 and 1980 in *SBSA*, they also tried to merge the past into the present in the setting of the narration. 'The setting in which the folktales presented here were recorded generally resembled the authentic folktale settings of the past, except for the presence of the tape recorder' (Muhawi and Kanaanaand, 1989: 4). Merging the past into the present is an indication of the need to revive not only the habit of telling stories but more importantly the setting, the feel and the memory. Palestinian connection to memory can be both mental and physical; by recreating similar physical sites, sensual and vivid images can be triggered, as well as a longing for a more stable past.

The tales were narrated in the Palestinian dialect and the compilers' annotations were written in Modern Standard Arabic. The fact that the tales in *Qul Ya Tayer* (2001) were not standardized has a significance that is worth highlighting here. In his discussion of the emergence of Palestinian nationalism, Meir Litvak (2009) compared Benedict Anderson's description of the formation of European nationalism, following the transformation of European oral vernaculars into written languages, with that of the Middle East. According to him, the vernaculars in Europe are different from the various Arab vernaculars, which will never evolve into written languages. Litvak bases his analysis on that of Haim Gerber (2004) who believes that 'the central and sacred role of literary Arabic as the language of the Qur'an stands in the way of such a process, thereby slowing down the evolution of distinct identities within a broader Arab nationalism' (Gerber in Litvak, 2009: 8). However, many Palestinian folklorists, Muhawi and Kanaana among others, argue against Gerber's claims since they have deliberately kept the tales in the Palestinian dialect, putting them into writing in their collection. Muhawi and Kanaana want to preserve the Palestinian dialect, drawing on its strong connection to the formation of an ongoing Palestinian sense of belonging and identity. Muhawi and Kanaana framed their intention clearly in the introduction of *SBSA*:

> The Palestinian folktale is part of the Arabic folk narrative tradition. The tales are told in the Palestinian dialect, with its two major divisions of *fallahi* (village speech) and *madani* (city speech). Most of the tales included were narrated by villagers only because tellers were more available in villages, where the tendency to preserve folk traditions is today much greater than in the cities. In times past, however, the folktale tradition was as popular in cities as in villages, perhaps even more so since city dwellers had more leisure time compared with peasants, who were tied to the cycle of the seasons. City dwellers tend to be more polished in their use of language than villagers, and are less likely to hold the variety of folk beliefs exhibited by village tellers. (Muhawi and Kanaana, 1989: 7)

Cultural forms of writing, including prose, poetry, visual and oral literature, have contributed to forming national symbols, idols and narratives that Palestinians can relate to in their pains and aspirations. In so doing, individual identity is partly constituted through 'acquired identifications, values, norms, ideals, models and heroes' (Ricoeur, 1990: 46). In both oral and written Palestinian literature we notice that the peasant *falāḥ* acquires a specific value and becomes a Palestinian national signifier. Idolizing the peasant in this way is not to rally an actual peasantry to the national cause but to constitute a unified people and nation and to endow it with an authentic history and culture. In fact, themes related to land, peasantry and rural life represented an innovated form in Palestinian literary culture, which previously had been rooted in the classical tradition (Parmentier, 1984; Jayyusi, 1984). The peasant has become 'the hero of national literature, whereas prior to 1948, the *falāḥ* – connoting someone lower-class, backward, and uneducated – was absent from official culture' (Swedenburg, 1990: 20). For instance, the tour of eight West-Bank artists in the United States led to the conclusion that 'the land, villages, and Palestinian people are preserved through [the painters'] art, as timeless expressions of a unique culture with rich history and traditions' (Cadora, 1988).

2

Palestinian Folktales: *Speak, Bird, Speak Again* (1989) and *Qul Ya Tayer* (2001)

Folktales: Reality versus imagination

Through folklore, art, music, oral literature and other forms, popular culture encompasses and manifests a collective effort to mediate people's responses, their desires, fears or anger. For Palestinians, as this book will highlight, popular culture, in this case folklore, paves the way for 'a narrative of continuity' which is at the heart of the discourse of Palestinian memory. As I discuss in the following chapters, Palestinian memory derives its force from Palestinians' collective effort of preservation across generations. Apart from being a means of expression, popular culture, in this case oral literature and folklore, can also act as forms of cultural resistance for Palestinians, a zone for affirming their identity against oblivion. Popular culture can be 'an arena of consent and resistance' (Hall, 1998: 15) through which different artistic forms of expression have the power to engender all forms of a nation's identity, whether cultural, national or historical.

Within the realms of popular culture, folklore can reveal much about a nation's cultural identity and heritage. Folklore is 'the collective name applied to verbal materials and social rituals that have been handed down solely, or at least primarily, by word of mouth and example, rather than in written form' (Abrams, 1981: 66). It includes proverbs, legends, folktales, folk songs and dances among other forms of expression. Within folklore, the focus of this book concentrates on a specific genre, the folktale. The latter has been generally defined as an output of imagination and fantasy: 'The folktale is a fabled poetry, a product of fantasy which does not require belief' (Bach cited in Dorson, 1972: 16).[1] In *Einfache Formen* (*Simple Forms*) (1929), André Jolles offers a humanist approach of genres, which treats folklore, legend, myth and riddle as 'primary verbal formulations of the basic mental concerns that preoccupy the human mind' (Jolles cited in Ashliman, 2004: 20).[2] In contrast, Lutz Rohrich constructs his own system of genres, predicated not upon the human mind but upon human reality. According to him, 'Folklore genres are verbal formulations of reality that encompass social life, religious beliefs, and natural laws' (Rohrich, 1991: 38). In Rohrich's usage, the term 'reality' has four different meanings, which can be distinguished as 'fictive reality', 'historical reality' and 'projected reality', each of which holds a particular relation to 'the reality of the narrator's world' (Rohrich, 1991: 40). According to him, fictive reality does not belong to the narrator's world but is part of his or her imagination. However, far from being purely imaginative, fictive reality can be part of a transformed historical reality. Rohrich talks about instances of transformation where customs, beliefs, social organization and material goods that were an integral part of a given historical reality 'have been eliminated, through a process of change from the narrators' world, and transformed into the fictive reality of folk narratives, where they survived' (Rohrich, 1991: 60). In other words, the components of a culture may undergo a transformation from history into fiction, from reality into fantasy, and thereby be preserved as part of the cultural record. The present, as well as the past, can become part of fictive reality; Rohrich refers to the outcome as projected reality. He examines aspects of culture, technology, social class and personal psychology as they are projected by narrators into the fictive realities of the different genres of folk narratives. The narrative variations that occur in the same tale type told by different people, he explains, are not 'necessarily a consequence of faulty oral transmissions, forgetfulness, and narrative improvisation that seeks to amend the story through invention or synthesis of different versions, but a projection of the personal and cultural realities of the narrators' (Rohrich, 1991: 66).

Rohrich's discussion of different realities within the folktale can help us to understand that the folktale is a social outcome, combining the narrator's world and the historical under the imaginary plotting of events. The folktale is a universal form and the Palestinian folktale is no exception, hence the interconnection between the Palestinian storyteller's environment, society and history, which are all projected in some way in the Palestinian folktale. Indeed, the environment in which the storyteller lives has a major influence appeared, of which the best known is perhaps Rank's *Myth of the Birth of the Hero* (1959). The psychoanalytic approach investigates folktales as a means of understanding the inner problems of human beings (Bettelheim, 1976, 1981). Adopting a different approach again, functionalists attempt to analyse the roles that folktales play in society, whether as transmitters of the past, as a form of entertainment, as a means of sanctioning and reinforcing established beliefs, attitudes and institutions or as a form of psychological escape from a repressive society (Hartland, 1900). Finally, some folktale analysts adopt a thematic approach. This involves focusing on specific themes, examining how they are represented in the plot and analysing their social significance (see, for example, Jennings, 1981; McGlathery, 1981 and Nollendorfs, 1981). Both Muhawi and Kanaana have adopted, for instance, the thematic approach in analysing the forty-five folktales in their compilation. Being involved in the selection and interpretation of these forty-five folktales, the compilers, as I will discuss later, are actively trying to safeguard this national heritage; however, they are also in control of what they want the readers to know and/or understand. It is here important to note that folklore is a fluid and evolving genre, subject to peoples' efforts, wills, desires and alterations. On the other hand, many folklorists, such as the ones under study, try to turn folklore into a fixed corpus of collected texts, or in this case folktales, attributing them with a number of cultural, social and national connotations.

Palestinian folk narratives

At a time when many anthropologists believe that folklore is dying out, that it has 'gradually been eroded by outside forces' (Dundes, 1969: 170), Palestinian folklore and popular culture are increasingly felt to be an important national resource. In fact, with the ongoing instability of Palestinian political and social structures and the constant threats to Palestinian cultural identity, it is incumbent upon Palestinians, as Kanaana says, to have 'a unified heritage and to have shared symbols, which will preserve their union like one cohesive nation more than any time before' (Kanā'na, 2000: 163). This is why the study of folklore, particularly folktales, is perceived as a necessary tool of resistance. Palestinian folklorists thus feel the need to document oral folktales as a record of the cultural identity of Palestinians. The collection and study of folktales has witnessed various phases and was carried out by different categories of Palestinian as well as non-Palestinian folklorists.

Traditional Palestinian narratives can be defined as narratives 'told by Palestinians who lived in the period of time leading up to 1948, the beginning of the *Nakba* or "Catastrophe" in a more or less stable, homogeneous and settled peasant agricultural society' (Kanaana, 2007). Traditional Palestinian folk narratives are to be found in three sources (Kanaana, 2007; Al-Sarīsī, 2004; Al-Khalīlī, 1977). One source is the folklore literature published by many European orientalists who did their research in Palestine, especially during the last quarter of the nineteenth century and the first quarter of the twentieth century. The German collection by Schmidt and Kahle, *Volkserzählungen aus Palästina* (1930), for example, is one of the most important and most frequently cited in Muhawi and Kanaana's compilation. Schmidt and Kahle compiled their material in the village of Birzeit in the years 1910–11. Their collection consists of 132 transliterated items in Palestinian rural dialect. The authors were mainly interested in the religious and linguistic aspects of the tales. Their introduction to the collection includes a fairly complete grammar of the Palestinian dialect and the footnotes to the tales tend to emphasize biblical parallels. The importance of this work lies in the fact that it makes the Arabic tales accessible to Western readers through facing-page translations into German. During the same period, a second important collection, by J. E. Hanauer, appeared in English entitled *Folklore of the Holy Land* (1935). The tales in this collection aim at showcasing Islamic, Christian and Jewish lore in Israel/Palestine; they revolve around beliefs about cosmology, the *Jinn*, plants and animals, and include saints' folktales, Juha[5] tales and proverbs. *Folklore of the Holy Land* is a rich descriptive record of Palestinian and Jewish traditions, but it tends, according to Muhawi and Kanaana, to 'embellish content for effect' (1989: 328).

A second source for traditional Palestinian folk narratives is the oral history recorded during the last sixty years by Palestinian men and women with a great range of knowledge of the traditional folklore (Kanaana, 2007; Al-Sarīsī, 2004; Al-Khalīlī, 1977). This includes collections by Palestinian and Jewish or Israeli compilers such as 'Abdil Laṭīf Al-Barghūthī (1979), Raphael Patai (1998) and others. Al-Barghūthī, for example, focused in his book *Ḥikāyāt Jin Banī Zaīd* (*Jinn Tales from Bani Zeid*, 1979) on tales from Birzeit, and more specifically its rural area, namely, the villages of Bani Zeid. The book is divided into two chapters; one is about personal experiences with the *Jinn* as recounted by Palestinians, including incidents related to the experience of being possessed by the *Jinn* and ways to get him or her out of the human body. The second chapter includes popular *Jinn* folktales in Bani Zeid, accompanied by folkloristic analysis. Al-Barghūthī analyses the tales from a religious perspective, foregrounding the interpretation of the *Jinn* in Islam. *Fariṭ al-rumān: al-mar'a al-Falasṭīnīa fī al-ḥikayāt al-sha'biya* (*Pomegranate Seeds: The Woman in the Palestinian Folktale*, 1997) is another collection produced by Israeli and Palestinian compilers, namely, Yoram Mirūn', Nimr Maṣarwa, Yahaīl Kara and Karmalā Shaḥada. Using both Palestinian Arabic and Hebrew, the compilers present a selection of folktales from the West Bank and Israel, most of which feature the woman as the heroine. The collection mainly addresses an Israeli audience, as can be seen in the fact that the footnotes are written in Hebrew.

The third source for Palestinian folk narratives is the folklore record collected by Palestinian folklorists who were trained by and worked with European orientalists and whose work is published mainly in English, German and French (Kanaana, 2007; Al-Sarīsī, 2004; Al-Khalīlī, 1977). Native Palestinian folklorists' interest in analysing the religious and social aspects of Palestinian folktales started mainly after the founding of two journals: *Al-turāth wa al-mujtama'* (Heritage and Society, 1974) and *Al-turāth al-sha'bī* (Folk Heritage, 1969). Both journals cover topics related to Palestinian culture, heritage and history. A number of Palestinian Arab scholars and writers, most notably Al-Sarīsī, Sirḥān and Al-Khalīlī, published important studies in the 1970s. In *Al-ḥikāya al-sha'biya fī al-mujtama' al-Falasṭīnī* (*The Palestinian Folktale in Palestinian Society: Texts and Analysis*, 2004), Al-Sarīsī devoted much attention to the social context of folktales in Palestine. He provides an insight into the nature, types and origins of folktales in Palestinian society, followed by an account of the methods adopted to analyse them, drawing on the functions as well as characteristics of folktales in Palestinian society. Al-Sarīsī includes seven groups of folktales: Stories from Social Reality, Legendary Stories, Humorous or Amusing Stories, Animal Stories, Stories about Beliefs, Stories about Personal Experiences and Stories about 'The Clever One' (*Al-shaṭir*).

Along the same lines, Nimr Sirḥān's *Al-ḥikāya al-sha'biya fī al-falasṭīnīa* (*The Palestinian Folktale*, 1974) 'focuses on the Palestinian customs and beliefs that underlie the tales' (Muhawi and Kanaana, 1989: 329). Sirḥān analyses the role of the hero and women in the tales and explains the importance of social relations in understanding Palestinian folktales in general. According to Muhawi and Kanaana, Sirḥān not only has shown that Palestinian social reality shapes the fictional aspect of the tales but also explains the importance of dialect in the Palestinian folktale. Finally, Al-Khalīlī published two important books: *Al-baṭal al-Falasṭīnī fī al-ḥikāya al-sha'biya al-Falasṭīnīa* (*The Palestinian Hero in the Palestinian Folktale*, 1979) and *Al-turāth al-Falasṭīnī w al-ṭabaqāt* (*Palestinian Folklore and Social Classes*, 1977). In *The Palestinian Hero in the Palestinian Folktale* (1979), Al-Khalīlī analyses the symbolism of heroism in universal folktales in general and Palestinian folktales in particular. In the second work, *Palestinian Folklore and Social Classes* (1977), the approach he adopts in analysing folktales is based on class struggle, which can yield useful insights, although the analysis focuses on only this one aspect of the culture. Al-Sarīsī, Sirḥān and Al-Khalīlī all offer folkloristic analysis from a largely social perspective, yet the three authors 'suffer from too much analysis, with the tales receiving relatively little space in the books' (Muhawi and Kanaana, 1989: 329). In 2001, Roshdī Al-'shhab published *Kān yā makān: ḥikāyāt sha'biya min madīnat al-Quds* (*Once Upon a Time: Folktales from Jerusalem*), in which he presents and analyses proverbs, legends, folktales, anecdotes, Bedouin and animal tales from Jerusalem. Ashhab adopts a scholarly analysis while maintaining the storytellers' dialect. He does not, however, explain the criteria for his selection or the logic behind his classification. Moreover, some tales do not have any explanation while others do not mention the names of their storytellers.

Most of these works have paved the way for the preservation of the essential cultural markers of Palestinian heritage and folklore. Nonetheless, they suffer from some gaps, such as not balancing content with analysis, focusing on one aspect only or addressing one specific audience. Unlike most Palestinian folktale compilations, *SBSA* and its corresponding Arabic collection *Qul Ya Tayer* are not simply a disinterested record of Palestinian culture, society and folklore but rather a subversive scholarly endeavour to empower the Palestinian voice before Western, Arab and Palestinian readers. My research examines the ways in which these collections frame Palestinian memory and cultural identity.

Ibrahim Muhawi and Sharif Kanaana are Palestinian anthropologists and folklorists who have published numerous scholarly articles and studies on the oral performance and translation of Palestinian folklore, much of it contemporary and political. These include Palestinian children's folklore; folktales of Jerusalem; legends of martyrs; Palestinian political humour, language, nation and identity and irony in Palestinian drama. The pre-*Nakba* stories in *SBSA* and *Qul Ya Tayer* are not political in nature, but are 'coherent and distinctive chunk of the culture' (Kanaana, 2012: 2, see Appendix 1) and society. Divided into such major groupings as *Individuals, Family, Society, Environment* and *Universe*, the folktales reflect the individual's passage through life and his or her relationship to society and the environment. Muhawi and Kanaana set out 'to ground the tales in the culture from which they arise' (Muhawi and Kanaana, 1989: 11), by examining for instance the role of women in strengthening the social fabric as well as the tradition of storytelling. The compilers give a voice to Palestinian storytellers, unlike other compilations, who are given prominence and identity throughout the process of storytelling while maintaining their Palestinian dialect, setting and narration skills. Both collections provide readers with extensive social, cultural and anthropological annotations: substantial introductions, cultural footnotes, analytical endnotes, indexes to tale-types and motifs and a bibliography of Palestinian folk narrative.

The society of storytellers in Palestine

The study of folktales usually requires an in-depth analysis of the conditions surrounding them, the tellers and the different social categories involved. As I discuss in the following chapters, identity is strongly communicated in Palestinian oral literature, mainly in the way it discloses settings, conditions and customs which are directly related to the formation of a Palestinian collective sense of belonging. In his research on Palestinian folktales, 'Umar Al-Sarīsī notes that Palestinian folktales describe the social sphere and setting of both villages and cities before 1948 or before the *Nakba*:

> The folktales represent different forms of Palestinian environment and social strata before they were expelled in 1948. They represent our villages at that time, cities and Bedouin life since every Palestinian cannot be detached

from his/her inherited knowledge, followed traditions, or literary arts. (Al-Sarīsī, 2004: 59)

The pre-1948 stories, as I will analyse in more detail later, are not only a manifestation of a nostalgic past but also the cornerstone of a nation's collective memory and identity: a collective Palestinian memory to be safeguarded and passed on from one generation to the next thanks to the role played by social groups of various ages, affiliations and backgrounds. As the focus of this book is on pre-*Nakba* folktales and their analysis, it is useful to look in more detail at the role the carriers[6] and tellers of Palestinian oral literature adopt in the development of Palestinian folk-telling tradition, which can contribute to consolidating Palestinian memory and identity.

The first category of tellers belongs to Palestinian rural areas, and, according to Al-Sarīsī, this group has been very keen on preserving the folkloric features of Palestinian culture. Their contribution to safeguarding Palestinian cultural identity, he explains, is apparent in the decorations of their houses, clothes, customs, songs and folktales. Following the *Nakba*, the harmonious social unity of rural areas was disrupted by dislocation and political instability, which led this social category to become more concerned and aware of the threat of losing one's collective cultural identity. As such, the agricultural/rural social class has made an effort to maintain a cultural continuum among Palestinians in spite of past and present difficulties. In Al-Sarīsī's words, 'When talking about Palestinian countryside, we refer to pre-*Nakba* society and settings' (Al-Sarīsī, 2004: 60). The main participants in storytelling in rural families are usually elderly women, who group everyone from the same extended family, mainly children, in circles, and then start telling folktales in Palestinian rural dialect. The role played by storytellers and the audience in this context, particularly when involving the younger generations, is perceived as fundamental for the transmission of Palestinian collective memory. Moreover, the folktales under study in the present book fall into the category of rural society, mainly made up of extended rural families, which, as we will see later, are very keen on carrying on the tradition of storytelling and preserving the pillars of Palestinian cultural and folkloric representations.

The second category of storytellers belongs to the city or to urban society which, according to Al-Sarīsī, has been affected by modernization and has therefore undergone changes in lifestyle and customs in comparison to rural society. People, however, still circulate the storytelling tradition and tell folktales. However, some differences can be seen in a number of aspects, such as the accent. The urban dialect tends to be softer as some sounds are modified, making strong sounds less difficult to say. Another difference is seen in the context itself. According to Ahmad Roshdī Ṣaleḥ, 'The content of the folktale within Palestinian urban society is less demonstrative of supernatural themes or subjects in comparison to the rural folktale style' (1995: 19). Both types of folktales, rural and urban, belong to literary nationalism, according to Al-Sarīsī, since rural oral literature is related to the significance of the land and peasants' direct contact with an agricultural way of life. In fact, the theme of the land and its strong symbolic relation to Palestinian identity and resistance is relevant to our analysis of the compilations under study, as I will discuss later in this chapter. Urban oral literature also bears the sense of nationalism and patriotism, according to Al-Sarīsī, since it discusses Palestinians' lifestyle in the cities, as well as the role of both domestic and international Palestinian trade in consolidating the union of Greater Syria (*Bilād al-Shām*) during the British Mandate era (Al-Sarīsī, 2004: 60).

Bedouins and refugees, among other social classes, play a role in perpetuating the storytelling tradition, as well as being active carriers of folktales in Palestine and in the diaspora. In the case of Bedouin society in Palestine, some Palestinian folklorists have observed that Bedouins are very keen on preserving all the elements of the folktales since many refer to old traditional Palestinian Bedouin rituals when it comes to themes of love and chivalry (Al-Jawahīrī, 1972). Bedouin folktales do not depict supernatural elements since, according to Al-Sarīsī, Bedouins were more interested in telling heroic accounts of tribal victories, fighting over land, honour and reputation. Finally, refugees have had a major influence on younger generations' awareness of the existence of a rich Palestinian oral cultural heritage. Their nostalgia for and memory of their homes and lands back in Palestine acts against forgetfulness, a motivator in safeguarding refugees' collective memory and embodying the hope of return in the near future.

The transmission of folktales within Palestinian society progresses from the older to the younger generations, as is the case in most societies. Elderly people usually have first-hand experience and more knowledge when telling stories. Moreover, there is an educational motive impelling parents to tell stories to their children, offering the chance to nurture their imagination, language and knowledge. In the Palestinian case, folktales are directly related to Palestinian identity and cultural representation, which pre-*Nakba* generations are trying to uncover and preserve. As I will discuss in more depth in the following chapter, collective memory or post-memory in the Palestinian context is realized by the efforts made by older generations to maintain the passing on of past events and unconsciously the pains of trauma to coming generations and to encourage the continuum of shared values, experiences and memories. While undertaking his research, Al-Sarīsī observed a concrete phenomenon of transmission over three Palestinian generations. He recorded the separate telling of the same folktale by the grandmother, the mother and the daughter. He noticed the following:

> The grandmother was better at remembering minute details and was very good at telling the story in the Palestinian dialect, maintaining a strong accent of the area she comes from. She was also very smooth and innovative in the plotting of the story. Most importantly, she was closer to describing the village setting and spirit before the expulsion in 1948 or *Nakba*. The mother, however, had some problems remembering the sequence of events and was mixing different stories. This is due to the fact that the mother's generation underwent displacement after 1948 and experienced the upheavals of the aftermath of the *Nakba*. The daughter, unlike the mother, was very good at maintaining storytelling rules and rituals. She only used more common and modern words. (Al-Sarīsī, 2004: 70)

Based on Al-Sarīsī's small experiment, we can deduce the importance of passing on stories from one generation to another. I think that the daughter was more successful than her mother in remembering the events and in preserving the storytelling rituals due to the need to be associated to a history, a culture and a collective identity that her generation is missing. The lack of a concrete harmonized Palestinian setting and the prevalence of the themes of 'resistance' and 'dream of return' have nurtured and intensified the daughter's desire to be faithful to the rules of telling a story, since storytelling tradition symbolizes her cultural and national belongings.

The power of transmitting folktales lies in 'the creative power of people' – *Al-qūwa al-ībdāʿiya lilshʿb* – as Al-Sarīsī explains. Folktales not just are circulated among individuals but are the product of a social endeavour, whether involving members of the same family, friends or professional storytellers, who all contribute to consolidating a sense of Palestinian belonging to both universal and Arab heritage and culture. The folktale usually starts its journey from the professional storyteller who enjoys telling his folktales to the public in groups, whose impact will remain in the public's mind. Reproducing and passing on folktales from one person to another will involve some changes and additions, or even omissions, depending on the new storyteller's capacity to remember or depending on his/her own circumstances. The folktale will be passed on to new storytellers, who will keep modifying the words, style and even sometimes the ending. According to Al-Sarīsī (2004) and Al-Jawahīrī (1972), this renewal process is enriching and more relevant to people's current conditions. The folktale in its new form is in harmony with popular experience and can trigger people's dreams and inspirations in their new cultural and social environments. As a result, this endeavour is part of a unified collective attempt to preserve of the storytelling tradition and creation of its new forms. As the soul of cultural Palestinian life, the folktale plays different roles and has a number of social and educational functions in Palestinian society.

Along the same lines, if we look at the Egyptian case for instance, we see that the Arab folk epic, namely, *Sirat Bani Hilal*,[7] is witnessing a regeneration and a growing interest following a previous decline, when many Egyptians became more interested in television, film, and Arab pop, and less familiar with epic and oral performances (Reynolds, 1995; Connelly, 1986). Egyptian folklorists and poets such as Jabir Abu Hussein and Abd Al-Rahman Al-Abnoudi endeavoured to record the epic tales, explaining the story of each section and making the performance accessible on radio and cassette tapes to audiences who are not necessarily familiar with specialized poetic language and plots. Al-Abnoudi has in fact worked on setting folklore in general and folk epic in particular in the now, establishing a bridge between the past and present while reconnecting the Egyptian masses, both rural and urban, to the heritage of storytelling and thus cultural identity.

The functions of folktales in Palestinian society

The folktale, as discussed, exists within different social classes and backgrounds and can represent the collective voice of a society, its culture and inspirations. According to some folklorists in the field of oral literature, the folktale plays an important role in shaping the identity of both the individual and society.

The question raised here is how the folktale can affect societies. Why does it play an important role in some societies, particularly the Palestinian one? To be able to answer this question, one has to start by looking at the different functions of the folktale. The meaning of function here, as defined by AR Radcliffe-Brown, and quoted in A'iz Al-dīn Ismā'īl's *Folk Telling in Sudan*, is 'what is presented by *the partial colour* of the colours of the activity or of the *whole activity*' (Ismā'īl, 1971: 174; emphases added). The 'partial colour' can refer to proverbs, folktales or popular song. The 'whole activity' here means the civilization under which the individual practises different activities. The function is also 'a study of all the social stages in life and their interactions; it is also the study of the individual, his/her lifestyle in a society, his/her adaptation and his/her development in it' (Granqvist, 1947: 14–15). Based on this, one can link the function to two major components: the individual or the subject and the society to which the individual belongs. The task of a folklorist in this sense is to stop and analyse the text and its components and to classify those components according to the text's social frame and nature. Then, the folklorist has to try and combine his/her observations into an overall picture of the society, which will give an idea of the kind of society the folktale is depicting. As the central unit, understanding the individual will help in understanding the social apparatus of a collective group. Most folklorists believe that the role of folktales is to consolidate people's cultural and belief values and to educate, both at the individual ethical level and at the collective social one. In this regard, I will describe the functions of folktales in Palestinian society following Al-Sarīsī's classification: belief function, psychological function and social function. In the following section, I briefly explain the abovementioned functions, which will become relevant to my discussion in the later chapters. Understanding the functions of folktales in general and Palestinian in particular will help us understand Palestinian culture and beliefs, hence will help in analysing Palestinian cultural identity and memory when examining some of the folktales or when elucidating the compilers' annotations.

The psychological function

Telling and hearing folktales can be a source of enjoyment. Human beings apparently seek to indulge in the duality of telling and/or listening to folktales, which affords them an opportunity to transgress the level of reality, while nonetheless subconsciously representing what they stand for. According to Friedrich von der Leyen in *The Fairy Tale* (1911, translated into Arabic by Nabīla Ibrahīm, 1990), there are two reasons why people enjoy telling and listening. Firstly, people are intuitively attracted to the pleasure, excitement and suspense of being a teller or a listener since the culture of narrating has long been established within families and educational institutions. Secondly, the style of narration or the artistic aspect is a very important motive for listening. The chain of events, characters' developments and a sense of humour can create diversified psychological dimensions for both listener and teller.

The folktale's psychological function lies in its power to trigger one's imagination and desires. Al-Sarīsī points out that 'folktales highlight individuals' and collective's hopes and wishes, which find room for expression in the world of imagination' (Al-Sarīsī, 2004: 311). Similar to dreams, telling folktales can release hidden desires and wishes, which meet the audience's desire for satisfaction and wish-fulfilment. Moreover, the storyteller, as Al-Sarīsī explains, has the ability to shape the plot of his/her story so as to motivate the audience to follow their natural instincts, to believe in the power of change and to be good human beings, since many moral messages can be embedded in a folktale. In other words, the folktale is not only a source of enjoyment and wish-fulfilment but can also be a motivator for changing negative social or ethical behaviours, hence making it instructive, constructive and educational. Here the role of Palestinian women storytellers is key. As I will elaborate in the following chapters, women are endowed with strong narrative skills, allowing them to reinforce Palestinian identity among younger generations. Folktales can also reveal the dark side of human beings, such as jealousy and rivalry, or they can give freedom of expression when it comes to social taboos, such as sex outside marriage.

The social function

Folktales express the voice of a group, community and society in different ways. Palestinian folktales can be a revealing source for understanding social traditions, structures and interactions among Palestinians. The frequency and insistence of perpetuating Palestinian folktales, according to Al-Sarīsī, is meant to expose the specificity of Palestinian social rituals among younger generations as a means of educating them about their history and culture. Among the most important social roles highlighted in most Palestinian folktales is the role of women. Women have leading roles in Palestinian society as mothers, wives, daughters and sisters. The majority of Palestinian folklorists, such as Al-Khalīlī (1979), Sirḥān (1974) and Al-Ghūl (1966), agree on the fact that Palestinian women are represented in the tales as strong partners, who are supportive and loving towards their husbands and families. As mothers, for example, Palestinian women are very devoted and charismatic; they can overcome their needs in order to sustain their sons or husbands. Both rural and urban Palestinian women are seen in the folktales as strong willed, determined and free to pursue their objectives and dreams. The Palestinian woman's dynamic role in her family is no exception to that of other women worldwide. Moreover, it is important to remember that this particular art or type of folktales in Palestine is narrated by women only (with very few exceptions of male involvement), which may explain why women in the folktales are usually attributed with very strong, feminine and positive characteristics. As I will discuss in more depth in the coming chapters, women's storytelling tradition and their portrayal in the folktales can be to some extent a reflection of the Palestinian patriarchal society, but it can also be a way for women to express their fears, conflicting desires and struggles. Another important point to bear in mind is that male storytelling is different from female storytelling, which means that the portrayal of women might differ depending on who is telling the tale.[8] Women, however, are not depicted as submissive or vulnerable in male storytelling. In her book, *The Warrior Women of Islam* (2014), Remke Kruk discussed the representation of women in Arabic popular epic tales, known as *Sīra*. Women were warriors and very strong usually, sometimes even stronger than men, she says:

> The fact that these heroic women are creatures of male fantasy, however, does not imply that the stories do not pay attention to emotions of women. Female sensitivities are regularly brought into focus, particularly in relation to matters such as motherhood, pride and jealousy. All we can say, however is that this tells us something about the attitudes and perceptions of the male narrators and their audience, and about the society in which they lived. (Kruk, 2014: 226)

Indeed, folktales share common points all over the world, whether narrated by male or female narrators; nonetheless, they highlight the specificity of a particular society, its history and aspirations, and hence cultural identity, as is the case with those from Palestine.

Following the role of women in Palestinian folktales, the importance of family and marriage institutions comes second, according to Al-Sarīsī. Hilma Granqvist explains that analysing the marriage institution in the Palestinian context shows 'the historical development of the village and its families, from which we can understand the social structure and family principles' (Granqvist, 1942: 25). In this sense, folktales reveal first the rituals and traditions of marriage ceremonies in both the countryside and the city. The storytellers are very faithful in describing marriage rituals in detail, mainly in the countryside, as those details are missing nowadays due to the diasporic situation or displacement. 'The full presentation of marriage rituals in the countryside around Jerusalem, as seen in the folktales, is meant to document those rituals as practised before the *Nakba*' (Al-Sarīsī, 2004: 191). Following marriage, the social function of Palestinian folktales is seen in the exploration of family relationships, in particular within the Palestinian extended family: husband and wife, parents and children, mother and children, father and children, brothers and sisters. The mechanism and division of roles is revealing, as once again it informs both the reader and the folklorist about the origin of many traditions and beliefs, Palestinian family rules and desires and most importantly the disclosure of cultural habits or rituals among family members which seem to have faded away because of political upheavals. Family interaction is well discussed and explored by Muhawi and Kanaana, hence additional discussion on the theme of family will appear later when analysing the folktales in *SBSA*.

Another feature of folktales that folklorists analyse is Palestinian work, wage labour and environment. Before the *Nakba*, social life in Palestine was harmonious and stable, which Al-Sarīsī believes is very important to highlight when analysing Palestinian folktales (Al-Sarīsī, 2004: 112). For instance, the reader gets to know more about village social life and the importance of agriculture and the land, which are crucial means for earning a living for Palestinian peasants. In fact, the folktale 'is a live descriptive movie of peasants' houses, activities in the fields, typical food and clothing' (Al-Sarīsī,

2004: 215). Moreover, there are minute descriptions of the land or fields where peasants plough and harvest, the most popular crops and fruit, and even musical instruments played by peasants or shepherds. The peasant and land have a significant association with Palestinian national belonging and resistance, which will be examined further in the following section. A number of professions and jobs are also described, including woodcutting, fishing, carpentry and blacksmithing. The reason for mentioning these professions in folktales, I believe, is to emphasize the beauty and richness of Palestinian landscapes before 1948. In other words, Palestinians were enjoying different professions across many forest and coastal areas, use of which by Palestinians after 1948 was minimized and restricted. Other folktales discuss the lives of traders or merchants, mainly in the cities, which reveal important aspects of Palestinian international and national trade and trading routes during the British Mandate when Palestine belonged to Greater Syria (Al-Sarīsī, 2004).

Folktales are not only descriptive of social life in Palestine; they can also be critical of social practices and norms. Under the guise of humour and entertainment, the role of Palestinian folktales is seen as both drawing attention to and attempting to rectify some examples of unacceptable behaviour of either the individual or the group in Palestinian society. At the end of every folktale, for instance, there is a lesson to learn or a moral to follow in real life – a common feature in folktales the world over. The most prominent examples found in many Palestinian folktales, as Al-Sarīsī explains, deal with tackling issues related to gender favouritism in Palestinian society, as males are considered by the family and society to be better and more gifted than females. Folktales may also try to prevent racial and social favouritisms, another social behaviour among many Palestinians considered to be unacceptable. Furthermore, Palestinian folktales aim to valorize and promote humanitarian values by encouraging people to be fair, just, honest, respectful to each other, helpful, generous and friendly. In fact, there is an urge to be critical and to promote important humanitarian values since after the *Nakba* 'people's humanitarian and Arab values were shaken by trauma as well as modernization' (Al-Sarīsī, 2004: 239).

Given the importance of portraying the family and social interaction, the reader is also exposed to important political rules and features in Palestinian society. The ruling system is symbolized by the king or sultan and ministers in the urban areas and by *Al-mukhtār*, the leader of a tribe, in the rural areas. Those ruling figures extend their authority and power through people's love and support; indeed, they are considered national patriotic figures whose sole aim is to protect the country and nation. While conducting his research on Palestinian folktales, Al-Sarīsī noticed that some storytellers deliberately mention the names of real kings or leaders who ruled Palestine in the past. For instance, 'The King of Al-Sukarīya' is a folktale that tells the story of a leader in the village of Al-Sukarīya, a village which existed before the *Nakba*, located between Gaza and Jaffa. In many instances, the folktales also refer to historical achievements and victories, such as the defeat of Napoleon when he tried to conquer the city of Acre. The reader (or listener) is given a historical, chronological account of battles of resistance from the Ottoman Empire up to the British Mandate era. 'Positive resistance is marked in the memory of people; heroic victories by particular individuals or groups are essential materials for Palestinian folktales' (Al-Sarīsī, 2004: 255). Hilma Granqvist (1942) also believes that following 1920 there was an urge among Palestinian storytellers to raise national awareness about secret Zionist plans for immigration to Palestine. In Al-Sarīsī's opinion, there are no Palestinian folktales about Israeli occupation (after 1948) since Palestinian folktales are the result of years of history, in addition to the fact that the Israeli occupation is still ongoing, meaning that people do not have to make the effort of remembering or/and retrieving it from their memories (Al-Sarīsī, 2004: 255).

In relation to political representation in Palestinian folktales, one has to highlight the symbolic significance of the land in Palestinian society. For years, there has been a strong connection between Palestinians and their lands. This is due to popular cultural and religious beliefs, maintaining the belief that one will always return to his/her land both in the denotative sense, by being buried, and in the connotative figurative meaning, symbolized in the dream of returning to the homeland. Palestinian folklorists have observed Palestinians' strong physical and emotional attachment to their land. This powerful link is seen in their connection to social practices related to farming, ploughing or harvesting, as discussed earlier, and also in the belief that protecting your land equals the protection of honour and dignity. Attachment to land is not unique to Palestinian folk literature as many folktales, particularly the ones originating from rural contexts, manifest the bond through descriptions of landscapes, caves, forests, trees, valleys, rivers and fruits. In the Palestinian context, the land is heavily emotionally charged with symbolism, particularly after 1948. It is in fact always associated with freedom, honour, steadfastness, heritage and hope. There is a passionate desire to concretize the descriptions in Palestinian folktales so as to connect the reader to the existence of the physical land, as well as to nurture the sense of nostalgia and memory among older generations, and to activate younger generations' passion for a land that some of them have never seen.

The belief function

In folklore studies, some folklorists, such as Alexander Krappe (1930), have maintained that folktales do not have any religious inspiration or spiritual philosophy. However, Krappe's belief should be questioned. Through the transmission of folktales from one culture to another and from one society to another, folktales will inevitably carry the social and religious beliefs of the original society, especially if the tales record the daily activities of a society. One cannot deny the existence of beliefs or religious allusions within the layers of Arabic folktales in general and Palestinian ones in particular, whether they aim at entertaining or educating the audience.

The presence of Islamic references can be seen, for example, in the style of narration, particularly in the opening and concluding expressions. Storytellers would usually start the folktale by saying 'in the name of Allah …' and end it by saying 'may Allah bless you and keep you healthy …'. Al-Sarīsī suggests that religion is present not only in the style of narration but also in the content. He is of the opinion that people's beliefs are part of their everyday lives and existence, which are both present in the style and content of storytelling (Al-Sarīsī, 2004). Hence folktales can project an existing reality of a particular society's religious beliefs and practices. Folktales can also play the role of educating younger generations about significant practices in Islam, for instance, the importance of charity, fasting, pilgrimage and praying. More importantly, Palestinian folktales refer to the existence of the three monotheistic religions: Islam, Christianity and Judaism. Fwzī' Al-'Antīl (1965) claims that the constant reference to the three religions is mainly related to the religious history of Palestine, as the sacred land and the cradle of religions. Palestinian folktales can reveal popular and cultural religious practices, which can be very specific and different from one society to another, such as visiting shrines, asking pious sheikhs for forgiveness and believing in talking to supernatural creatures, such as *Jinni*. In fact, the geographical location of the most popular shrines occurring in Palestinian folktales tends, according to Al-Sarīsī, to highlight the historical background and richness of the history of Palestine which is manifested in the Canaanite[9] era and folklore. I will elaborate on the belief function and the other functions in greater detail when analysing the folktales under study in the subsequent chapters.

Paratextual material in *Speak, Bird, Speak Again* and *Qul Ya Tayer*

Apart from containing some of the most popular folktales in Palestine, Muhawi and Kanaana's compilations (both English and Arabic) stand out for their comprehensive scholarly apparatus, giving the reader, whether ordinary or expert, detailed linguistic and folkloric explanations, as well as cultural and historical contextualization. The materials around the folktales, known as framing tools or paratextual materials, disclose the compilers' agenda as well as encouraging the reader to view the folktales through a specific lens. Framing[10] can be an active process of signification 'by means of which we consciously participate in the construction of reality' (Baker, 2006: 167). It can also be an interpretive power to grant agency to the individual for a conscious intervention 'to organize experience and guide action' (Benford and Snow, 2000: 614). The interactant, in this case Muhawi and Kanaana, will use specific devices to influence other interactants' or readers' understanding of what is going on. One of the main framing devices worth reviewing briefly is the notion of paratext[11]:

> The verbal frame, or paratext, may enhance the text, it may define it, it may contrast with it, it may distance it, or it may be so disguised as to seem to form part of it. In fact, the frame by necessity defines a relationship different in quality to that between the text itself and its audience. (Maclean, 1991: 274)

Paratexts refer to those elements which surround a literary text and which help 'a text to become a book and to be offered as such to its readers and, more generally, to the public' (Genette, 1997: 2). In other words, a text is 'a long sequence of verbal statements' and paratexts are perceived as certain 'productions' that decorate, reinforce and promulgate it (Genette, 1997: 1). Genette describes paratexts as 'zone[s] between text and off-text' and as 'a fringe of the printed text which in reality controls one's whole reading of the text' (Genette, 1997: 2) – in other words, as elements which 'frame' the main text. The use of paratexts enables the text to be interpreted following a specific motive, ideology or agenda. The most important role of paratextuality is 'to ensure for the text a destiny consistent with the author's purpose', which can also involve the decision of other agents (Genette, 1997: 407).[12] Thus paratexts can actively control and mobilize the audience's understanding. Paratexts in fact consist of all the extra-textual material that immediately surrounds a text or is scattered throughout it, including titles, the author's or translator's name, introductions, footnotes, book covers, postfaces, glossaries, blurbs and images or illustrations,[13] all of which have specific functions.[14]

The two collections address different audiences, an English-speaking audience (mainly in the United States) and an Arabic-speaking audience. The tales that feature in each collection are supplemented by extensive paratextual material, which help English- and Arabic-speaking readers, respectively, understand the relevant cultural as well as social context. I discuss here the paratextual material in the two collections, following the order in which this material is presented in the English collection, given that *SBSA* appeared first, and may therefore be used as a point of reference in the following description.

The paratextual material in the English collection consists of the following elements in this order: 'Foreword', 'Acknowledgements', 'Note on Transliteration', 'Key to References'; I will refer to these three elements as Pre-Introduction Paratextual Material. These are followed by an Introduction which consists of fifty pages and is divided into six parts. The Pre-Introduction Paratextual Material and the Introduction together constitute the front matter of the volume. The main body of the text, that is, the tales themselves, is separated from the front matter with a blank page and preceded by 'Notes on Presentation and Translation'. The tales are also accompanied by 'Afterwords' and 'Footnotes'. Finally, Post-Tales Paratextual Material consists of a section entitled 'Folkloristic Analysis' and a number of appendices. I will indicate below where relevant any differences in the content and order of paratextual material in the Arabic collection.

Pre-introduction paratextual materials

Following the table of contents in *SBSA*, five pages are dedicated to Alan Dundes's foreword. Slightly different from the English collection, the translation of Alan Dundes's foreword in *Qul Ya Tayer* follows *Taqdīm al-mū' lifīn lil ṭab'a al-'rabīa* (The Authors' Introduction to the Arabic Edition) and *Taqdīm al-ṭab'a al-'rabīa* (The Introduction of the Arabic Edition).

Foreword

Muhawi and Kanaana launched their compilation in 1989, giving the opening words to Alan Dundes's introduction for the Western reader. Analysing the foreword discloses a key point in the way *SBSA* was initially introduced. Being written by a prominent scholar like Alan Dundes, the foreword added credibility to Muhawi and Kanaana's work and facilitated readers' reception to what would be considered as a subversive narrative in the West, particularly in the United States during the late 1980s. In fact, the power of intellectuals, such as Dundes, lies in being 'endowed with a faculty for representing, embodying, articulating a message, a view, an attitude, philosophy or opinion to, as well as for, a public' (Said, 1996: 11). The art of representing is articulated by the use of framing devices, such as paratexts (Genette, 1997). The power of framing and paratexts can alter the main text and mobilize readers (Baker, 2006; Gürçağlar, 2002).

Forewords, similarly like prefaces, expose the 'why' and the 'how' behind the writing of a work, except that the preface is written by the book's author, translator, publisher or other agent. The foreword, however, must be written by a credible person in the field, rather than the author.[15] Genette (1997: 196–209) divides the functions of prefaces into 'themes of the why' and 'themes of the how'. The former aims to tell readers why they should read the book by emphasizing its importance and value. The latter aims to instruct readers about how they should read the book, in an attempt to ensure that the book is read as the preface writer wishes it to be read. As with the preface, 'themes of the why' and 'the how' as described by Genette exist in my analysis of the foreword in *SBSA*, except that they are introduced by another agent and not the author. Forewords, like prefaces, can direct the reader to understand the text, especially a translation, from a specific angle. Gürçağlar (2002), unlike Genette, believes that a translator's preface is not necessarily 'allographic'

(Genette, 1997: 179), that is, merely presenting the aims of the translation of the work; a preface in her view can be part of an institutionalized ideology.[16]

Dundes starts his foreword by introducing Muhawi and Kanaana's collection as a remarkable work that 'offered a rare combination of ethnographic and literary glosses on details that afford a unique glimpse into the subtle nuances of Palestinian Arab culture' (Dundes in Muhawi and Kanaana, 1989: ix). He establishes the status of the work as pioneering, 'destined to be a classic and will surely serve as a model for future researchers in folk narrative' (Muhawi and Kanaana, 1989). He then compares *SBSA* to different works written mainly during the eighteenth and nineteenth centuries. According to Dundes, *SBSA* has a similar status – popular as well famous – to the Brothers Grimm[17] collections. It is even more distinctive in his opinion as it reflects 'the efforts of the collectors to preserve unaltered the precious folkloristic art forms of the local peasantry' (Muhawi and Kanaana, 1989). The collection is non-elitist and not addressed to a special category of intellectuals. Dundes believes that in spite of eighteenth- and nineteenth-century Western folktale collections' fame, they failed in being truthful to the cultures they arose from, since collections at the time were confined and conformed to 'the higher canons of taste'(Muhawi and Kanaana, 1989: x):

> They [the eighteenth- and nineteenth-century folktale compilers] actually rewrote or otherwise manipulated the materials so assiduously gathered. One reason for this intrusiveness was the longstanding elitist notion that literate culture was infinitely superior to illiterate culture. Thus the oral tales were made to conform to the higher canons of taste found in written literature, and oral style was replaced by literary convention … The Grimms and their imitators were trying to create a patrimony for purposes of national pride (long before Germany was to become a nation in the modern sense), and tampering with oral tradition suited their goals. Texts that are rewritten, censored, simplified for children, or otherwise modified may well be enjoyed by readers conditioned to the accepted literary stylistics of so-called high culture. (Dundes in Muhawi and Kanaana, 1989: x)

Dundes, as an intellectual, 'questions rather than just communicates' (Said, 1996: 37), which is essential when establishing the difference between elite culture and popular culture. The collection under discussion is, in fact, suitable for all social and intellectual levels in the Arab world and the West. Moreover, the language, unlike world-renowned collections over recent centuries, is not beautified (Kanaana, 2012, see Appendix 1),[18] changed or falsified. The language, mainly the Palestinian dialect, has been authentically represented and transmitted to the reader. The interconnection between language and national and cultural identity will be fully developed over the coming chapters.

Another important feature highlighted by Dundes in his foreword is the academic value and scientific weight of *SBSA*, arguing that the latter is distinctive for its scientific apparatus. Once again, he compares *SBSA* to the majority of nineteenth- and twentieth-century folktale collections arguing the latter's deficiency in 'meeting the minimum criteria of scientific inquiry' (Dundes in Muhawi and Kanaana, 1989: x). They also lacked information about the tellers, and there was 'rarely concerted attempt made to compare a particular corpus of tales with other versions of the same tale types' (Muhawi and Kanaana, 1989). Most tales at the time were presented with no cultural context or analysis of their meaning, according to Dundes. By scientific inquiry or scholarly apparatus, Dundes refers to the extensive paratextual materials needed in the framing and grounding of the tales. Another reason for the inadequacy of nineteenth-century folktales, mainly those representing non-European countries, according to Dundes, is the fact that the collectors/compilers were not originally from the place where the tales were told. Many compilers, who happened to be 'colonialist administrators, missionaries and travellers' (Muhawi and Kanaana, 1989) recorded stories they liked or found amusing. However, the majority of the recorded tales underwent modifications and omissions of details that those compilers found inappropriate. Dundes questions the authenticity and honesty of those tales as they had to be modified to suit the standards of the recipient culture. *SBSA* is a breakthrough in the sense it is written in the native language (Palestinian dialect) and by Palestinians, who are acquainted with their folk culture, representing a genuine effort to portray truthfully the culture of the tales.

Dundes goes on to discuss Muhawi and Kanaana's background as compilers, translators and anthropologists, highlighting their academic expertise in the field of anthropology, translation and cultural studies. He then describes their encounter at Birzeit University and the roots of their project. The compilers not only collected but also got involved in efforts to transcribe, translate and contextualize the tales both linguistically and culturally:

> Collecting the tales proved to be only the first step. Transcribing and translating the tales took many, many hours of arduous, meticulous work. Then, to make the tales intelligible to readers unfamiliar with Palestinian society, Muhawi and Kanaana elected to prepare a comprehensive yet succinct cultural overview with special emphasis on family dynamics. (Muhawi and Kanaana, 1989: xii)

Being a pivotal paratextual element in highlighting the intentions of Muhawi and Kanaana's project, Dundes's foreword praises and stresses the importance of the paratextual elements around the tales in *SBSA*:

> The ethnographic portrait provided in the introductory essay is a remarkable achievement, and it certainly facilitates a better understanding of the tales that follow. ... The anthropological influence is also felt in the very organization and sequential order of the tales. ... The anthropological bias, however, is always balanced by attention to literary topics; the poetics of opening and closing formulas, for example, are discussed in depth, and careful comparative annotations relate these tales to other Arabic folktales as well as to the international folktale scholarship in general. ... It is precisely because such close attention was paid to the concerns of the humanist and the social scientist alike that this collection of folktales is so special. (Muhawi and Kanaana, 1989)

Resembling a double framing or one paratext within another, the paragraph quoted above highlights the importance of reading the tales within their scholarly apparatus, namely, introduction, afterwords and footnotes. In fact, the distinctiveness and originality of *SBSA*, as described by Dundes, are attributed mainly to the compilers' anthropological and literary expertise in grounding the tales within Palestinian culture, identity and continuous memory, turning hence *SBSA* into 'a landmark entree into Palestinian Arab ethos and worldview' (Muhawi and Kanaana, 1989).

The key point stressed by Dundes towards the end of his foreword is the political motive behind the collection. There is emphasis on the existence of a strong national Palestinian identity in spite of political dislocation. For Dundes, the establishment of Israel in 1948 cannot deny Palestinians' voice and right to preserve their culture, expressed in this case with the telling of folktales. The notion of homeland, no matter how problematic it is to define, represents an unavoidable existential question for Palestinians, who were and are still suffering from occupation, displacement and uprooting. As I will elaborate in more depth in the coming chapters, Dundes's statement reinforces the continuity of Palestinian collective memory on the one hand and post-memory (Hirsch, 1996, 1997, 1999 and 2008; Hirsch and Smith, 2002)[19] on the other:

> There was once an area of the world called Palestine, *where the Arab inhabitants had – and have* – a distinctive culture all their own. It is that culture that is preserved so beautifully in the magical stories contained in this volume. (Dundes in Muhawi and Kanaana, 1989: xiii, italics added for emphasis)

The notion of 'collective memory' can be seen in his use of past then present tenses – *where the Arab inhabitants had and have* – as he words it. Dundes gives the reader the understanding that Palestinian culture has always been alive, is not dead because of the establishment of Israel and will never be. Dundes's message stresses the importance of allowing Palestinians to revive the distinctiveness of their cultural and social identity, urging against forgetfulness. The foreword itself is a form of highlighting Muhawi and Kanaana's intention in compiling, documenting and translating for Western, Arab and mainly Palestinian coming generations, with the aim of guaranteeing continuation and revival.

Not only is the collection a valuable scholarly work with a scientific apparatus of analysis, via the usage of comprehensive paratextual elements, it is also a source of enjoyment and pleasure. Dundes's final point is to show that the collection is suitable for any kind of reader; both scholars and folktale lovers will enjoy reading it:

> Some readers may choose not to refer to the scholarly apparatus, preferring instead to enjoy only the tales themselves, but scholars will surely be grateful for the thoughtful notes and 'afterwords' the authors have provided. (Muhawi and Kanaana, 1989: xiii)

He also insists on the survival of folktales, in spite of the claims that folktales are limited to the past or that they are disappearing:

> I have repeatedly heard literary folklorists claim that the fairy tale genre is dead. These misguided academics continue to pore over such purely literary collections as the *Arabian Nights* or the celebrated collections of Perrault

and the Grimms, not realizing that the fairy tale is alive and well in the modern world. (Muhawi and Kanaana, 1989)

Dundes once again emphasizes the importance and survival of Palestinian tales, which 'will be told as long as birds sing!' (Muhawi and Kanaana, 1989).

Acknowledgements, note on transliteration and key to references

In the 'Acknowledgements' in *SBSA* Muhawi and Kanaana express their gratitude to the storytellers, whose tales they compiled, and to colleagues at the University of California, and they acknowledge the support of organizations such as the American Palestine Educational Fund and the Ford Foundation, among others. The Arabic collection does not include an acknowledgements section. Instead, there is a note about the aims and profile of the Institute for Palestine Studies,[20] which published *Qul Ya Tayer*. This is followed by a thank-you note from the Institute to the Qattan Foundation,[21] the main and only sponsor of this project. The fact that the volume was published by the Institute for Palestine Studies and funded by the Qattan Foundation is significant since it highlights the importance of the Arabic collection as a national project.

The 'Acknowledgements' is followed by the 'Note on Transliteration' in the English collection, which explains the system adopted for transliterating the Palestinian dialect. This is of course only included in the English collection, and its use is largely confined to the transliteration of individual words and expressions in the English text of the tales. However, it is indispensable to deciphering one fully transcribed tale in Appendix A (Tale 10). Finally, the last section before the introduction is the 'Key to References', where explanations are given of abbreviations that appear in footnotes and tales; for example, 'TM' stands for the journal *Al-turāth w al-mujtam '* (Heritage and Society). These sections, 'Note on Transliteration' and 'Key to References', do not appear in the Arabic collection. Instead, the compilers introduce two sections on presentation in *Qul Ya Tayer* namely *Taqdīm al-mū 'lifīn lil ṭab ' a al- 'rabīa* (The Authors' Introduction to the Arabic Edition) and *Taqdīm al- ṭab ' a al- 'rabīa* (The Introduction of the Arabic Edition). These are discussed under 'Paratextual Material within the Tales' later in this section.

Introduction

The English and Arabic collections both include a comprehensive introduction by Muhawi and Kanaana. Both introductions address the same issues and offer readers background information about Palestinian society, culture and beliefs. In the English collection, the introduction extends to fifty pages and in the Arabic collection to fifty-four. Both English and Arabic introductions are divided into six sections, in the following order: 'The Tales', 'The Tellers', 'The Tales and the Culture', 'The Tales and Authority in Society', 'Food in Society and Tales' and 'Religion and the Supernatural'.

In the section on 'The Tales', the compilers explain the criteria for selection, which are based on 'popularity and excellence of narration' (Muhawi and Kanaana, 1989: 7). In other words, 45 tales were chosen out of 200 because, according to Muhawi and Kanaana, these tales were, in the opinion of their raconteurs, very popular. Excellence of narration is also a determining criterion when variant versions of the same tale were found by the compilers. Muhawi and Kanaana then explain the differences between the terminology of *ḥikāya* or *khurāfya* (both meaning 'folktale'), as opposed to fable or fairy tale in English. *ḥikāya* puts the emphasis on the mimetic or artistic aspect of narration, whereas *khurāfya* stresses the fictitious aspect (Muhawi and Kanaana, 1989: 8). Muhawi and Kanaana argue that folktales are told mostly by women and are associated in Palestinian society with 'old wives' tales'. Men, on the other hand, prefer to listen to and tell epic stories in diwan gatherings. This distinction leads the compilers to examine gender differences in the manner of delivery. Men's performance, for example, relies more on physical movements, whereas 'women rely on their voices and the power of the colloquial language to evoke a response' (Muhawi and Kanaana, 1989). Muhawi and Kanaana give credit to women for developing the art form of the folktale in the Palestinian context and go so far as to argue that 'men who tell folktales must adopt the narrative style of women' (Muhawi and Kanaana, 1989: 11). In addition to the different manners of delivery, the setting and the language distinguish the folktale from the epic story. To achieve effective narration, 'the same conditions of past settings have been established while recording the present collection, which involves evening times, small audiences and dim light' (Muhawi and Kanaana, 1989: 12). The compilers believe that social gatherings were important in the past in Palestine and reflect the culture's heavy emphasis on the oral tradition and verbal ability. The language used in the tales, mainly 'the opening formula, creates an air of expectation as the session unfolds'; hence 'the setting requires a special style and narrative attitude' (Muhawi and Kanaana, 1989). Finally, in this first section on 'The Tales', the compilers describe the difference between rural and urban dialects in Palestine, alluding to the context of the tales in the past, which was part of the social life of a stable peasant community:

> The folktale tradition we have been describing falls within the context of the extended family and forms part of the social life of a settled and flourishing peasant community. With recent displacement of the Palestinian people, the social and geographic bases for the tradition have been severely disrupted. (Muhawi and Kanaana, 1989: 14)

Muhawi and Kanaana then move to a discussion of 'The Tellers' and give details of their gender, social status and age. The seventeen storytellers, who do not think of themselves as such, are mostly women. Fourteen are housewives who can neither read nor write, and only two out of the seventeen live in the cities of Gaza and Jerusalem; the others have lived in villages all their lives (Muhawi and Kanaana, 1989: 15). The most distinctive tellers, in the opinion of the compilers, are Fatema from Galilee (Tales 1, 9, 11, 23, 24, 26, 36, 38 and 43), followed by Shafiʻ. Unlike Fatema, Shafiʻ is one of 'four or five [people] in any village community who shows an intense personal interest in preserving and transmitting the practice' (Muhawi and Kanaana, 1989: 10). According to Muhawi and Kanaana, 'His sense of plotting and double plotting is superb' (Muhawi and Kanaana, 1989: 16). Shafiʻ contributed Tales 5, 8, 10, 15, 25 and 44. There is also ʼlmāza, Shafiʻ's wife (Tales 14, 18, 37), who uses rich language and whose stories come from a wide variety of sources. Im Nabīl (Tales 17, 19, 28, 30 and 39) is the archetypal old woman. Finally, there is Im Darwīsh, who is 'responsible for two of the best tales in the collection (Tales 21 and 45)' (Muhawi and Kanaana, 1989: 10).

In the section entitled 'The Tales and the Culture', Muhawi and Kanaana set out to ground the tales in their culture, by examining the cultural pillars that constitute Palestinian society and that are reflected in the tales. The first cultural aspect referred to is the role of Palestinian women in structuring social institutions. Their gender does not mean that they have no power in Palestinian society. On the contrary, they are considered to be credible eyewitnesses of life and history. In fact, the power of women is realized in their role as storytellers in reality and as heroines in fiction: 'These tales almost always concern, not heroes, but heroines: mothers, daughters, and wives' (Muhawi and Kanaana, 1989: 18). The discussion then moves to the household in which the tales are told, the setting being that of the extended family. This leads to explanations of polygamy, patrilineality, endogamy and patrilocality, which represent important social Palestinian themes in the tales, as when a polygamous situation signals conflict or when endogamy is shown to disrupt family unity. Patrilocality can be problematic, because when a woman marries outside her family her in-laws will always consider her a stranger. Muhawi and Kanaana's aim here is not to state that Palestinian society is polygamous or patrilineal, but mainly to show that these themes serve an educational function, especially given that children constitute the majority of the audience. The final parts of this section are dedicated to an outline of family structure and relationships. The analysis focuses on the role individuals play within the context of the family, rather than as individuals themselves. This involves a discussion of father–son, mother–daughter, sister–brother, husband–wife, sister–brother's wife and wife–mother-in-law relationships.

The following section, 'The Tales and Authority in Society' focuses on the interconnection between the teller and the tale itself from the perspective of authority. Three main elements of authority in Palestinian society are analysed by the compilers: age, gender and sexuality. Age and gender regulate individuals' behaviour. For instance, age commands respect and should command obedience to parental authority (Muhawi and Kanaana, 1989: 31). In terms of gender, old women's narration constitutes a form of authority; moreover, the social structure itself, which is the material for basic plot situations, provides models for the authority that regulates individual behaviour in the tales. Through respect for tradition and age, individuals are brought up to harmonize their will with that of the family. At the same time, undertaking or initiating an individual action that involves breaking the rules of the family and social norms 'is interpreted as an act of heroism' (Muhawi and Kanaana, 1989: 32). Finally, sexuality represents an important resource for power and authority in the tales. On the one hand, the tales reflect prevailing moral standards, but, on the other, they also articulate attitudes and practices which are in total contradiction to social norms. To explain the importance of sexuality as perceived in the tales, the compilers devote parts of this section to the role played by the Palestinian family and society in preserving what is considered as the foundation of a good reputation and honour. Within the domestic sphere, sexuality is closely connected to the family's honour and reputation, and families 'do restrict, channel, and control the sexual activity of their members' (Muhawi and Kanaana, 1989: 33). At the social level, 'the preservation is witnessed through the separation of sexes, which starts early in schools and social gatherings' (Muhawi and Kanaana, 1989: 33). This does not mean that denial or discreetness is the prevailing ethic in many of the tales. On the contrary, the role women play in the tales is more complex, active and influential than those of men. Men's portraits, however, 'are usually restricted to their social roles as sons, brothers, fathers and authority figures, whereas the women's are more complex' (Muhawi and Kanaana, 1989: 33).

Since most of the tales are told in villages, they portray a peasant society which relies heavily on agriculture. In the section on 'Food in Society and Tales', Muhawi and Kanaana explain that 'the cultivation, consumption, storage, sale and distribution of food are the family's primary concerns. Therefore, food plays an important role in the tales' (Muhawi and Kanaana, 1989: 37). Food is considered, for example, the basic motivator of action in all the *environment* tales, and it figures prominently in several others (Tales 1, 9, 14, 15, 27, 29, 34, 36 and 45; see below for the classification of the tales). Goods are the patriarch's belongings, and his permission must be sought before anything is given away. The patriarch's wife, on the other hand, is responsible for the food's distribution. Also food is associated in the tales with 'the expression of love in all its forms' (Muhawi and Kanaana, 1989: 37); for instance, the rituals of love are always accompanied by rituals of food, as in weddings. However, it can sometimes lead to envy, jealousy and conflict when not distributed equally to members of the extended family. At the social level, the giving and sharing of food 'symbolises hospitality and generosity' (Muhawi and Kanaana, 1989), though it can also trigger competition for social prestige among families, which take advantage of ceremonial occasions to earn recognition for their wealth. In fact, all stages of a person's life and those of the family, whether involving joy or mourning, are celebrated with the sharing of food. Muhawi and Kanaana thus conclude that food can be part of one's identity and sense of belonging.

To clarify the source of supernatural beliefs in the tales, the compilers explain in the section entitled 'Religion and the Supernatural' how in reality 'peasants in Palestine do not distinguish between official religion and its teaching on the one hand and the beliefs and superstitions of folk religion on the other' (Muhawi and Kanaana, 1989: 42). In fact, no clear distinction exists between the supernatural and that of everyday life. Supernatural forces take 'specific shapes in the form of *Jinn*, ghouls, giants, or other supernatural beings (e.g. Tales 5, 6, 8, 16, 17, 18, 19, 22, 29, 30, 32, 34, 35, 36, 37, 40)' (Muhawi and Kanaana, 1989: 44). At other times, they remain as an abstract force, like chance or predestination. Muhawi and Kanaana then discuss the influence of supernatural forces on the characters' actions in the tales. For example, there is the concept or motif of the journey, during which the characters have to go through many experiences until they achieve their goals. During this journey, 'actions are carried out, by the concretization of the non-material, the interpretation of the physical and the supernatural, the distinction between good and evil, and the balance of forces between them' (Muhawi and Kanaana, 1989: 47). Moreover, the notions of 'reward' and 'punishment' as aspects of daily life and the doctrine of predestination, the compilers explain, control the plot in most of the tales. Finally, the action is not necessarily physical but can be carried out through the medium of language, which 'becomes a silent "actor" in the drama of the tales' (Muhawi and Kanaana, 1989: 48). As I will discuss in more depth in the following chapters, the compilers' introduction is aimed at guiding the reader's understanding of the social and cultural infrastructure of Palestinian identity. Being comprehensive in addressing detailed aspects of Palestinian rural society, the introduction, I argue, highlights the scholarly nature of the endeavour carried out by the compilers.

Paratextual materials within the tales

The introduction is followed in the English collection by one and a half pages of 'Notes on Presentation and Translation'. Here, Muhawi and Kanaana explain briefly the logic behind the strategic decisions they made when translating the tales, taking into consideration issues of register and style. They discuss linguistic and stylistic considerations for dealing with oral performance, for example, arguing that 'literary oral narrative, when translated for print into another language, obviously undergoes in reality a process of double translation. The first is from one language to another, and the second is from one medium into another' (Muhawi and Kanaana, 1989; 1989: 51). Muhawi and Kanaana's aim is to provide their target readers with natural texts, which nevertheless follow the original very closely. In other words, there is little room for 'interpretive intrusions' since, according to them, the translation assumes that the tellers must tell their own tales. An attempt is made where possible to replicate the narrative rhythm and grammatical structure of the original, and also to avoid word-for-word translation (Muhawi and Kanaana, 1989: 52).

Unlike the English collection, where 'Notes on Presentation and Translation' is included after the Introduction, in the Arabic collection the introduction is followed by two 'presentations'.

The prefaces to the Arabic compilation Qul Ya Tayer

It is worth remembering here that the latter was published twelve years after the publication of the English collection in 1989. Because *SBSA* achieved popular and academic success among Western readers, scholars in anthropology and folklore studies, and Arab and Palestinian natives in the diaspora, the compilers decided to publish the folktales in their original language. This is unusual in that works are usually first published in the source language then translated into target languages. In my interview with Sharif Kanaana in 2012, I was curious to know the motive behind such a decision. Kanaana stated that both he and Muhawi were driven initially by a national desire to carry out the project, addressing a Western audience. The purpose, according to him, was to advocate the Palestinian cause, not politicize it, through a transparent reflection of Palestinian culture and society (see section 'Appendix 1'). The compilations might not contain explicit references to the political situation; however, the compilers are driven by political and national aims. When asked about the publication of the Arabic edition, Kanaana did not say if it was deliberately timed after the English one. However, following the publication of *Qul Ya Tayer* (2001), Kanaana was surprised by its popularity among Palestinians. 'I did not think that Palestinians needed a book like our project. However, ... I found out that both Arabs and Palestinians need them too.' The urge to 'read and tell' Palestinian folktales, particularly among Palestinians in the diaspora, is 'like a compensation of what Palestinians lost, it is a form of retrieving some of what they lost'. Since the Arabic edition addresses Arabs in general and Palestinians in particular, Muhawi and Kanaana provide two prefaces or 'presentations'. The first preface is *Taqdīm al-mū'lifīn lil ṭab'a al-'rabīa* (The Authors' Introduction to the Arabic Edition) by Muhawi and Kanaana, followed by *taqdīm al-ṭab'a al-'rabīa* (The Introduction of the Arabic Edition) by Ibrahim Muhawi and Jābir Sulaymān.[22]

Taqdīm al-mū'lifīn lil ṭab'a al-'rabīa *(The Authors' Introduction to the Arabic Edition)*

Muhawi and Kanaana first offer an account of the previous two publications of the same collection, that is, *SBSA* and a French translation published in 1997, based on the English compilation. Both compilers then move to highlight the motives behind their project. They firstly discuss the importance of preserving the Palestinian dialect which 'is one of the most important features of the identity of Palestinians' (Muhawi and Kanaana, 1989: xv). The fact that the tales in *Qul Ya Tayer* were not standardized but kept in Palestinian dialect is connected directly to the preservation of a distinct Palestinian identity. Many Palestinian folklorists, including Muhawi and Kanaana, aim to disprove Haim Gerber's claims concerning Arab vernaculars[23] since both have deliberately kept the tales in the Palestinian dialect, as orally told, then transcribed in their collection. According to both compilers, keeping the folktales in the Palestinian dialect has a national dimension by reconnecting the culture that those tales come from with both the Arab world and the world at large. Asked whether it was a deliberate choice to have less Palestinian dialect in the latest edition of *Qul Ya Tayer* published for children in 2010, Kanaana replied the following:

> To be honest, I was not happy with the new Arabic edition. The agreement with The Institute of Palestine Studies was that one page should be in the original Palestinian colloquial facing or opposite a simplified version in Modern Standard Arabic. However, the new edition has only one page with simplified MSA. I was very disappointed since the whole point was to reinforce the cultural bond Palestinians have through the Palestinian dialect. My aim was to keep the spirit of Palestinian culture and its identity through the telling of Palestinian folktales in Palestinian dialect! (Appendix 1)

Clearly, the whole aim, particularly with the latest simplified children's version of *Qul Ya Tayer*,[24] is to preserve the cultural identity of Palestinians manifested in their dialect. It is even more important in this case as the audience of the latest edition is the younger generation, who more than the older generation is in urgent need of a detailed portrait of their culture, language and history, especially if never experienced in reality. The importance of Palestinian dialect for future generations will be highlighted more below, since it is a recurrent theme in Muhawi and Kanaana's introduction.

Like Dundes, Muhawi and Kanaana explain in their introduction to the Arabic collection their aim of addressing two kinds of audience: ordinary and expert readers. Both categories, according to the compilers, will enjoy the content of folktales, even more so as the folktales are accompanied by detailed paratextual analysis. Each section of the analytical apparatus or paratextual element of the Arabic collection is then described in 'The Authors' Introduction to the Arabic Edition', namely, *Al-muqadima* (Introduction), *Al-ta 'qīb* (Afterword), *Al-ḥawashī* (Footnotes) and *Taḥlīl ' nmāṭ al-ḥikaya al-sh 'biya* (The Folkloristic Analysis). Because they shed light on the stories from different angles, the Introduction, according to Muhawi and Kanaana,

> aims at contextualising the stories within their cultural and social frame. It connects the art of storytelling to the social environment they aroused from. Moreover, it helps the reader to understand the hidden meanings of the tales as well as to be able to enjoy the tales in a literary way. (Muhawi and Kanaana, 2001: 18)

The footnotes have, according to Muhawi and Kanaana, ethnographic and linguistic purposes. By helping the reader to understand Palestinian culture, the footnotes play the role of explaining to the reader the nuances of meaning of many Palestinian words related to particular popular and cultural beliefs and traditions. The scientific or scholarly role of footnotes, in their view, will help experts in different fields, such as ethnography and anthropology, to analyse the cultural references. The explanation will help in elaborating and expanding research on particular traditions and rituals mentioned in the tales. Hence, more room is provided for a more elaborate ethnographic study. The Afterword, the explanatory section following every group of tales, explains the logic adopted by the authors in dividing the tales into groups. For Muhawi and Kanaana, the Afterwords aim to treat the tales as literary texts, relating them again to the social environment.

The final paratextual and most important scientific apparatus, according to the compilers, is the 'folkloristic analysis', as it has two essential dimensions: scientific and national. The scientific dimension is the adoption of the universal analysis of folktales in analysing the forty-five tales under study. The use of folkloristic analysis in *Qul Ya Tayer* is the first of its kind to be applied to Arabic folktale collections in general and Palestinian in particular. According to Muhawi and Kanaana, the use of the folkloristic analysis is a remarkable achievement in the field of folkloric studies in the Arab world. Since the current collection addresses 'ordinary as well as expert readers' (Muhawi and Kanaana, 2001: xvii) both Arabic and English collections have specific national aims. The first national aim is to provide readers with a comprehensive picture of Palestinian society, its traditions and culture. Secondly, as the English publication has succeeded in becoming a reference for teaching anthropology of the Middle East – its folklore, society and literature – in both the Arab world and English-speaking countries, the compilers want to duplicate the exemplary nature of the English publication in Arabic, targeting Arab students of anthropology.

The last national aim is seen in Muhawi and Kanaana's contribution to folkloristic analysis and the classification of folktales. Both compilers have followed Aarne and Thompson's types of the folktale, drawing on Thompson's motif index of folk literature[25] in order to produce a list of motifs relevant to the forty-five tales. Their effort aims to reveal the link between Palestinian heritage and Arab heritage and to link both to universal and human civilization. Being a positive and insightful model of analysis, Muhawi and Kanaana's approach was, a few years after the publication of *SBSA*, also adopted in Hasan El-Shamy's *Folktales of Egypt* (1995). The latter, according to Muhawi and Kanaana, relied on the *SBSA* folkloristic analysis in documenting the folktales and linking it to the Arab heritage. Aarne and Thompson's types and El-Shamy's research, however, have not yet been translated into Arabic. Thus, *Qul Ya Tayer* is the first collection in the Arab world to undertake scientific folkloristic analysis of tales in Arabic. In other words, Muhawi and Kanaana intend to see the Arabic publication become a reference for studying Palestinian folklore in Arabic and in Arab universities. The purpose in doing so is not only to preserve folktales for coming generations but also to reinforce and emphasize Arab self-determination and cultural cohesion.

Taqdīm al-ṭabʿa al-ʿrabīa *(Introduction of the Arabic Edition)*

The 'Introduction of the Arabic Edition' was written by Muhawi and Jābir Sulaymān, credited with translating and revising the Arabic collection. The introduction offers the reader background information about the different regional dialects in Palestine and the difference between Modern Standard Arabic (MSA) and the Palestinian dialect. The methods used to signal dialectal variation between, for instance, urban and rural accents in a number of tales are then explained. As in 'The Authors' Introduction to the Arabic Edition', Sulaymān and Muhawi reiterate the scholarly achievement and originality of having the 'Folkloristic Analysis' for the first time available in Arabic. It is vital, according to them, to write in Arabic in order to ensure that *Qul Ya Tayer* functions as an accessible scholarly reference that can be used by Arabs, whether students or scholars. More importantly, Sulaymān and Muhawi end their introduction of the Arabic edition by reinforcing the main objective of the project, the preservation of Palestinian collective memory and the highlighting of Palestinian cultural identity, particularly among future Palestinian generations, who endured occupation, diaspora and arbitrary attempts at uprooting their traditional society (Muhawi and Kanaana, 2001). Reviving collective memory and ensuring a cultural continuation, otherwise known as 'post-memory', as I will discuss, is an aim pursued by both ordinary Palestinians and intellectuals. As folklorists and intellectuals, Muhawi, Kanaana and Sulaymān devote their efforts not only to documenting Palestinian oral literature but also to establishing a bridge, a continuum allowing the re-emergence of Palestinian cultural memory, particularly if the aim is to also turn future Palestinian generations into active carriers of Palestinian folk literature, as their introduction says.

Afterword

Each group or sub-group of tales is followed by an 'Afterword' (*Al-t 'qīb*) in both collections. For example, the first group, *Individuals*, consists of eighteen tales divided into four sub-groups, namely, *Children and Parents, Siblings, Sexual Awakening and Courtship* and *The Quest for the Spouse*. Each of these sub-groups is followed by an afterword. According to Muhawi and Kanaana, the afterwords, which are similar in both collections, aim to explain the logic behind the tales' classification, drawing on literary criticism. The elaborate afterwords are used by the compilers to establish a link between the tales and social reality, the storytellers' imagination and culture. Indeed, the role of afterwords is described as one of establishing a bridge between fiction and reality, which is assumed by the compilers to exist.

Footnotes

Footnotes (*ḥḥwāshī*) in both volumes offer detailed cultural, ethnographic and linguistic explanations of specific words or expressions. The English collection features 412 footnotes, most of them clarifying cultural references related to modes of life in Palestine, customs and beliefs that might be unknown to the target reader. Framing the tales with footnotes, as will be seen in my analysis, aims at reinforcing the narrative of Palestinian collective and cultural memory. For example, the tale 'Lady Tatar' starts with the sentence: 'There were three sisters, and each of them had a hen.' A detailed footnote explaining the cultural connotations of the word 'hen' reads,

> In Palestinian villages families ordinarily raised animals in the yard. The mothers would designate a hen or two for each of her marriageable daughters so that they could sell their eggs to buy beads, thread, and other embroidery items in preparation for marriage. Because the hens were left to roam freely in the fields, when one was lost the girls would first search the abandoned wells for them. The villagers searched the wells for other lost animals and children. (Muhawi and Kanaana, 1989: 178)

The Arabic collection features more footnotes than the English one: a total of 440. The discrepancy in the number of footnotes may be explained by the fact that the tales in the Arabic volume are written in a mostly rural Palestinian dialect; hence it is necessary to add cultural explanations and linguistic clarifications in MSA. In 'Ghazale', Tale 17 in the section entitled 'Individuals', the Palestinian colloquial word for the verb 'to stare at' is *baḥara*, which is quite different from *am ʻana* in MSA (Muhawi and Kanaana, 2001: 141). Consequently, an Arab reader from Tunisia, for example, would need a linguistic explanation in MSA to be able to understand this verb. There are also discrepancies in the number of footnotes attached to individual tales. For instance, 'The Golden Pail' features seventeen footnotes in *SBSA* and twenty-six in *Qul Ya Tayer*.

Post-tales paratextual materials

Both collections feature a post-tale section of extensive 'Folkloristic Analysis' (*Taḥlīl al-ʼnmāṭ al-fulklūrya*), in which the English and Arabic titles of each tale are given, followed by the name and age of the teller and her or his place of residence. The tales are then identified according to type, following the Aarne–Thompson system of types of the folktale. Moreover, the compilers list Arabic parallels to the tales according to their geographic proximity to Palestine. As mentioned above, the 'Folkloristic Analysis' and Thompson's types are important in the sense that they link Palestinian heritage and folk tradition to a more universal heritage of orality within an academic frame. In the Appendices (*malāḥiq*), the English collection, unlike the Arabic one, includes a transliterated version of Tale 10 as the first appendix. Finally, both collections end with an 'Index of Folk Motifs' (*Fahras al-waḥadāt al-sardya*) which appears as Appendix B in the English collection and Appendix A in the Arabic.

The tales

The two collections, as mentioned, each consist of forty-five tales, which are divided into five groups: (1) Individuals, (2) Family, (3) Society, (4) Environment and (5) Universe. Unlike in previous Palestinian compilations, the compilers of both collections group the tales thematically, ordering them according to a pattern that reflects an individual's life cycle from childhood to old age.

The first and largest group of tales is included under 'Individuals'. The eighteen tales in this group are divided into four sub-categories: Children and Parents, Siblings, Sexual Awakening and Courtship and The Quest for the Spouse. The first five tales in 'Children and Parents' deal with different aspects of the relationship between parents and children, specifically highlighting 'the theme of individual freedom' (Muhawi and Kanaana, 1989: 82). The tales in this group reflect mother–son/daughter and father–daughter/son relationships, drawing on the emotional bonds, challenges and authority narratives within Palestinian families. The five tales under 'Siblings' focus on relationships among siblings in different contexts. Siblings of the same sex generally develop relationships characterized by conflict, competition and jealousy, as in the tales 'Half-a-Halfling' and 'Little Nightingale the Crier'. Other tales in the same category reveal the strong bond among siblings from the opposite sex, showing a prevailing relationship of love, tenderness and mutual cooperation (Muhawi and Kanaana, 1989: 110–12). In the 'Sexual Awakening and Courtship' sub-category, the predominant theme conveyed in all five tales is the importance and development of sexual desire prior to formal arrangements for marriage (Muhawi and Kanaana, 1989: 144). In 'The Little Bird', 'Sackcloth' and 'Jummez Bin Yazur, Chief of the Birds', the power that women possess through their sexuality is revealed. The last sub-category of 'Individuals' is The Quest for the Spouse. Unlike the previous set of tales, which deal with subjective emotions associated both with hidden and open desires towards the lover or the family, 'the three tales of this category explore the quest for a bride interplayed with social forces' (Muhawi and Kanaana, 1989: 168). In all three tales, the initiation of the quest is constrained by the Palestinian social system. The authority figure, which aims in Palestinian culture to preserve traditions and customs, is highlighted in these tales.

The second group of tales is categorized under 'Family'. The fourteen tales in this section are divided into three sub-categories: Brides and Bridegrooms, Husbands and Wives and Family Life. The whole group of tales 'explores the existing interaction, way of living and challenges between newly married couples in the extended family' (Muhawi and Kanaana, 1989: 203). The Brides and Bridegrooms sub-category deals mainly with the marriage relationship, focusing on new couples and the pressures they experience with respect to their choice of mate and their sexuality. The five tales in this sub-category explore forms of successful marriages, especially in the initial phases of the relationship. The first two tales focus on the problems that women face, whereas the third and fourth deal with the pressure faced by men (Muhawi and Kanaana, 1989: 204–5). Similar to Brides and Bridegrooms, Husbands and Wives, which consists of four tales, addresses issues revolving mainly around the theme of sexuality. The difference in this category, however, lies in Palestinian women being more open and explicit about their feelings in comparison to men. Moreover, the category addresses the relationship between husband and wife at a certain stage in the marriage, highlighting the causes of stagnation in a relationship, which, according to the compilers, often lies with the absence of children. Solution to the conflict lies in fulfilment realized through children in 'The Seven Leavenings', finding the right partner in 'The Golden Rod' or in a change in character (Muhawi and Kanaana, 1989: 228). The last category in the Family group of tales is Family Life. The five tales in this category treat conflicting loyalties among the extended family. The conflict, as described by Muhawi and Kanaana, usually centres on the male, whose position as the head of his own household or extended family requires dedication and a sense of responsibility (Muhawi and Kanaana, 1989: 249). It reveals the challenges the man faces when trying to balance between 'his conjugal and natal family' (Muhawi and Kanaana, 1989: 250).

The section entitled 'Society' includes only five tales, which focus on the relationship between the individual and society. The tales feature a broader zone of interaction in which family bonds and obligations do not control the plot or actions. According to the compilers, 'the notions of collectivity and harmonious unity are predominant themes, manifested in people's values of helping those in distress and neighbors' (Muhawi and Kanaana, 1989: 277). But this group also shows how disorder can arise when individuals attract envy and negative forces because of their children or wealth, which are sources of envy in Palestinian society. The group entitled 'Environment' consists of four tales, 'The Little She-Goat', 'The Old Woman and Her Cat', 'Dunglet' and 'The Louse'. This group is quite different from the previous ones since it does not reflect Palestinian social reality in the same way the other tales do. Rather, the tales serve 'an analogical function and as models of that reality' (Muhawi and Kanaana, 1989: 290). According to Muhawi and Kanaana, the tales are a 'reflection of the existing harmonious interdependence and connection between the individuals and their environment, both animate and inanimate' (Muhawi and Kanaana, 1989: 290). Themes of collaboration and support prevail in these tales, symbolizing and promoting values of collectivity, and solidarity among Palestinians. The last group is Universe, a theme that transcends the familial, societal and physical environment. The four tales in this group deal with 'the relationship between the human and the divine; a relationship based on the acceptance of the will of God' (Muhawi and Kanaana, 1989: 324). The tales in the group address the way Palestinian society perceives folk religion and official religion. Moreover the tales highlight the notion of wisdom and its difference between Palestinian men and women. Wisdom is shown to be acquired through self-acceptance and understanding the forces of life and social constraints. Fate can be also a source of reward or punishment.

3

Palestinian Women and the Preservation of Memory in Palestinian Folktales

Given the ongoing Palestinian struggle, traumatic experiences are not just lived and experienced once within a specific time frame and generation; rather, their effect can persist, be transmitted and documented. Trauma, as discussed previously, can take different shapes and even create a source of regeneration in an attempt to reconcile the past with present, which can be seen in literature or cinema. The main question posed is how folktales can transcend, then transform, the trauma of the *Nakba* into 'a narrative of continuity' (Jayyusi, 2007) and into a revived cultural identity. At this point, it is important to think of the agents who not only witnessed the historical and political transformation of Palestine but, most importantly, have lived through social and cultural developments across three generations. The agents, in this case Palestinian women, I argue, represent credible and powerful sources for preserving as well as transmitting Palestinian memory and identity. In *SBSA*, the folklorists used the medium of literature, specifically folktales, to explore, study and document Palestinian social reality and culture. Indeed, 'they have discussed the dynamic and dialectical relationship between Palestinian society and the tales' (Peters, 1991: 441). This is true; however, their discussion would have been relatively impoverished without Palestinian women's position as storytellers in reality and protagonists in the folktales.

It is women's voices as mothers, daughters, sisters and wives in the folktales which, I think, merge memory, identity and history with their personal narratives and private spheres. Hence I intend to look at narratives of Palestinian women within their families as mothers, sisters and wives. The discussion focuses on a selection of folktales where the roles of Palestinian women reveal a resilient discourse of strength, continuity and heritage. Through the voices of Palestinian women, Palestinian collective memory and cultural identity gain momentum, disclosing women's narrative of home and family interaction as well as social criticism. Through storytelling and roles in the folktales, the division of roles – as mothers, sisters or wives – plays an important part in informing both the reader and the folklorist about the origins of traditions and beliefs, highlighting Palestinian family rules and desires, and most importantly cultural habits or rituals among family members, which are at stake because of political upheavals. Hence, in order to understand Palestinian social dynamics, it is important to look at the roles of Palestinian women and narratives within the family, merging their positions as storytellers in reality with their projected roles in the folktales.

Because folktales express the popular voice of a group, community and society, as discussed in the first chapter, Palestinian folktales can be a source for understanding social traditions, structures and interactions. As observed by a number of Palestinian folklorists and anthropologists, such as Al-Sarīsī (2004), Al-Jawāhirī (1979) and Al-Khalīlī (1977), Palestinian folktales reveal customs, rituals and marriage traditions, among other rural and urban social practices, which I will expand on when I discuss marriage and sexuality. Like other forms of narrative, folktales 'thrive on conflict and its resolution' (Muhawi and Kanaana, 1989: 13), which originate from real social milieux; thus 'tellers don't have to invent situations of conflict' (Muhawi and Kanaana, 1989). Similarly, Palestinian colloquial language, 'with all its expressive potentials, is seen in the linguistic environment' (Muhawi and Kanaana, 1989). The similarity in the ways themes and language are derived from a vivid reality emphasizes the survival of social and linguistic identity. Hence the plots, themes and language are rooted in present social and family structures. The kinship system, which is explained extensively in the compilers' introduction, helps the reader to understand themes of conflict and harmony in Palestinian folktales. Moreover, it helps to define social position, roles and modes of interaction:

> The family occurs in all the tales without exception, either as theme or as background. And because our concern is to explore the relationship between the tales and the culture, we must examine the whole system of family relationships in order to provide the necessary cultural background to the tales. We thus avoid the pitfall of looking at the tales as mere reflectors

of the culture but rather see them as aesthetic transformations – miniature portraits of an existing social reality. (Muhawi and Kanaana, 1989: 20)

Since family relationships constitute the core of Palestinian culture, Palestinian mothers, who represent the majority of storytellers in the present compilation, use language and plot in order to portray their roles in the family and society, reinforcing Palestinian cultural identity as well as collective memory. For instance, if we look at the titles of the majority of tales in *SBSA* and *Qul Ya Tayer*, we notice 'the prevalence of grammatically feminine titles, many of which are women's names (Tales 3, 13, 17, 18, 20, 26, 27, 31, 33, 42, 45),[1] and even those that do not have feminine titles, such as Tales 14 and 43 ("Sackcloth" and "The Rich Man and the Poor Man"), have women as the major characters' (Muhawi and Kanaana, 1989: 18). Because most of the storytellers are women, the tales express women's insights, thoughts and desires; in short, the tales reveal their inner world and narrative:

> Women's personal narratives ... illuminate the significance of the intersection of individual life and historical moment; they address the importance of frameworks of meaning through which women orient themselves in the world. (Personal Narrative Group, 1989: 22–3)

To understand how Palestinian collective memory is both gendered and engendered by women within the Palestinian family, the following discussion will be divided into five parts, namely: mother–daughter narrative, mother–son narrative, sibling narrative, courtship/sexual awakening and marriage narratives. Palestinian women's narrative, as I will examine, is not only descriptive of their social positions or roles but can also be critical of some social norms and cultural attitudes. Their narrative, can also be educational, targeting younger Palestinian generations in order to reinforce in them social integrity, identity and culture. Their voice through the folktales is embedded with a mix of personal, cultural, historical and national narratives.

Mother–daughter narrative

The role of mothers is important in Palestinian society because they control the dynamics of the whole family, including, particularly before 1948, the extended family: hence mothers were and are still considered to be influential familial figures, who not only control many household matters but are also shaping the power relations in the family and are acting as mediator between the father and other members of the family. The popularity of the first tale in *SBSA*, 'Tunjur, Tunjur' (*Ṭunjur Ṭunjur*) among Palestinians stems from its representation of the strong bond between mother and daughter. The tale emphasizes an important theme, the importance of having children in Palestinian society; this is because children are considered a source of economic stability as well as security for the family. 'Tunjur, Tunjur' starts with the mother who is sad because she has not borne children. Consequently, she keeps praying to have a daughter, even if it were a cooking pot. The mother's wish is fulfilled, and she gives birth to a cooking pot, which is feminine in Arabic (*ṭunjara*). Tunjur continually leaves the house in order to bring all kind of goods to her mother. The daughter, according to the compilers, demonstrates the economic value of children for the Palestinian family. In the absence of the father, the daughter, in spite of her appearance, has a duty towards her mother to get food and money. The tale shows how children in Palestinian society provide financial support to their elderly parents; it is in fact their duty to help their parents:

> In addition to the emotional bonds that hold mother and daughter together, an economic motive is operating in the tale as well. The mother's initial wish is not only for a daughter but also for a source of income, and her willingness to let her daughter out of the house is conditioned by her poverty. (Muhawi and Kanaana, 1989: 82)

There is also an important emotional and cultural aspect behind the mother's wish, following a Palestinian cultural belief as evinced by 'Palestinian sayings, confirming appreciation – for example, "Girls are kind" *Il banāt ḥanāyin* and "Daughters will help you [literally, 'you will find them'] in your old age; they will take pity on you" *Il banāt bitlāqīhin bikabarak, byshfaqū 'līk*' (Muhawi and Kanaana, 1989: 21). The mother–daughter relationship in Palestinian society is based on strong emotional bonds, trust and understanding. Daughters are expected to be affectionate and kind with their parents, especially mothers. The daughter Tunjur symbolizes a daughter's dedication, attention and love in making her parents comfortable and cared for. Daughters are also initiators of action, looking for food or income to help the mother. The assumption here is that the mother of Tunjur is a single mother, hence the girl's freedom in leaving the house is 'intertwined with that of economic necessity' (Muhawi and Kanaana, 1989: 82). The freedom granted to the daughter in 'Tunjur, Tunjur' can be morally ambiguous by conservative rural Palestinian standards. It would have been different and more difficult to have this kind of freedom had the daughter had brothers, as the compilers explain in the foreword. The folktale, among many others, introduces the plot and roles under the frame of Palestinian cultural identity, which is transmitted via the language used by the storytellers.

The interconnection between language, plot and the position of the storyteller in 'Tunjur, Tunjur' is also significant. Upon realizing that Tunjur brought treasure to her mother and not the usual food, the mother became annoyed and surprised at the same time. The mother realizes that her daughter's freedom can be risky since she is getting into the habit of taking other people's belongings to satisfy the mother economically. Here the voice of the storyteller is merged with the voice of *Tunjur*'s mother, saying,

> 'Yee! *May your reputation be blackened!*' يي يا مشحرة!' منين هاظ جبتيه؟
> She cried out. 'Wherever did you get   (Muhawi and Kanaana, 2001: 68)
> this?' (Muhawi and Kanaana, 1989: 59;
> italics for emphasis)

The mother's reproach stands for her worry for her daughter's reputation; her freedom is not acceptable in a conservative village. Being upset, she reproaches her daughter using a very common expression among Palestinian women only. The expression 'May your reputation be blackened!' (*Yī ya mshaḥara*) the compilers deemed important to explain in a footnote, saying,

> *Ya mshahara* – literally, 'O you who smeared herself with soot!' is a popular expression used among Palestinian women in order to reinforce a specific storytelling style attributed to Palestinian women. A woman blackens her face as a sign of mourning when someone dear dies. Hence, metaphorically when a woman does something she is not supposed to do, her honour dies and her reputation becomes black. The expression, however, need not always carry connotations of ominous wrongdoing; it is frequently used, as in the present context, as a form of mild reproach. (Muhawi and Kanaana, 1989: 59)

The dramatic situation created by Tunjur led the storyteller to use the power of language in order to authenticate the role of the mother as well as to add a stronger effect. The framing of this particular expression by the compilers serves two functions. On the one hand, it empowers the narrative of Palestinian women storytellers, attributing the art of storytelling to them. On the other hand, the reader, particularly the non-Palestinian, realizes the fears of a Palestinian mother over the reputation of her daughter in a rural pre- and/or post-*Nakba* environment. The roles of mother and daughter and their interaction in 'Tunjur, Tunjur', I argue, are inseparable to Palestinian cultural and social identity, which the *Nakba* narrative constitutes an important part:

> They [*Nakba* memories] focus on the family and the domestic space of home. Since caring for the family has been the primary role of Palestinian women, their memories of the *Nakba* are often inseparable from family life and their identity as daughters or mothers. (Humphries and Khalili, 2007: 219)

The whole tale revolves around the mother and her daughter Tunjur within a Palestinian domestic setting. Even when the daughter is out searching for goods, such as honey (*'sal*), meat (*laḥma*) and the bride's jewellery (*sīgha*), the storyteller shapes the plot based on Palestinian domesticity, to which a rural[2] Palestinian mother would relate to. Not only does the storyteller shape the plot of the story, but she uses language to empower her authority as a storyteller as well as to trigger a sense of collectivity among the audience. For instance, the first time Tunjur is found by a passer-by, he shouts, saying,

'Eh!' He exclaimed, 'who has put this pot in the middle of the path? *I'll be damned*! What a beautiful pot! It's probably made of silver. (Muhawi and Kanaana, 1989: 56; italics for emphasis)	إه! مين حاططها هاي بنص الدرب؟ يخرب بيت هالطنجرة ما أشلبها! كنها فضّة! (Muhawi and Kanaana, 2001: 66)

Using a phrase used to express surprise and disbelief in Palestinian dialect, the passer-by said *ykhrib bayt*, which literally means 'may a house be ruined' and idiomatically the equivalent of 'damn it' in English. The phrase in the folktale is translated as 'I will be damned' is not used in an insulting way but added in this context to dramatize the flow of narration by the storyteller. Being usually used by Palestinian women, the compilers have added a footnote to the Arabic compilation but not to the English one, explaining that 'since the use of such phrases is most of the time attributed to women, it endows the folktale with a distinctive narration style not suitable for men' (Muhawi and Kanaana, 2001: 66).

Another device used by the storyteller, that of interrupting the flow of narrative, to express surprise and 'alert the listeners that something out of the ordinary is about to occur' (Muhawi and Kanaana, 1989: 55), is the use of the word 'behold' in English, *wuīla* in Palestinian dialect:

| A day came and a day went, and behold! She [the mother] was ready to deliver. (Ibid.) | روح يا يوم تع يا يوم و الّا هي صارت بدها تجيب. (Muhawi and Kanaana, 2001: 65) |

The fact that the folktales contain such devices or phrases of surprise not only contributes, in my opinion, to enriching the narrative style and flow but also serves to emphasize the linguistic identity of Palestinian women and their culture, specifically the Palestinian dialect, which needs to be preserved from one generation to the next. As will become apparent in the coming sections, Palestinian storytelling via women's agency aims at highlighting also 'the importance of the social aspect of oral tradition, in which listening to and watching the teller and reacting collectively cannot be recorded' (Barhoum, 1990: 71). The experience of storytelling, as one can see, is rich and interactive, maintaining shared experiences among listeners and storytellers. As Brand (2009) notes in her discussion of women's discourse of collective memory, the voice of collectivity starts with women's accounts of narrative style in rural pre-*Nakba* Palestine. 'It begins idyllically with such words as "hand in hand", "together" and "closer", stressing the strong community atmosphere' (Brand, 2009: 178).

In 'The Cricket' (*Al-khunfusa*), the mother plays an important role in her daughter's marriage. She advises her daughter to choose the most suitable partner, revealing the degree of love and trust the daughter feels for her mother, which is a natural reflection of the trust and reliance mothers and daughters share in Palestinian society. 'The Cricket' also reveals the degree of wisdom and experience that mothers have in life, giving them the credibility to be consulted by both son and daughter. The tale shows a harmonious and affectionate relationship between a mother and her daughter, who, no matter what she looks like, will always be loved and protected by her mother. Motherly love can be seen as a universal theme in the majority of folktales; the distinction in this case lies in grounding the love and image of motherhood within Palestinian culture and according to Palestinian beliefs about the family institution.

The love and advice extended by the mother to her daughter, I argue, is related to the position of the storyteller in reality. The majority of storytellers in *SBSA* were over sixty years old when the tales were recorded, and in Palestinian society such women are regarded as being endowed with experience and excellent skills of narration. Palestinian women, in their maturity, are at the apogee of their authority in the society, as perceived by the society. Having been through a complete cycle of life, often within extended families, Palestinian women are regarded as very good teachers in terms of experience, knowledge and advice. Furthermore, in Palestine older women are often seen as being able to see through hypocrisy, making them particularly able to create stories that critique society. Storytelling for Palestinian women is also a form of expressing authority and extending wisdom to younger generations:

> The tales are themselves empowering and constitute a form of authority for the old women who narrate them. The narrative style and method used draw their authenticity from the rules and conventions handed down by the Palestinian tradition in folk narrative. Similarly, the individual tellers, who already enjoy social authority through their special position as old women, derive moral authority from the tradition, which serves to validate the act of narrating the tales to the young, thereby providing them with *heroic models for behaviour*. (Muhawi and Kanaana, 1989: 29, italics added for emphasis)

Older Palestinian women, mothers and grandmothers, are not only seen as reliable sources of narration due to their maturity and experience but also perceived as examples to be followed by younger generations, who consider their mothers or grandmothers as inspirational and *heroic models for behaviour*. The parallels and extension of roles between the mothers in 'Tunjur, Tunjur' or 'The Cricket' and the storytellers in reality are their sharing of cultural identity and social structure. The latter supplies material for basic plots and also provides models for the authority that regulates individual behaviour in the tales. Gender and age create a form of authority for women heroines as well as storytellers. The authority position that Palestinian women are endowed with controls behaviour in the family; knowing how it works helps the reader to understand the plot of the tale as well as reinforcing the sense of belonging and identity extended to younger generations.

As individual identity is partly constituted through 'acquired identifications, values, norms, ideals, models and heroes' (Ricoeur, 1990: 46), the younger Palestinian generation would identify with and relate to the national role of storytellers as well as seeing themselves in the characters of most of the tales. Spreading pre-*Nakba* culture, symbolized in the harmonious family structure and roles found in the tales, is a national duty perceived by many women storytellers. The latter become national symbols through an active fusion between memory and history. The past and its setting, as I discuss in more depth below, constitute sites of memory, giving rise to Palestinian national and cultural identity. Symbols, past periods or heroes become a repository from which not only a unified collective memory can be regenerated but also a collective national aspiration to safeguard cultural identity. Given the role of mothers in Palestinian families, I have briefly discussed the daughter–mother interaction in some tales, showing how significant their relationship is to understanding cultural traditions, social roles and even fears. To gain a broader understanding, it will be important to look at the mother–son relationship, which will reveal other aspects of Palestinian cultural identity.

Mother–son narrative

The mother–son relationship is prevalent in many of the tales, such as 'The Woman Who Married Her Son' (*Ilī tzawajat ibinhā*) and 'Shwesh, Shwesh!' (*Shwish shwish*). This type of relationship is remarkably strong but complex in Palestinian society. In 'The Woman Who Married Her Son', the tale revolves around the mother–son relationship and the jealousy created once the son gets married.[3] The conflict arises when the son replaces his mother's attention and protection with that of his wife. In a patrilocal extended family, 'when the son marries, both mother and daughter-in-law have difficulties' (Muhawi and Kanaana, 1989: 82) adapting to the new changes. It is the mother's possessiveness and control which lead her to get rid of the wife so that she can be both mother and wife to her own son. In spite of the dramatic plot, the language used by the storyteller invites the reader to enjoy the authentic sense of Palestinian cultural identity through poetic language. As an example, when the wife took refuge at the neighbours' house, the mother (disguised as wife) was pregnant and so sends her servant to ask the neighbours for sour grapes. The real wife, sad and upset, answers the servant as follows:

| My mother gave birth to me in the wilderness, and over me birds have built their nests. The king's son has taken his mother to wife, and now wants to satisfy her craving at my expense! Come down, O scissors, and cut out his tongue, lest he betray my secret! (Muhawi and Kanaana, 1989: 61) | أنا أمي ولدتني في البرية   و الطيور عششت عليه
و ابن السلطان يوخد امه   و يحكم وحامه عليه
طيح يا مقص قص لسانه   قبل ما يكذب عليه
(Muhawi and Kanaana, 2001: 70) |

Disputes between daughter-in-law and mother-in-law are common in many societies. In the Palestinian case, particularly in Palestinian popular culture and oral literature, the distinctiveness lies in the artistic and linguistic form of expressing the conflict. The poetic pattern used is known as *Zajal*, a popular form of rhymed poetry based on improvisation and use of Palestinian dialect. The art of *Zajal*, according to Asadi, 'characterises the language of a Palestinian mother, the language of the land and heritage; it carries Palestinians' hopes, pains, aspirations and dreams' (Al-Asʿadī, 2008). *Zajal* not only is attributed to women and mothers in particular but also has the power to transform the plot and themes in this tale into a cultural representation of a national heritage. It is an art that transmits a collective, national and cultural specificity into the memory of the reader and listener, as well as nurture memory across younger generations, particularly the post-*Nakba* generations.

Because time and memory are interconnected, the passing of time can create memories but can also lead to forgetfulness, nurture nostalgia and threaten distortion. In this regard, the pre-1948 generation is threatened with being forgotten and erased from present generations' memories, which is especially significant given that this generation bears the memories, stories, history and life of a very specific phase, referred to among Palestinians as 'the days of the lost paradise'. To avoid the fear of amnesia growing in the Palestinian context, playwrights, novelists, poets and folklorists are urged to make the effort to register, record, film, store and document Palestinian collective memory. Some Palestinian intellectuals rely on using, for instance, the device of storytelling in novels, plays or films. This device, as we see with Palestinian women storytellers, helps to bridge the gap between two phases and/or generations. The link between pre- and post-1948 in the Palestinian case is maintained through what is referred to by Sa'di and Abu-Lughod (2007: 19) as 'generational time':

> Yet in time-reckoning, the *Nakba* has embodied an unbridgeable gap between two qualitatively different periods: pre and post *Nakba*, often experienced as generational difference. Generational time is a key dimension of memory for Palestinians. There are processes of transfer from one generation to another – of stories, memories, foods, and anger; there is inheritance of the identity and burden; but there is also some resistance across the generations to the great significance of the past.

Because traumatic experiences and catastrophe tend to break the flow and transmission of memories, individuals are threatened by the loss of identity and sense of belonging. Their link with the past, represented in archives, possessions, records and artefacts, could be destroyed. In other words, the continuity of normal transmission between the individual, family, community and cultural heritage is disrupted and broken. To counter this fracturing of memory transfer and to preserve a continuum of transmission, second and third generations play the role of nourishing post-memory[4] work in order to process the experience of the first generation and to mend and reactivate the damaged memorial structures. Post-memory can be useful in understanding how pre-*Nakba* and post-*Nakba* generations communicate their griefs, hopes and memories, as post-memory is distinguished from memory by 'generational distance and from history by deep personal connection' (Hirsch, 1997: 22). In other words, memory is more connected to the past; nonetheless, it can be mediated. 'Postmemorial work strives to reactivate and re-embody more distant social/national and archival/cultural memorial structures by reinvesting them with resonant individual and familial forms of mediation and aesthetic expression' (Hirsch, 2008: 112). Storytelling could be in this case a form of 'aesthetic expression' mediating between present and past; it is 'a structure of inter- and trans-generational transmission' (Hirsch, 2008: 111).

The manifestation of prosthetic memory and post-memory are seen within different modes of representation, particularly cinematic and literary. Alison Landsberg sees the reproduction as a positive development, arguing that 'the mimetic, bodily experience of the historical past afforded by the mass media can make particular histories or pasts available to people across existing stratifications of race, class, gender, and generation' (Landsberg, 2004: 19). Drawing on Landsberg's explanation, we see that Palestinian cinema and film production, for instance, are influenced by the practice of storytelling of the *Nakba*. Even the structure of the films is deeply affected by the storytelling function. In his article on 'The Continuity of Trauma and Struggle', Haim Bresheeth discusses the use of storytelling in some Palestinian films as 'an Ethnotopic device'. He argues that storytelling, in the films he analyses, not only functions as a device for delivering historical detail and personal memory but also 'revive[s] and reclaim[s] for Palestinian memory ... constructing a possible space for national and individual existence and identity today' (Bresheeth, 2007: 165). When asked about the rationale for telling a political story as a myth in the Palestinian film *Ustura* (Myth), the director, Nizar Hassan relates it to his own childhood and to the important role his mother played in strengthening his sense of belonging and identity through her stories.[5]

Hassan's use of storytelling both in his own reality and in fictional film production helps to underline the importance of storytelling in Palestinian society, as an expression of continuation, existence and affirmation, using mass media in this case as a prosthetic medium for transmission and identification. One can argue that storytelling forges the individual, family and society into a wider national spectrum. In other words, the story translates a person's vision and identity as a part of a larger unit. The story of family meets and overlaps with the story of nation; hence, it represents in the Palestinian context the anchor for both personal and national identity. In the instance of Hassan, for example, post-memory is seen as a residual type of memory, a recollection of an event or a past not personally experienced but socially felt. Moreover, since we are discussing the narrative of mother and son in the folktales, one can deduce the importance and credibility of the mother figure, particularly of the first generation, in connecting and affirming subsequent generations' communal, collective and social identities.[6] By reinforcing the distinctiveness and longevity of Palestinian culture and history, Palestinian women secure a transition for Palestinian cultural memory over generations:

> Indeed, the very survival of the tales as a tradition with a recognizable narrative structure, a coherent moral universe, and a set of assumptions immediately understandable to audience and narrator alike confirms the cultural continuity of Palestinian social life. (Muhawi and Kanaana, 1989: 12)

Women's role and narrative, whether as storytellers or heroines, empower pre-*Nakba* history, social structure and cultural traditions. Nationally speaking, their narrative is a form of resistance against oblivion and change since they represent a model of wisdom for younger generations to follow and respect. Artistically speaking, the popularity of Palestinian folktales is attributed to women's developed storytelling style, which men learn and duplicate:

> The Palestinian folktale is a highly developed art form. Its style, though not artificial, follows linguistic and literary conventions that set it apart from other folk narrative genres. It relies on verbal mannerisms and language flourishes not used in ordinary conversation, especially by men. Women were largely responsible for developing this style, and they carry on the tradition. To sound credible, men who tell these tales must adopt the narrative style of women. (Muhawi and Kanaana, 1989: 3)

Having only three male storytellers out of seventeen in the present collection, female storytellers rely more on linguistic expression than epic stories. Palestinian men usually prefer epic stories in the diwan, which differs in the manner of delivery as men tend to use physical movement while women use certain stylistic features, which give the tales their particular character. Women's speech is direct and earthy, and Palestinian women are considered to be reliable observers of their society since there is an immediate connection with their own lives and the overall social structure. Age also constitutes an important consideration. Palestinian women narrators gain credibility through old age, which is considered to be marked by wisdom and trust.

In their introduction, the compilers establish a distinction between 'passive' and 'active' storytellers. The former 'is someone who doesn't normally tell tales, nor is he/she known in the village as a teller' whereas the latter 'is one of four or five in any village community who show an intense personal interest in preserving and transmitting the practice of tale telling' (Muhawi and Kanaana,

1989: 9–10). The way this division is made endows Palestinian women storytellers with a level of responsibility and the position to carry the tradition from one generation to another, despite being uneducated.

Mother–son narrative in the folktales seems to be dependent on the mothers' authority over the son's marriage in Palestinian society. The son's choice for a bride is dependent on the mother's choice and opinion, as it is the case in 'Shoqak Boqak!' (*Shūqak būqak*). In this tale both sister and mother play an important role in finding a suitable wife for the son, even providing him with a critique of his wife-to-be. The mother and sister's control of the situation can arise partly because of the degree of social and gender separation in villages. And because of the strong matriarchal role enjoyed by a Palestinian mother in her extended family, the bride has to gain her full approval and satisfaction. In 'Shoqak Boqak!' the following dialogue reveals the agreement between the son and his mother over finding a bride:

He said: 'You must look for a bride for me whose face is like blood on the snow.'	قالها:' بدي تدوريلي على عروس يكون وجهها مثل دم عالثلج.'
...	...
Rushing home, she said to him, 'Son, what a bride I've found for you! In all my life I've never seen anything like her.'	روّحت قالت لابنها: 'يمّا شو لاقيتلك عروس! بعدني بتاريخ حياتي ما شفت مثلها.'
(Muhawi and Kanaana, 1989: 182)	(Muhawi and Kanaana, 2001: 167)

In rural areas the custom still persists today that the mother is the one who searches for a bride, checks on her, proposes and may even test her, as in 'Jummez Bin Yazur' (*Jūmiz bin yazūr, shaykh al-ṭuyūr*). In this tale, the mother asks the bride to thread a needle (to test her eyesight) and crack a nut with her teeth (to test her strength). Although shown in an exaggerated way, these trials persist to some extent in some conservative rural areas in Palestine. In both tales, the reader is shown a number of real elements from Palestinian social and cultural habits. As mentioned before, mothers extend their role through the authority granted to them by the society and family. As Hilma Granqvist (1931, 1935) observed while analysing the status of Palestinian women in villages, mothers and sisters usually try to find a bride for their son/brother who is also from their own extended family. In this way, the bride will be considered as an insider.

Remaining within the fusion of mother and storyteller narrative, 'Shwesh, Shwesh!' (*Shwish shwish*) takes a different angle on mother–son relationships in Palestinian society. In this folktale, the mother tries to break free from her role because she wants to remarry. The son is not pleased with this and decides to punish her. In Palestinian society, mothers over the age of fifty are expected to dedicate their full attention to their sons and daughters, especially if the father is away or dead. This tale shows how mothers in Palestinian society represent symbols of sacrifice and dedication to their offspring. The fact that the mother in 'Shwesh, Shwesh!' wants to think of herself and choose a new man is culturally unacceptable, particularly in rural Palestine. The narrative of the mother, nonetheless, is ambivalent. On the one hand, 'the mother seems to have achieved what all women are supposed to dream about: loving and obedient sons and grandchildren and dutiful daughters-in-law' (Muhawi and Kanaana, 1989: 67, footnote). The footnote follows this part in the tale:

> His (the son's) wives organised themselves so that one of them was always rocking her while another was doing the work. His mother spent all her time in the hammock, and his wives were always rocking her. (Muhawi and Kanaana, 1989: 66)

The image depicted by the storyteller could reveal to some extent the inner desire of a Palestinian single mother, who within a particular social, polygamous and rural environment (before 1948) could have enjoyed this ideal situation. On the other hand, the storyteller's narrative shows the social restrictions on women who are past childbearing age and who are not allowed to act on their sexual desires. The narrative of Palestinian women in this tale relates to the tension between her desires and social expectations and duties.

An important question raised by the compilers in their introduction, on whether women are indulging in fantasy or wish-fulfilment, is worth looking at, particularly within the gender differences and restrictions imposed by some social beliefs in the Middle East. According to the compilers, the pertinence of fiction and fantasy in folktales does not deny that the tales present a portrait of the culture, and that in spite of gender and social constraints, Palestinian women are endowed with a level of objectivity, wisdom and authority. I think that Palestinian women storytellers mirror their society with its worst and best aspects, regardless of whether they are indulging in fantasy or wish-fulfilment. They are active observers who weave plots for the folktales from their day-to-day life experience. As noted earlier, Palestinian women's roles are continuously manifested through artistic and literary representations. Even if they suffer from lack of public presence or from patriarchal kinship restrictions, Palestinian women try their best to define their roles in society themselves without seeking male input, and this can be seen throughout the tales. James Scott's notion of the 'hidden power' or 'resistance' (Scott, 1985) among peasants can be relevant when referring to Palestinian rural women's form of power. According to Scott, who opposes Gramsci's idea of hegemony,[7] peasant and slave societies use cultural forms of resistance rather than political forms of rebellion. Indeed, forms of power do not have to be manifested within a public sphere but can be better expressed through art and orality for Palestinian rural women,

> and in other forms of folklore that in Palestine are traditionally their domain: embroidery, basket weaving, pot making, and verbal arts like wedding songs and laments for the dead. Women provide a large measure of the creative and artistic energy in the society, as these folktales amply demonstrate. (Muhawi and Kanaana, 1989: 19)

I would further argue that women's role in preserving the transmission of Palestinian popular and oral culture, whether as contributors to folkloric activities or as active carriers of Palestinian storytelling, is a form of narrating Palestinian collective memory in a social, rather than political, story. As Hanita Brand (2007) argues in her article 'Palestinian Women and Collective Memory', Palestinian women's way of expressing collective memory reflects their roles, aspirations and efforts within the Palestinian social institution. Storytelling, in fact, acts as a compensation for what Palestinians lost; it is a form of retrieving their past. Storytelling can even be seen as a prosthetic device,[8] through which Palestinian memory is revived and reclaimed through 'constructing a possible space for national and individual existence and identity today' (Landsberg, 2004: 18). Prosthetic memory can be seen as the medium between historical events and our personal experiences, the replaced missing link between the first and second generation. Combining as it does personal and historical narratives in an 'experiential site',⁹ I argue that prosthetic memory could be manifested in women's storytelling. The latter, I think, is not just a means to reinforce group identity and pass on memories; it also enables, as Landsberg explains, 'the transmission of memories to people who have no "natural" or biological claims to them' (Landsberg, 2004).

Despite the traumatic and unstable political situation, which still exists today, Palestinian cultural structures have developed over generations and thus cannot simply disappear. Some changes have taken place, no doubt, but the main markers of behaviour and cultural norms are still present in their social milieu, which need to be passed on from one generation to the other. Here the voice of Palestinian women becomes very important, turning the political narrative of cultural and collective memory into a social one. I would further argue that Palestinian women confirm the pertinence of social and cultural values in the tales, which exist in a context of strong familial, social and cultural integration among Palestinians:

> The tales assume a stable social order, which no doubt characterized Palestinian society for hundreds of years before the advent of the British Mandate in the early 1920s; the current situation for most Palestinians, however, is one of Diaspora and exile, requiring adaptation and cultural change. This is not to say that the cultural assumptions informing the tales and those prevailing in modern Palestinian society have been severed. Ideals of behaviour that have developed through the institutions of the culture over countless generations do not simply vanish overnight. (Muhawi and Kanaana, 1989: 12)

Although the ideals of behaviour are persistent, the tales are not simply mere reflectors. The tales, through women's narrative, are rather a representation of family reality, interaction and cultural existence throughout different generations. For instance, women's narrative of authority in choosing their sons' brides, as I discussed in 'Shoqak, Boqak!', or mothers' vulnerability to their sons' opposition to remarriage as in 'Shwesh, Shwesh!' among other examples, highlight the role played by women storytellers in transforming Palestinian narrative of memory from the political into the social. The transformation happens through, I argue, their constructive voice in educating younger generations as well as their role in criticizing or exposing social problems. In other words, both compilers and storytellers frame Palestinian cultural memory, whether by analysing family relationships or by addressing conflicts in society that when translated into tales 'become the existential realities of the heroines and heroes' (Muhawi and Kanaana, 1989: 20). For instance, polygyny is a recurrent theme but, in spite of being out of proportion to its incidence in the society, the frequency serves an educational function, especially if children are listening every time these tales are told.

To better understand the generational mediation and continuum between past and present, it is useful to look at Jan and Aleida Assmann's distinction between 'communicative memory' and 'cultural memory' (Hirsch, 2008)[10]. 'Intergenerational memory' known also as 'communicative memory' is constructed through the effort of individuals to pass on their biographical recollections from one generation to another generation in informal and oral conversations. The transmission of memories can be directly manifested within individuals, mainly with the family as the main unit of transmission, who can pass on their bodily and affective connection to that event to their descendants, over three to four generations. 'Cultural memory', also called 'trans-generational memory', however, is associated with the national/political and cultural/archival memory. Being a national and institutionalized form of memory, cultural memory is manifested through traditional archiving of memories seen 'through monuments, days of remembrance and other structures or institutions that together form a shared identity for a group' (Hirsch, 2008: 111). The combination of both communicative and cultural memory I think exists in *SBSA* and its Arabic version. Thanks to the compilers' anthropological observation of the Palestinian family over three generations, throughout their introduction, footnotes and afterwords, Muhawi and Kanaana formally document the heritage of a vibrant oral culture within its social reality and cultural memory. Moreover, women's narrative as storytellers and heroines reinforces social bonds of communicative memory through their informal and conversational role within the family.

Returning to the three tales I have so far discussed, 'Tunjur, Tunjur', 'The Woman Who Married Her Son' and 'Shwesh, Shwesh!', the reader of *SBSA* and/or its *Qul Ya Tayer* not only enjoys the plot and characters' interaction but, more importantly, appreciates the cultural and social reality, characterized by trust and dependence between mother and daughter or by love and protection (and even jealousy) between mother and son. In addition to presenting reality, women's narrative of memory, I argue, is educational for younger Palestinian generations given that children are among the main readers or listeners to the tales. For instance in 'Tunjur, Tunjur', the child learns to accept him/herself in spite of any differences, and so do his/her parents:

> [The tale] makes the child aware and reassured of his value and important role in maintaining a continuation of life. Moreover, the tale teaches parents to accept their child the way he/she is, without regret or wishes. As many tales start with a childless mother, who wishes to have a child at any expense, the mother once having a child learns to accept and raise him/her, even if it were a cooking pot or a cricket. (Fayād, 2010: 40)

Through women's narrative, storytelling can perform a therapeutic function in popular culture, acting as an aid to emotional and social growth. 'Such tales help children move from one level of consciousness, guided by "the pleasure principle", to a more adult level, guided by "the reality principle"'[11] (Bettelheim cited in Hinds et al., 2006: 71). Hence, through both inter- and transgenerational memory, Palestinian reality is extended to younger generations to help them grasp vital cultural practices and social identities. The fusion of cultural and communicative memory helps to raise awareness, in the case of oral literature, that both culture and art are not reducible to, or deducible from, each other. Tales on mother–son/daughter relationships not only expose familial interactions but reveal a portrait of the culture or of part of the culture which the reader will relate to when similarities in form occur or cultural details are adapted by local tellers. As I will discuss in the coming section, siblings' relationships highlight different social, cultural and national paradigms.

Sibling narrative

The process of remembering is not simply a retrieval of stories or images out of the storehouse of memory; it extends and transmits stories, memoirs, feelings and aspirations among people or children who do not have firsthand experience of such events (Hirsch, 2002, 2008). Palestinian women play an important role in paving the way for a smooth transition of cultural values in Palestinian society and family. Women's roles, I argue, as mothers or sisters, engender as well as gender the preservation of cultural memory, which is manifested through their roles and narratives. Sisters, like mothers, play a major role in consolidating family bonds and establishing harmony. The narrative of siblings as portrayed by the storytellers and the compilers consists of one of the most fundamental bonding ties in a Palestinian family, and one with the greatest potential of growth. Culturally, the sister has great influence in choosing her brother's bride. As discussed previously in 'Jummez Bin Yazur', together with the mother, the sister searches for a suitable bride, with whom they can get along, as they will probably be sharing the same household. The sister also shows her joy in her brother's wedding by expressing publicly through dancing at his wedding and singing songs of praise for his wife.

The sister can even replace the mother's protectiveness and affection as seen in 'The Orphan's Cow' (*Baqarat al-yatāmā*)[12] where the sister is faithful and loving to her brother in hardship. Poor treatment by the stepmother strengthens the relationship between brother and sister. Even after being enchanted, the brother in the form of a gazelle is very affectionate and caring with his sister when the latter is thrown in the well by the sultan's family. Through hardships, the death of the mother and the bad treatment of the husband's family, the relationship between sister and brother becomes stronger – the very survival of both sister and brother depends on their mutual love and cooperation. The narrative of siblings, in my opinion, is related to the role of sisters in the Palestinian family and social institutions. Cultural identity becomes causally tied to the Palestinian social institution. In other words, individuals identify with Palestinian social structure and norms, hence adhere to their social identity. Moreover, the importance of the bond between brother and sister is connected to the sense of collective identity, family solidarity and unity. The narrative also draws on the specificity of Palestinian cultural institutions, where the brother is regarded as responsible for his sister even when she is married; 'He remains her protector *sanad* or *'izwa* for the rest of her life' (Muhawi and Kanaana, 1989: 24). As Inea Bushnaq noted,

> Idealized brother and sister relationship in the stories is a reflection of the patrilineal bond that makes father and brother responsible for a woman even after she marries and goes to live in her husband's house. (Bushnaq, 1990: 133)

In this regard, Hasan M El-Shamy discusses the way he classified Arabic folktales which he compiled between 1969 and 1972 following his 'Brother–Sister Syndrome' theory[13] in his book entitled *Tales Arab Women Tell* (1999). El-Shamy believes that all folktales are governed by familial interaction and that tales should be grouped into sections under kinship-bound labels. Most importantly, that 'brother–sister relationship plays a decisive role in the generation, development, and continuation of a specific pattern of family structure and a host of other related social and cultural institutions' (El-Shamy, 1999: 3). I would add further that the narrative of siblings can be very powerful and a means for not only cultural work on memory but also national work, as is the case in 'The Green Bird' (*Al-ṭayr al-akhḍr*).[14] This is one of the most popular tales among Palestinians, glorifying once more the bond between the brother and his sister. At the beginning the sister has a leading role as mediator between the stepmother and her father, following the death of her mother. Later on, in spite of being manipulated and badly treated by her stepmother, her faithfulness and devotion to her brother revives him. The tale shows

> the level of solidarity between a brother and his sister, which cannot be compared to the husband and wife relationship. Blood-relationship has a crucial role in shaping siblings' relationships, which reflects the dimension of kinship in Palestinian rural society. (Naṣir, 2002: 20)

The bond between the sister and the brother reveals according to Muhawi and Kanaana 'a meaningful clue concerning the cultural emphasis on first-cousin marriage. First-cousin marriage in Palestine ideally combines both brother/sister and husband/wife relationships' (Muhawi and Kanaana, 1989: 113). The metaphoric representation of the brother–sister relationship or the narrative of Palestinian storytellers in this particular tale is meant to idealize endogamy/first-cousin marriage in Palestinian society, since ideally the cousin combines the brotherly tenderness and protection with sexual attraction.

In addition to promoting among younger generations love and care between brothers and sisters, as well as the social and cultural importance of first-cousin marriage in Palestinian society, the tale has deeper layers worth highlighting. As the story unfolds, the reader finds that the bird is the reincarnation of the dead brother, who was murdered by his stepmother and eaten by his father (without the father's knowledge). At the end of the story, the bird comes back to his human shape after punishing his parents and paying tribute to his sister's loyalty. When the bird makes his appearance at the wedding his sister was attending, he says:

I am the green bird	أنا الطير الأخضر المزيّن المحظر
Who graces this gathering!	خالتي ذبحتني و أبوي أكلني
My stepmother slaughtered me	و أختي الحنونة حنّ الله عليها
And my father devoured me	لملمت عظاماتي و حطتن بجرن الرخماتِ
Only my kind sister	(Muhawi and Kanaana, 2001: 101)
(Allah shower mercy on her!)	
Gathered up my bones	
And saved them in the urn of stone.	
(Muhawi and Kanaana, 1989: 101)	

In disbelief at seeing a bird speaking, the guests keep on repeating: 'Speak bird! How beautiful your words are!' (Muhawi and Kanaana, 1989) and the bird repeats the same poem until he becomes human again. Birds appear frequently in Palestinian folk culture, particularly in songs and proverbs. They symbolize women's femininity and sexuality, as I will discuss in the coming section, as well as being an important folkloric symbol in Palestinian popular and folk culture.[15] As Granqvist observes (1935), the green bird occurs in many of the songs sung at wedding celebrations.

Further to the bird's folkloric and cultural significance, I would argue that the bird symbolizes Palestinian cultural heritage in general and women's narrative in particular. In other words, the bird in the tale keeps on singing until life is brought back to the son. In the same vein, Palestinian storytellers are urged to revive their memory and safeguard their cultural and national identity. This explains also why the collection under study is entitled *Speak, Bird, Speak Again* or *qūl ya ṭayr* literally meaning 'speak bird' in Arabic. Both titles invite the readers to listen to the bird's singing, a symbol of stories which stand for vibrant heritage, love for life, regeneration and resistance against denial and oblivion. One could even say that the title of the compilation represents the folk and oral literature of a nation which is asking for recognition and identity affirmation from the whole world. In the interview I conducted with Dr Sharif Kanaana in 2012, he stated,

> Yes – it [the title] is symbolic of course. The title comes from a tale in the collection entitled 'The Green Bird' (*Al-ṭayr al-akhḍar*). The bird represents

Palestinians and *Speak Again* refers to revival, regeneration also to hope. (Appendix 1)

In the realms of memory, 'The Green Bird' also symbolizes narratives of continuity that mark not only the past within the present but also the past still at work within the present, actively changing and reshaping it into the future. Even more, the narrative of continuity becomes Palestinians' unavoidable duty to secure a cultural continuum between past, present and future.

Furthermore, the narrative of continuity is embedded within the voice of women as storytellers, seen again in the symbolism of the bird. As I mentioned earlier, the bird's significance not only is national or political but also, in my opinion, represents the voice of Palestinian women, symbolizing the power of their femininity. The latter will become more apparent in my discussion of sexuality and marriage. The way birds are connected to storytelling and women's narrative is seen in the way Palestinian women storytellers end some tales. As I discussed at the beginning of the chapter, Palestinian women are endowed with the skill of telling folktales; it is one of the arts they master. The folktales have specific forms of narration at the beginning and at the end, otherwise known as closing and introductory formulas. Among other closing formulas, some storytellers end their folktales by saying,

The bird has flown and a good evening to all (Muhawi and Kanaana, 1989: 65).	وطار الطير و تتمسو بالخير. (Muhawi and Kanaana, 2001: 74)

The presence of the bird in women storytellers' style, I believe, attributes to Palestinian women the power of regeneration and of preserving cultural identity. Palestinian women represent the voice of the bird who tells stories of collective memory, history and identity to younger generations. It is their responsibility as mothers, sisters and wives to transmit the essence of Palestinian cultural identity to those who 'grow up dominated by narratives that preceded their birth' (Hirsch, 1997: 22). Palestinian narrative, whether by mother or sister, shapes Palestinian post-memory, through which storytelling fuses 'cultural' and 'communicative' memories at the inter- and trans-generational levels (Assmann, 2006; Hirsch, 2008). In other words, folktales encapsulate a whole cultural system portrayed by Palestinian women, who safeguard heritage through preserving the transmission of Palestinian communicative memory at the family or the intergenerational level. The framing of the folktales by Muhawi and Kanaana is, on the other hand, a national project of documentation to reinforce Palestinian cultural memory, thereby promoting trans-generational continuity.

Because the Palestinian extended family is characterized as 'patrilineal, patrilateral, polygynous, endogamous and patrilocal' (Muhawi and Kanaana, 1989: 13), it is inevitable that conflicts arise. Once more women's narrative of cultural memory, as I have discussed with regard to Palestinian mothers, gains strength as a means of education for younger generations, as well as of social criticism. Through women's voice as sisters or storytellers, folktales not only are descriptive of social life in Palestine but can also be critical of social practices and norms. Under the guise of humour and entertainment, Palestinian women's narrative aims to draw attention to and rectify unacceptable behaviour by either the individual or the group in Palestinian society. Within sibling relationships, love, affection and mutual cooperation can turn into conflict, competition and jealousy. The main problem tackled, in women's narrative in this case, is gender favouritism, as males are considered by the family and society to be better and more gifted than females. Forms of racial and social status privileging have also been challenged in some folktales and women's narratives.

One of the best examples and one of the best-loved tales in Palestine, maybe because it dramatizes a situation that can occur in any family, is 'Half-a-Halfling' (*Nuṣ nṣīṣ*).[16] Within a polygamous environment, the tale firstly shows how the husband can sometimes be unfair with one of his wives, treating the non-blood-related wife better than the cousin wife. Endogamy, otherwise known as first-cousin marriage, can be regarded in Palestinian society as 'the ideal marriage because it exercises a positive pull toward family harmony' (Muhawi and Kanaana, 1989: 16). Nonetheless, competition among brothers tends to act against a family background of polygyny and first-cousin marriage. As a result, the sons of one of the wives compete for attention causing harm and distress. The educational element is felt throughout the tale; it reinforces the idea that heroism lies in actions not in appearances. The most important elements in a hero are his virtues of courage, truthfulness and resourcefulness, seen in the character of 'Half-a-Halfling'. The latter has successfully helped his half-brothers to escape from the Ghoul, which demonstrates 'generosity of spirit by rising above the pettiness of sibling rivalry' (Muhawi and Kanaana, 1989: 111).

The question one might pose is how can women's narrative against favouritism contribute to engendering Palestinian cultural memory? I argue that it is related to developing the identity of younger generations, whom we know constitute the majority of the audience, and heroism is embedded within women's narrative so as to help children develop their identities within the family and society. Identity development, as the tales reveal, starts from understanding the rules of society, mainly the notion of 'authority'. The latter implies learning more about the system of rewards and punishments in Palestinian culture, seen, for example, in respect for tradition, old age and obedience to parental authority. On a higher level, the question of authority is relevant for understanding the individual's relationship to society, and hence to the meaning of heroism in the tales. In other words, women's narrative, whether as storytellers or heroines, promotes the idea of respecting authority and co-existence among patrilineal, patrilateral, polygynous, endogamous and patrilocal Palestinian rural society. Because it can be difficult to achieve harmony and agreement, it is necessary to make younger generations avoid the act which triggers problems, namely, favouritism. Moreover, by constant repetition of tales, children develop an understanding of the structure of extended families in Palestine, mainly prior to 1948, in which collective identity was stronger than nowadays. It is, I think, important to highlight the collective social milieu and its connection to respect for age and gender throughout the tales, ensuring that collective identity is inherited, whether consciously or subconsciously, in the construction of younger generations' cultural memory and identity:

> Heroic action in the tales also concerns the idea of identity in the society. Again, from the perspective of the extended family, identity is collective. Through respect for tradition and deference to age, individuals are socialized from childhood to harmonize their will with that of the family. They are encouraged to perceive themselves as others see them and to validate their experience in terms of the approval of others. (Muhawi and Kanaana, 1989: 31)

As mentioned earlier, heroism is related to the development of identity, which means that the hero does not necessarily start as a hero in the tale, as in 'Half-a-Halfling' but learns to become one by the end. In an interview conducted with Sharif Kanaana by Robin Myers and Shadi Rohana (2011),[17] Kanaana comments on the link between Palestinian folklore and identity, saying,

> I feel that humanity is losing so much these days by not resorting to folk tales in the raising of its children. Folktales are universal, they assure the child that one day he or she is going to grow up and be as strong as the hero.

Both Kanaana's observation and women's narrative throughout the folktale compilation, I argue, reinforce one main characteristic within cultural memory, known as 'the concretion of identity' or the relation to the group (Assmann, 1995). Being the store of knowledge from which a group gains awareness and unity, cultural memory acts as an identificatory system of signification. Integrity and collectivity in the process of developing younger Palestinian generations' identities are supported by the 'capacity to reconstruct' (Assmann, 1995: 130). No memory can preserve the past without an actual effort to criticize, preserve or transform. In other words, through the valorization and promotion of human values, such as cooperation, truthfulness, faithfulness and humbleness, or heroic actions in the tales, women's narrative helps to unify the integrity of individual identity within collective, social and cultural memory. I would even say that women's narrative acts as a post-memory mode aimed at promoting important human values, since after the *Nakba* 'people's humanitarian and Arab values were shaken by trauma as well as modernisation' (Al-Sarīsī, 2004: 239). The transmission of post-memory, as such, connects generational experiences also through the bridging of social and human values, rendering memory more of a personal than historical experience (Hirsch, 1997). One should also not exclude the downside of post-memory as it can burden coming generations with a lack of closure regarding their political identity and future. This is particularly seen within the oral narrative of Palestinian history told by refugees in Palestinian camps in Lebanon, who form their collective memory through 'individual stories told and re-told in refugee gatherings' (Sayigh, 2007: 140); nonetheless, they feel bitter about their present circumstances:

> First generation refugees were blamed by their children and blamed themselves for leaving Palestine, possibly as a reflection of Lebanese

accusations of cowardice. A common formula for expressing this guilt and anger was, 'if only we had died in our country rather than come here!' (Sayigh, 2007: 156)

In all of the above, Palestinian women are endowed with strong characteristics; 'Their values, in fact, depend a lot upon their personality' (Granqvist, 1935: 169). The narratives of Palestinian women represent authority and respect as well as symbolizing love, wisdom, affection and support. Palestinian women do not only act as heroines in folktales but as heroines in real life, as mothers, wives, daughters and sisters. The relation to male social identity can, as in real life, affect women's social identity, resulting in either harmony or conflict. Palestinian women, whether as sisters or mothers and through the voice of women storytellers, not only manifest their cultural roles but also try to represent the social struggles and pressures many of them endure, such as social restrictions over women's sexuality before marriage and tensions once the newly-wed is introduced to the husband's extended family. For Palestinian women, conflict is inevitable in the structure of the system which she tries to challenge or co-exist with. These tales as the compilers confirm 'almost always concern, not heroes, but heroines: mothers, daughters, and wives' (Muhawi and Kanaana, 1989: 18).

To complete women's circle of narrative in the compilation under study, I deem it essential to shed light on their identity development and the way it is once again projected in the tales, in this case as a lover and a wife. A decisive and crucial transitional period through which each individual gains maturity is known as 'sexual awakening' or 'development'. During this phase the individual becomes emotionally and physically attracted to someone else. The development of sexual awakening and identity is prevalent within the tales and, I argue, is also part of women's narrative to engender cultural memory and identity.

Sexual awakening

Maintaining the argument of identity development in relation to cultural memory, 'The Little Bird' (*Al- 'uṣfūra al-ṣaghīra*) is a pertinent example. Being one of the most popular and first stories told to Palestinian children, the tale is basically about a bird that is getting ready for marriage. The bird goes through a preparatory state and readiness, which symbolize sexual awakening for young Palestinian girls. The latter, as the bird shows, prepare the make-up, henna and trousseau. So by beautifying and putting herself on display, she arouses the interest of the sultan's son. The tale, on the one hand, reveals women's sexual awakening, maturity and open desire to find a husband or going out and actively pursuing one. On the other hand, the bird symbolizes the woman's preparation and desire for marriage. The tale, in spite of its brevity, is culturally rich and denotative of women's inner world and desires. Reality in this tale is seen from the woman's perspective; even if not able to publicly express her interest in sex, the woman actively looks for her match within a Palestinian cultural context. This transitional stage, although always informed and controlled by Palestinian patriarchal and conservative society, shows the woman's eagerness to pursue a husband and desire to have a family. An expected identity is dictated to her by a male-dominated environment, through which the tale showcases two paradoxical states. On the one hand, because Palestinian women, mainly in villages, have little freedom to express their sexual desires, one can argue that the tale's popularity implicitly reveals woman's awareness of her beauty, sexuality and desire to be chosen by a man. On a less idealistic view, the tale portrays the confined narrative a woman in that context is expected to do or be for her to be appreciated and valued among her family and society.

For educational purposes, the storyteller has adopted a style of narration full of humour so as to attract her audience, mainly children. The reconstruction of cultural memory as discussed previously can be achieved through the power of narration, hence language. Language, as I will discuss later, is a fundamental constituent in the construction of national identity as well as collective memory. Spivak argues that 'language works as a negotiation of the public and the private' (2007: 9). The negotiation between private and public in this case is aimed at disclosing the hidden voice of Palestinian women and their desire to finding the right mate, as well as targeting younger generations in order to transmit and preserve customs and values. The implied educational function is realized through the medium of humour and language as the tale shows:

She [the female bird] sat awhile. Then, my little darlings, came the son of the sultan, who was roaming the neighbourhood looking for something. Meanwhile, she was singing:

> 'I am wearing my very best!
> Ya-la-lal-li
> And this is the day of my feast
> Ya-la-lal-la.'

'Eh!' he thought. 'Who is singing like that?' He listened carefully and behold! It was the little bird singing. Aiming his gun, he fired and shot her. She sang her song:

> 'What a sharp shooter!'
> Ya-la-lal-li
> What a sharp shooter!
> Ya-la-lal-la.'

He then plucked her feathers, and she was singing:

> 'A fine feather-plucker!
> Ya-la-lal-li
> A fine feather-plucker
> Ya-la-lal-la.'

Then he cooked her, and still she chirped:

> 'What a good cook!
> Ya-la-lal-li
> What a good cook
> Ya-la-lal-la.'

Putting her into his mouth, he chewed her until she was soft, then swallowed her. She went down into his stomach. In a while, he got up and shat her. She then sang out:

> 'Ho! Ho! I saw the prince's hole,
> It's red, red, like a burning coal.'

(Muhawi and Kanaana, 1989: 116–17)

قعدت. قام بيجي ابن هالسلطان, داير يغوي, و هي قاعدة تقول:
لبست جديدي, يلاللي   و اليوم عيدي يلالا

قام قال: ' إه ! شو هاي اللي بتحكي هيك!'
صار ينصت عليها و إلا هي العصفورة بتحكي. قام اطلع عليها, طخ! قوسها. صارت تقول:
قواس شاطر, يلاللي   قواس شاطر, يلالا

قام إجا معطها. صارت تقول:
مغاط شاطر, يلاللي   مغاط شاطر يلالا

إجا طبخها. صارت تقول:
طبّاخ شاطر, يلاللي   طباخ شاطر, يلالا

إجا أكلها, لاكها, نعمها و صرطها و نزلت على بطنه. شوي قام شخها: قامت صارت تقول: 'هو!هو! شفت صرم ابن السلطان و هي حمرا حمرا, مثل الجمرة'
(Muhawi and Kanaana, 2001: 114–15)

Although sexual subjects are taboo in polite conversation, Palestinian folk culture is accepting of language related to bodily function, making the tales more humorous and appealing to children. Humour has the power to make the content of the language memorable, enriching the heritage of oral literature as well as empowering women's narrative of femininity within their social identity. The symbolism of birds, as discussed before, is versatile and significant to engendering as well as gendering memory. Birds stand for women's power, freedom and cultural identity as well as sexuality.

Because folktales belong to people and their lives in all its forms, the tales showcase Palestinian popular culture, which 'reinforces the existing cultural attitudes and lifeways' (Harmon, 2006: 69). One aspect of Palestinian folktales, I would argue, in general and this collection in particular, is aimed at projecting the image of harmonious life before the *Nakba*. For instance, the reader gets to know about village social life, wedding customs, clothes and cultural practices. The tales, however, and via the women's voice, can also raise questions about the social norms, traditions and pressures a woman suffers from in a patriarchal and conservative society which I will discuss shortly. One feature of women's narrative could be the maintaining of a continuity of folklore and heritage, a state of normality Palestinians are longing for. In both 'The Little Bird' and 'The Green Bird', for instance, women's narrative and the compilers' cultural framing aim to expose readers to Palestinian cultural customs so as to appreciate the flow of the story and understand the significance of weddings in Palestinian society. This is mainly done for two reasons: The first is to document the oral heritage of a very unstable part of the world, hence highlighting the specificity of Palestinian culture and identity to non-Palestinians. Secondly, the aim is to work on developing young Palestinians' cultural and national identity and to enlighten them from an early age about the cultural stages and preparations the bride has in the Palestinian context, seen in 'The Little Bird'. Describing the bridal seat and wedding procession in Palestine, the compilers explain in a footnote:

> The bridal seat (*masmade* مصمدة) is usually an elevated seat, composed of several folded mattresses, where the bride sits after having been led in the wedding procession (*zaffe* زفة) from her father's house to that of the groom with all the female wedding guests singing, dancing and ululating (*zaghareet* زغاريد) around her. The groom usually joins her later in the evening, and the couple sit together in the midst of the dancing and singing. (Muhawi and Kanaana, 1989: 116)

Likewise, in 'The Green Bird', the dead brother appears as a bird while his sister is at a wedding. When the bird starts talking, the storyteller says, 'the guests forgot about the wedding procession and turned their attention to the bird' (Muhawi and Kanaana, 1989: 101). Muhawi and Kanaana deemed it important at that moment to add a footnote explaining Palestinian wedding processions:

> The wedding procession (زفة) *zaffe* is an essential part of the Palestinian wedding ceremony in which relatives and friends of the couple sing and dance in the street in celebration of the marriage. See Granqvist, Marriage II: 35–137. (Muhawi and Kanaana, 1989: 101)[18]

Palestinian storytellers are very faithful in describing marriage ceremony rituals in detail, mainly in the countryside, as those details are missing nowadays due to the diasporic situation or displacement. According to Al-Sarīsī, 'The full presentation of marriage rituals in the countryside around Jerusalem, as seen in the folktales, is meant to document those rituals as practised before the *Nakba*' (Al-Sarīsī, 2004: 191). Through symbolism, humour or cultural reference, the discourse of continuity, regeneration and affirmation is attributed to Palestinian women.[19]

Being narrators and active carriers of the Palestinian folk tradition in reality, as well as heroines in fiction; the compilers throughout the paratextual elements aim at empowering the image of Palestinian women and address the assumptions of otherness, weakness and submissiveness interpreted by the West:

> Western readers will be struck as much by the tone of the tales – the narrative voice that speaks through them – as by their style, for the tales empower the women who narrate them to traverse, in their speech, the bounds of social convention. (Muhawi and Kanaana, 1989: 12)

The questions one needs to address here are, first, to what extent are the storytellers and folktales detachable from the compilers' interpretations? And has their motive affected the choice of the selection of tales for inclusion? In their introduction, the compilers justify the selection of the forty-five tales to excellence of narration and popularity. Although true, I think that the folktales were selected also to satisfy the authorial agenda of the compilers. This is clearly seen in the way they interpret and present the folktales to their readership. One cannot deny the prevalence of stereotypical images about Arab women in the West and the compilers' aim to rectify this image through empowering their roles throughout the collection. I however think that the compilers are still exercising some power on the voice of Palestinian women storytellers, and albeit benign, it is still a form of control and manipulation. Remke Kruk, in her book *The Warrior Women of Islam* (2014), described the role of warrior women in Arabic popular epic, which are adventure and heroic tales about male and female champions. These tales were composed by men for a male audience, ignoring women's ambitions, and was designated to satisfy a male audience. Shedding more light on women's roles, as strong, wise, courageous heroines, Kruk also discusses what the West would usually expect from such epics:

> A striking point in the epics, in particular the 'Bedouin' ones, is that gender roles are often reversed, or at least run counter to what the average Western reader would expect. Women defeat and humiliate men on the battlefield, causing not anger but passionate love. Daughters protect fathers or take bold initiatives. ... We must assume that epic literature (*sīra*) was originally composed by men for a male audience, to be recited in the public space, a predominantly male domain. Accordingly, the martial women do not represent the female angle in the male discourse, but embody the perceptions, anxieties and desires of men. (Kruk, 2014: 225)

Popular epic tales are different from folktales in content, delivery and storytellers. The former are created by men for a male audience featuring the adventures of women, which means that the male is the one controlling the way women appear in popular epics. Folktales, on the other hand, are told by women storytellers to a mixed audience, portraying women's roles and lives. The folktales, although purely attributed to women, are not free from males' interpretation and/or selection in *SBSA*.

As I mentioned before, the folktales are not only descriptive of harmonious life and environment, but they can also showcase the fears, anxieties and social pressures women go through in a conservative milieu. In spite of being a natural aspect of maturity among young men and women, sexual awakening can create conflict within the family. When a girl's identity transforms into that of a woman, her physical appearance becomes her tool to attract men. This beauty, however, can trigger jealousy and tension, as in 'Jummez Bin Yazur,

Chief of the Birds' (*Jumīz bin yazūr, shaykh al-ṭuyūr*).[20] The tale, similarly to 'The Little Bird', reveals the sexual awakening of Set Al Hussun, who metaphorically asks her father to bring her a man to marry. Both tales use the bird as a metaphorical disguise so to convey a culturally complex message that can hardly be mentioned or communicated directly. Both tales highlight the eagerness for marriage among young women, who have started to understand the complexity of their sexual feelings. On the one hand, Set Al Hussun's beauty will help her to pursue the man she loves; on the other, it creates hostility and harmful jealousy among her sisters and her lover's sisters, who all try to create obstacles for her. Sexual jealousy can appear more prominent among sisters than brothers. In real life, having the freedom to actively pursue a man is very difficult; as it could put at stake the woman's reputation and honour. Some tales, such as 'Jummez Bin Yazur' and 'The Little Bird', are not always representations of real social situations but can express wishes, inner struggles and fears. Cultural identity, in this case, I believe, embraces fears versus wishes, pressures versus freedom, desires versus restrictions, which are all part and parcel of the identity development of an Arab woman in general and a Palestinian one in particular. Hence one can say that both tales reinforce the cultural identity of a woman, within the customs of Palestinian society, while shedding light on her conflicting desires related to sex and marriage.

Marriage

To be able to understand the Palestinian social structure, one has to understand family and marriage institutions. Here the role of Palestinian women as storytellers is important since it reveals their inner or private world, as well as their family and marriage institutions. Hilma Granqvist explains that analysing the marriage institution in the Palestinian context shows 'the historical development of the village and its families, from which we can understand the social structure and family principles' (Granqvist, 1942: 25). Following sexual awakening, there is a life-changing personal, familial as well as cultural phase that both men and women have to experience in relation to choosing the suitable husband or wife. The quest for a partner in Palestinian society does not depend on the individuals only; there is interplay of social forces during the quest. Both parties in this stage will have the personal readiness and willingness to carry out the quest for a socially and personally appropriate husband or wife. Women's narrative throughout the tales merges both public and private spheres, as I will show shortly, defining the position of the Palestinian woman in relation to society, symbolized by authority and duty towards the extended family, as well as shedding light on the woman's inner desires, maturity and conflicts. In fact, women in most tales instigate actions, their roles developing from lovers to wives, affecting as such the dynamics of conjugal and family relationships.

For instance, some of the tales, such as 'The Brave Lad' (*Al-shāb al-shujā'*),[21] tackle the problem of authority at the family and societal levels. In other words, the freedom to choose the right partner in Palestinian society does not only depend on the individuals' desire but is obstructed by the requirements of the social system. Firstly, the daughter's choice of marrying the brave lad is rejected by the father or king. As the story unfolds, we realize that for the lad to have the king's daughter he has to kill the Ghoul, which is a public duty. The Ghoul can also represent an authority figure against the choice of two people. In order to achieve their objective, both the king's daughter and the brave lad have to face authority by challenging the Ghoul. According to the compilers, authority figures preserve tradition by hindering both sexes' personal freedom:

> Because in traditional Palestinian and Arab culture the choice of a mate is of vital importance to the community, it cannot be left entirely up to the individual, the interests of the whole family must be taken into account as well. Those who insist on choosing for themselves, then, must be willing to make sacrifices to achieve their goals. In the 'Brave Lad', the young lad must have enough courage to face the Ghoul. (Muhawi and Kanaana, 1989: 168)

Authority figures are part of the cultural pattern of Palestinian society. It can act as a constructive voice of wisdom and balance between the young couple's desires and social expectations; alternatively, it can control and limit individual's freedom. The fact that the choice of a mate is also important to the community highlights collective responsibility towards the young couple and their families, since marriage is not only dependent on the individual's choice in a Palestinian rural society but shared and approved by the main male figures in the family as well as extended family, friends and neighbours. It is important to note that in pre-*Nakba* rural Palestine, as the folktales reveal, the notion of collective identity was very strong, as I will explore in greater detail in the next chapter. Women's narrative, therefore, shows how marriage and choice of partner transcend the private sphere and become a public collective responsibility. In spite of the limitations imposed on individual choices, the intervention of the community can reinforce collective identity among people through showing care and protection. Another important element in reinforcing the cultural pattern of Palestinian rural society is seen in the storyteller's realistic narration style. It is characterized by 'the absence of magic and the supernatural, giving a meaningful cultural context to the quest pattern' (Muhawi and Kanaana, 1989: 168). At the beginning of the tale, the storyteller describes,

> A lad in love with the girl but too poor to become the king's son-in-law … (Muhawi and Kanaana, 1989: 148).

> 'و كان فقير و بحب البنت و بقدرش يناسب الملك'
> (Muhawi and Kanaana, 2001: 139).

Social status differences are a universal theme in folktales; however, the storyteller's narration harmonizes the choice of words to fit within the Palestinian cultural context. In the Palestinian Arabic version the storyteller chose to use the verb *nāsaba* meaning literally 'to be suitable for/in accord with'. In this particular context, the verb *nāsaba* means 'to become part of the in-laws' family' or to 'become the son-in-law' as the English translation shows. This particular verb within the storyteller's sentence carries a strong cultural connotation for the Arab reader in general and the Palestinian in particular, emphasized by the compilers' use of a popular proverb in a footnote:

> The lad could not possibly have been able to afford the costs of the wedding, which are borne entirely by the bridegroom's family, since for a king's daughter the festivities would have to be lavish. A Palestinian proverb says, 'He who has money can have the king's daughter for his bride.' (Muhawi and Kanaana, 1989: 148)

Combining the narrative of the storyteller and the compilers' framing, cultural memory is nurtured through the use of a popular proverb. Using proverbs to consolidate a particular situation as is the case in this tale relates reality (finding the right partner) to oral culture and heritage. The cultural framing, added by the compilers, can act as one of the characteristics of cultural memory, namely, 'obligation':

> The relation to a normative self-image of the group engenders a clear system of values and differentiations in importance which structure the cultural supply of knowledge and the symbols. (Assmann, 1995: 131)

Through the voice of the compilers, the narrative of women in relation to the choice of the suitable partner is strengthened. In fact, the footnote adds, I believe, credibility to women's storytelling and mainly shows obligation to reflect the cultural institution of a whole group. Conversely, in the tale 'Clever Hassan' (*Al-shāṭir Ḥasan*)[22], women's narrative shows how figures of authority and newly-weds may clash in the course of the latter's identity development and harmony can only be achieved through cooperation and by having sufficient strength of character to be independent. The tales as mentioned previously do not only reflect cultural realities but also criticize existing cultural restrictions and educate future generations on how to become self-reliant, wise and independent.

Once the new partner is chosen, the couple encounter considerable changes, challenges and lessons to learn. Some of the tales in Group II (Family) explore the challenges faced by newly-weds, who try to establish patterns of communication and learn to deal with each other's needs and limitations. Suitability is a key theme discussed in many tales that reveal personal, social and cultural contributors to marriage. Throughout the tales, we are shown how the insight of Palestinian women helps to establish a successful marital life. A successful marriage can only be achieved if both partners are suitable for each other. Mutual suitability and choice, 'given the dynamics of the Palestinian social system, is of utmost importance in the lives of the newlyweds' (Muhawi and Kanaana, 1989: 203). In this regard, 'The Cricket' (*Al-khunfsa*)[23] is a perfect educational tale, and one of the most popular children's tales in Palestine highlighting the importance of choosing a compatible partner in order to achieve happiness and harmony. Unlike 'Clever Hassan', 'The Cricket' stresses the importance of first consulting with parents, particularly mothers, before taking any decisions related to marriage. The choice of the individual's mate is dependent on parents' advice, recommendations and consent. The cricket, which is looking for a suitable mate, keeps asking her mother for advice until her mother approves the right one. The folktale uses symbolism to introduce a fundamental issue in the Palestinian marriage institution, namely, the suitability or compatibility of mates. The perfect choice of a mate, as women's narratives show in the folktale and in the narration, is based on a compromise between individual desire and family requirements. A successful marriage involves 'an agreement not between two individuals but between two families in Palestinian villages' (Granqvist, 1931: 53). While looking for the right husband, the cricket came across the mouse and the following dialogue takes place between the cricket, her mother and the mouse:

She [the cricket] went away, and walked and walked until a little mouse found her wandering about and chirping: 'Tzee, tzee, tzee.' 'What're you looking for?' he asked. 'I'm wandering around looking for a bridegroom.' 'Will you marry me?' he proposed. She answered: 'Cricket, cricket, your mother! And you are cousin to the whore. I'll put the gold in my sleeve, And talk to my mother some more.' 'O mama!' she said to her mother. 'His eyes are wee, his head is wee, and his ears are wee. All of him is very small.' 'Yes,' said the mother, 'this one's your size. Marry him.' So back to the mouse the cricket went. 'Yes,' she said, 'I'll marry you.' (Muhawi and Kanaana, 1989: 200)	راحت صارت تمشي تنّه لاقاها هالفار الزغير, و هي ماشية و بتقول: 'سي, سي, سي' قالها الفار: 'عليش دايرة؟' قالتله: 'دايرة أدوّر على عريس' قالها: 'تتجوزيني' قالتله: خنفس خنفس إمك و القحبة بنت عمك لاحط الذهب بكمي و أروح أشاور إمي قالتها: 'يما عينه زغير زغير. و راسه زغير وغير. و ذانه زغير. و كلياته زغير زغير' قالتها: 'أه , هاظ على قدّك. اتجوزيه' راحت قالتله: 'بتجوزك'. (Muhawi and Kanaana, 2001: 181–2)

Because folktales mature with age, Palestinian storytellers, according to the compilers, 'are considered asexual and hence beyond the operative social taboos concerning speech and other forms of outwardly acceptable politeness' (Muhawi and Kanaana, 1989: 3). This could be the case in some parts in Palestine, mainly rural areas, where they would consider women who are past childbearing age to have no sexual desires, giving them the green light to use sexual or taboo language in order to add humour to the narration. On the one hand, Palestinian society gives elderly Palestinian women credit for their narration skills since they are perceived to possess authority, knowledge and wisdom. On the other hand, Palestinian women seem to be victims of a projected social belief, making them act as asexual, using deliberate references to sex or body parts while narrating so as to trigger a sense of humour.

As discussed earlier, the popularity of most of the tales in *SBSA*, such as 'The Cricket' and 'The Little Bird', is attributed to narrative style and humour. Humour for a child, according to Kanaana, 'consists of breaking the rules and the taboos of adult society' (Kanaana, 2008),[24] be it in mentioning sexual parts of the body or comic language. Kanaana in his article on 'Stories Told by and for Palestinian Children' believes that 'crude terms used by storytellers from illiterate, traditional, oral societies do so to entertain and amuse children and should be deemed quite legitimate' (Kanaana, 2008). In other words, humour functions as a device to smooth educational transmission of identity for children in general and Palestinian children in particular, who end up remembering, enjoying and appreciating, accepting and identifying with cultural institutions. Moreover, a child, unlike an adult or literary critic, does not analyse a story logically and try to find the message behind it. A child rather lives out the story by identifying with one of its characters, usually the hero. The child, as I discussed earlier, identifies with the authority image, thus developing the image of a hero in him/her. Heroes, as models of behaviour for younger generations, help to develop the child's identity. At the same level of identification, the narratives of Palestinian women reinforce their cultural position and authority, which the child learns to respect and relate to.

Because cultural memories, identities and practices do not flow simply or predictably from one generation to the next or from the homeland to diasporic communities, intellectuals, folklorists and ordinary storytellers try to make efforts to reproduce the missing transition between past and present, between lived experiences and the recreation of effect and between loss of authentic memory and the chase for a replacement. In the work of Daniel and Jonathan Boyarin (1993), the structural logic of diaspora emerges as a progressive model for maintaining cultural identity across geographical ruptures. Indeed, some memories and traditions even develop and become stronger in the diaspora than they are in the homeland. Thus the efforts in recreating or investing (Landsberg, 2004), as seen in mass culture or literature, emphasize the idea that prosthetic memories are not intrinsic to any individual, and not limited to the organic experience of any person or group, but equally available to everyone. Referring to the Holocaust, Hirsch says that

> the children of exiled survivors, although they have not themselves lived through the trauma of banishment and the destruction of home, remain always marginal or exiled, always in the Diaspora. 'Home' is always elsewhere. ... This condition of exile from the space of identity, this diasporic experience, is a characteristic aspect of postmemory. (Hirsch, 1997: 243)

The same applies to many exiled Palestinians living in the diaspora, with the difference that their past is not over yet nor is it forgotten. The bridge between generations cannot be pain-free or smooth, as the wound of trauma is still open for Palestinians; nonetheless, the memory work, particularly prosthetic, can highlight and safeguard the cultural and family institutions that third generation or Palestinian diaspora communities have not experienced. One can argue that art and oral literature are the best media to transgress post-*Nakba* pain. Through women's narrative, be it critical, humorous or educational, and through the compilers' framing, trans- and intergenerational transmission of heritage, cultural identity and self-identification become fundamental for later generations. For instance, the fact that the cricket puts gold in her sleeve is culturally significant for Palestinians. According to the compilers, 'the gold' refers to the bride's wealth, and the word 'cousin' refers to husband. I would argue that 'the gold' can also stand for 'the bride's dowry'; moreover, it is common to call a husband 'cousin' (*ibin 'am*) because traditionally cousin marriage is encouraged in Palestinian society. The gold is placed in her sleeve because 'traditional Palestinian women's dress has long, flowing sleeves in which small objects can be placed' (Muhawi and Kanaana, 1989: 199). The additional explanation helps contextualize the search for a mate in a specified cultural, societal and familial setting. Through exposing and framing the tales, I think that post-memorial work strives, in Hirsch's words, 'to reactivate and re-embody more distant social/national and archival/cultural memorial structures by reinvesting them with resonant individual and familial forms of mediation and aesthetic expression' (Hirsch, 2008: 112). In fact, for many second-generation Palestinians films and literary works, including folktales and storytelling, have become the main vehicle through which Palestinian post- and prosthetic memories are articulated, understood and made alive.

Following the challenges of choosing the right partner, issues emerge in the conjugal life between a husband and his wife, specific to the Palestinian context. One of the most recurrent themes is 'sexuality' and its impact on the development of the individual before and after marriage, within the codes of Palestinian culture. The vitality of sexuality is crystallized in the husband–wife relationship, which is the most prominent relationship in the tales, featuring as a theme in nearly all of them. In spite of the restrictions on sexuality imposed by the family and society on young women before marriage, sexuality remains an essential motivator and enhancer of feelings in relationships between newly-weds and mature married couples. Given the authority allowed to storytellers in expressing themselves freely, women's narrative of cultural memory throughout the folktales is gendered and engendered also around the lives of husbands and wives, through which both undergo identity development, disappointment and regeneration. Throughout the narration and plot, Palestinian women may express their desires and feelings openly. Even more, women storytellers can act as spokeswomen for other Palestinian women, expressing how they may feel about their inner needs and emotions. We find in fact that in many tales women's sexuality and their emotional needs are being affirmed, whether directly or indirectly.

Women's narrative tries to transcend social restrictions regarding expressing romance, by which we find an affirmation of romantic love before and after marriage. As seen in some tales, such as 'Jummez Bin Yazur' (*Jumīz bin yazūr*), 'Sackcloth' '(*Bū al-lababīd*), 'The Brave Lad' (*Al-shāb al-shujāʿ*) and 'Lolabe' (*Lawlaba*), romance is fundamental to the development of a relationship into marriage. To be more specific, women's narrative throughout the compilation, I think, is juxtaposing parental authority and social intervention[25] regarding the girl's choice before marriage with women's inner desires and wishes, which the society will not allow in public. The heroines, for instance, in 'Jummez Bin Yazur' and 'Sackcloth', are playful and creative in their ideas of how to pursue a mate, showing their strength of character and beauty. In 'Shahin', the heroine is more mature than the man, showing more wisdom and responsibility in dealing with the emotional upheaval stemming from the first stirrings of sexuality. Being the main initiators of actions as they try to pursue the right husband, sexuality lies at the heart of female power in the majority of tales.

Some tales expose possible problems between a husband and a wife, mainly because of sexual insecurity and lack of trust, such as in 'The Golden Rod in the Valley of Vermilion' (*Qaẓīb al-zahab biwadī al-'qīq*)²⁶ and 'The Seven Leavenings' (*Im al-saba' khamayr*).²⁷ The relationship between husband and wife at a certain stage is characterized with tension as a result of mistrust of the wife or sexual insecurity. According to Muhawi and Kanaana, some tales reveal 'the dark side of sexuality, where men's fear or anxiety about their virility is projected as the women's sexual voraciousness' (Muhawi and Kanaana, 1989: 227). The lack of harmony and increase in tension are also caused by the absence of offspring. The problem is seen in the way women and men associate sexuality with fertility and virility in Palestinian society. The absence of offspring makes a man more vulnerable to social criticism, and he would be forced to marry another woman as a result.

Since both husbands in 'The Golden Rod in the Valley of Vermilion' and 'The Seven Leavenings' feel inadequate because of the infertility of their marriage, they start to question their manliness and as a result vent their frustration by beating their wives. The lack of offspring, as the tales reveal, can be more problematic for Palestinian women than for men. Socially and culturally speaking, male children represent a form of security for mothers, as they constitute an essential part of her identity. A mother without a son in rural Palestine can be seen sometimes as having no security in life. This attitude to male offspring is socially constructed since in Palestinian society male children represent manliness and virility for the mother. In both tales, the resolution to problems is realized either through a positive transformation in the husband's character by admission of error or through conceiving children: the wife in 'The Seven Leavenings', for example, gains her respect back only once she claims that she can conceive. The tales, in fact, show how cultural approaches to sexuality differ between men and women and between generations in Palestinian society. The problem, in my opinion, lies in how society defines women according to particular roles, in which their identities need first to satisfy the patriarchal society. Tales such as 'The Golden Rod in the Valley of Vermilion' and 'The Seven Leavenings' implicitly raise awareness of the consequences of men's anxiety and fear, which can negatively affect relationships, leading to lack of trust and separation.

The discourse of sexuality throughout the narratives of Palestinian women in *SBSA* crystallizes in 'Im Eshe' (*Im 'aysha*).²⁸ Once more, the language reveals the power of women's narration, combining humour and a wife's revelation concerning the importance of her husband's virility. In most of the tales, reference to sexuality is present as a theme but not explicit in the language. In 'Im Eshe', however, the wife is given more freedom to express her feelings, giving the reader a more culturally subversive approach to sexuality. The husband slaughters their chickens and the cow and spills the oil, but the wife tolerates everything except the loss of his sexual organs:

> 'To hell with it [the oil]! Just open!'
> 'No. You will kill me!'
> 'What did you do?'
> 'I said to the cow give me some food! But she wouldn't. So I slaughtered her.'
> 'Let it be a sacrifice! You're worth everything. Just open!'
>
> 'You'll slaughter me!'
> 'Why? What did you do?'
> 'The camel was chewing his cud. I said to him, 'Give me some food!' but he wouldn't. He came at me, and I covered my pecker with a cauliflower leaf. He goes and bites me, eats the leaf and eats my pecker tool!'
> 'Alas! Alas!' cried Im Eshe. 'Nothing in the world matters like your balls, and now you're a gelding!' (Muhawi and Kanaana, 1989: 227)

> قالتله: 'عمرها! افتح!'
> قالها: 'لأ بتقتليني'
> قالتله: 'شو سويت؟'
> قالها: 'قلت للبقرة إطعميني, مقبلتش. قمت ذبحتها'.
> قالتله: 'فداك افتح الباب'
> قالها: 'بتذبحيني'
> قالتله: 'ليش؟ شو سويت؟'
> قالها: 'الجمل قاعد يلوك. قلتله إطعمني, مقبلش. يشّن عليّ. حطيت ورقة القرنبيط على زبرتي. قام يخمشني, يوكل و رقة القرنبيط و يوكل زبرتي'
> قالتله: 'كل شي فداك, غير بيظاتك و اخصاك!'
>
> (Muhawi and Kanaana, 2001: 204)

The tale shows that the couple can tolerate the loss of any material possessions but the one loss the marriage cannot sustain is that of husband's virility. The Palestinian woman's voice throughout the tale reveals her power in managing her household as well as her marital life. Unlike 'The Golden Rod in the Valley of Vermilion' and 'The Seven Leavenings', where men's frustrations are more apparent, 'Im Eshe' reveals women's frustration concerning men's lack of virility. As a matter of fact the source of frustration, whether for men or women, is related to their social position in a conservative rural community. On the one hand, both women and men have to abide by cultural constructs imposed by society, in which they have to perform their public roles. This means that women are expected to be fertile and men to be virile. On the other hand, women's narrative sheds light on the dark sides of marital life, giving deeper insight into the fears of men and women within their private sphere. Once more the negotiation between public/cultural and private/home spheres is combined in this folktale and its narration, reinforcing the power of language in expressing cultural identity and therefore memory. The latter is realized through what Assmann, translated by Czaplicka (1995: 130), would refer to as 'formation', in which cultural memory features through 'the objectivation or crystallization of communicated meaning and collectively shared knowledge'. The sharing of knowledge helps to turn cultural memory into 'the culturally institutionalised heritage of a society'. In other words, women's narratives throughout the tales and the compilers' notes do not only describe, for instance, the institution of marriage in Palestinian society but also relate it to Palestinian collective and cultural identity and hence the institutionalized heritage of Palestinians.

In addition to the importance of sexuality in marital life, symbolizing fertility and productivity, its lack can cause disharmony or even divorce. The disruption of harmony between a wife and her husband, as exposed in most of the tales and as women's narrative of cultural identity within the family reveals, comes from pressure inflicted by the extended family or from rivalry as a result of polygynous situations. In both cases, the wife tries to be in control of the situation and wants to win the husband's attention and love, pushing her to become manipulative. Particularly in a polygynous situation, women fight and conspire against one another so to win the attention and affection of her husband. The competition can be, for instance, over the production of male heirs. In other words, the more sons one wife has, the more privileged she is by her husband. A clear example is seen in 'Precious One and Worn-Out One' (Al-ghālya w al-bālya) and 'Half-a-Halfling' (Nuṣ nṣīṣ); in the former tale the wife has fewer male children therefore is considered to be 'the worn-out one' and in the latter tale, the second wife shows off her sons who are, in comparison to the son of the first wife, Half-Halfling, stronger and bigger. Hence, problems intensify because of divided loyalties in a polygynous situation. The jealousy and hostility are created when the woman is replaced by another woman or when the women compete for attention.[29] This situation is observed in many cultures and is ubiquitous in the Palestinian. The tensions rising from polygamy and/or mothers-in-law coexisting for a married woman are issues that Hilma Granqvist (1935) observed when she carried out her study on *Marriage Conditions in a Palestinian Village* (II, 380):

> At marriage, when a woman leaves her father's house, her greatest care is to adjust herself to her mother-in-law and to her co-wives should her husband have other spouses. The position of an old wife when a new wife is brought into the house is often difficult and frequently leads to her leaving her husband and returning to her father's people. There is no necessary disgrace attached to such a procedure, and frequently her flight forces the husband to change his behaviour.

The conflict between husband and wife can also worsen over 'conflicting loyalties' (Muhawi and Kanaana, 1989: 248). Some tales, such as 'The Woman Whose Hands Were Cut Off' (*Muqaṭaʿit al-dayāt*),[30] show how the husband is torn between his loyalty to his natal family and to his conjugal family. In the tale, the man is caught between his wife and his sister, making the situation more complicated as he chooses his wife over his sister. The male is usually in a difficult situation vis-à-vis the females for whom he is responsible. Once more, Palestinian cultural identity is exposed through the dynamics of marital life. Palestinian family structure seems to be more dependent on collective identity, namely, the extended family and the phenomenon of polygamy in rural Palestine. From the perspective of Palestinian women, the extended family and polygamy threaten the harmony and peace of conjugal life. It might be frustrating for individual Palestinian women and men; nonetheless, the folktales through the women's and compilers' narratives show society in its best and worse: a stable and long-established cultural system, which Palestinians want to relate to even more today, particularly amid political instability and threats of identity loss.

Moreover, and as discussed throughout this chapter, it seems that the compilers and storytellers are aware of the importance of transitional generational time, whether consciously or not. Muhawi and Kanaana, for example, have tried to facilitate and reinforce the process of transfer from one generation to another highlighted in both the content of folktales and their effort to describe and frame them. The aim in their collections (both Arabic and English) is to draw a continuation of the past into the present, as well as to raise awareness among younger Palestinian generations of the existence of a homeland, culture and history through the transmission of Palestinian folktales. In the Arabic collection *Qul Ya Tayer*, the compilers stress in the introduction the importance of their book-functioning as an accessible scholarly reference for Arabs, whether students or scholars. The power of post-memory is that its connection to its object or source is not mediated through recollection but 'through an imaginative investment and creation' (Hirsch, 1999: 22). Creation and investment are well expressed in literature, particularly oral literature, and can serve post-memory by changing reality and the past or by consolidating the existence of culture and history. In any case, the compilers, Muhawi and Kanaana, and the Palestinian women storytellers, have their own agendas and motives, which may be similar or different, behind the framing of post-memory transition. Finally, both post- and prosthetic memories can either burden future generations with a complex past or can be perceived as a salutary development since they pave the way for strong community, shared past and for new collective frameworks that cut across existing social divisions.

4

Cultural Identity and Sites of Memory in Palestinian Folktales

In the same vein, the present chapter extends important notions of memory, collective and cultural, and collective identity to looking at folktales, mainly in Group III (Society), Group IV (Environment) and Group V (Universe). I intend to discuss specific sites and agents of Palestinian memory, which, I argue, mobilize Palestinian cultural identity and collectivity across geographical space and time. In so doing, I look at the peasant discourse in the folktales, featured in particular examples related to setting, people and lifestyle, which reinforce, and call for the regeneration of, pre-1948 communal identity (hence post-memory). The discussion will allow me to elaborate on the role of language as a bridge between Palestinian cultural identity and memory in the folktales under study, connecting communicative with cultural memory (Assmann, 2006, 1995; Hirsch 2008, 1996, 1999). Palestinian cultural identity, as I will show, maintains its existence and force through a mixture of religious and folk beliefs, prevalent in Palestinian dialect, which I argue empower a collective spirit and unity among Palestinians.

The third part of my chapter will focus on an important site of memory and component of Palestinian cultural identity, namely, food. Like religion and peasanthood, food is a productive area for exploration. References to food in the folktales, I will show, can act as bearers of Palestinian memory. Food operates as a means for strengthening Palestinian social interaction, giving prominence to the distinctiveness of Palestinian cultural identity. My discussion on food touches upon relevant notions in memory and food studies, such as prospective memory (Sutton, 2008), sensuous memory (Holtzman, 2006) and gustatory nostalgia (Sutton, 2001). Nostalgia can be seen as a form of reminiscence about a glorious past, a form of escapism from the present, or as a driving force to renew cultural identity. Finally, role of Palestinian women cannot be ignored when discussing food's interconnection with memory and identity. Palestinian women, I argue, are agents of memory via the mediation of culturally related food symbolism in some tales and their titles. Women's storytelling tradition, as I aim to show, relates to transactive memory (Smith, 2007), through which Palestinian women promote essential cultural values in Palestinian society. Women's food discourse engenders Palestinian memory and cultural identity where there may be, for example, folkloric references to beauty, sexuality, conceiving children and craving.

Peasantry as a site of memory and identity

As discussed previously, the context of Palestinian folktales is sourced in a rural environment and villages. The setting, as I described it and as the compilers explain it in their paratextual notes, originates in a pre-*Nakba* context. All the tales describe a harmonious and agricultural pre-1948 setting, most prominently in tales in Group III (Society) and Group IV (Environment). The tales in these groups reveal the dynamics of Palestinian society and take a closer look at people and neighbourly interaction in rural villages. Unlike tales in Group I (Individuals) and Group II (Family), in Groups III and IV 'family bonds and obligations do not necessarily dictate the standard of conduct' (Muhawi and Kanaana, 1989: 277). This means that the level of interaction between individuals in the last groups of tales transcends family boundaries, integrating the individual into wider relationships with his/her community, environment and religion. The interaction between the state of peasantry and Palestinian lifestyles cannot be ignored when analysing the main pillar of Palestinian memory, namely, cultural identity, in *SBSA* and *Qul Ya Tayer*. Under the umbrella of cultural identity, people's way of living, traditions and food rituals can be major markers in forming their national identity and therefore their collective memory. It is important to look at how peasantry, whether in setting or lifestyle, combine both communicative and cultural memory (Assmann, 1995), turning the Palestinian peasant into a national signifier (Swedenburg, 1990) and hence peasantry into a national discourse of Palestinian cultural memory.

Recreating the homeland

Like memorial books which focus on maintaining place names (Davis, 2007; see below), the folktale, I argue, can represent a folkloric landmark for Palestinians' cultural memory. In his discussion on memory, Pierre Nora proposes a useful way to think about how humans relate to places in their past as: 'lieux de mémoire' (sites of memory). As Nora explains,

> The moment of lieux de mémoire occurs at the same time that an immense and intimate fund of memory disappears, surviving only as a reconstituted object beneath the gaze of critical history. This period sees, on the one hand, the decisive deepening of historical study and, on the other hand, a heritage consolidated. ... Lieux de mémoire are simple and ambiguous, natural and artificial, at once immediately available in concrete sensual experience and susceptible to the most abstract elaboration. Indeed, they are lieux in three senses of the word – material, symbolic, and functional. (Nora, 1989: 12, 18–19)

For Palestinians, physical spaces and rituals carry the emotive charge of nostalgia concerning pre-1948 history and communal life. As I discussed in Chapter 1, nostalgia is triggered when one suffers from a drastic change in the physical environment or 'built environment' (Goffman, 1959), this disruption resulting in identity discontinuity. Because Palestinians' present is not improving, nostalgia can work either way: a curse or bliss. Given the paradoxical nature of nostalgia in the Palestinian case, nostalgia not only can be a form of longing or reminiscence, locking memories into an idealized past as a way to escape the present, but can also act as a buffer against forgetfulness and denial. One way to look at nostalgia is as a motivator to recreate new identities or to affirm old ones (Charmaz, 1994; Davis, 1979; Milligan, 2003). Because pre-*Nakba* places or lifestyles are related to collective social practices, places turn into a live story of collective history. Through recalling places and their repetition in the folktales, Palestinians can connect with their pasts, strengthen cultural memory and preserve identity, perpetuating a strong sense of collective memory. If 'the land, villages, and Palestinian people are preserved through [the painters'] art, as timeless expressions of a unique culture with rich history and traditions' (Cadora, 1988: 11), folktales, similarly, mobilize collective, cultural and social continuation.

Combining Halbwachs's approach to memory and the group and Warburg's treatment of the language of cultural forms and memory Assmann (1995) attributes cultural memory with 'the concretion of identity' and 'capacity to reconstruct' (Assmann, 1995: 130) among other characteristics. Assmann's discussion enriches my analysis of the portrayal of peasantry and peasants in the tales and their accompanying footnotes or paratext. Both ordinary Palestinians, such as the storytellers, and folklorists, such as Muhawi and Kanaana, merge communicative memory, meaning the daily communication, language, habits and lifestyles, with the will to officially document and preserve Palestinian culture and identity seen in the compilers' efforts. For instance, in Tale 26 'Minjal' (*Minjal*), Minjal bakes bread outdoors in her clay oven (*ṭabūn*). The compilers found it necessary to explain the architecture of Palestinian village houses:

> The 'clay oven' (*Tabun*) is a small structure housing an earthen oven used for baking bread and for some cooking. Villagers usually build the oven at some distance from their living quarters in order to avoid its smoke, most commonly at the edge of the road closest to the house. The *Tabun* is a circular structure a yard high and which diameter of about a yard; its smooth clay walls house two compartments, the lower for the fire and the upper (usually lined with pebbles over a metal sheet) for baking the bread. (Muhawi and Kanaana, 1989: 219)

The elaborate footnote, both in Arabic and English, not only is aimed at informing the reader of the general layout of the lower part of the house but also serves to trigger the visual imagination, conveying a more vivid image of real places that no longer exist. In her article 'Mapping the Past, Re-Creating the Homeland', Rochelle Davis (2007) describes Palestinian memorial books with maps of pre-1948 villages, as 'dossiers of evidence: land records, genealogies, photographs, and stories all aimed towards showing the villagers' relationship to the places in the village' (Davis, 2007: 58), demonstrating the existence of a shared history and physical existence among Palestinians. The *ṭabūn* description not only is informative but also, in my opinion, maps out Palestinian memories and national belonging to tangible sites. Similarly in Tale 40 'Dunglet' (*Baʿirūn*) and Tale 3 'Precious One and Worn-Out One' (*Al-ghalia w al-balia*), the reader is informed or reminded of the architecture

Cultural Identity and Sites of Memory in Palestinian Folktales   119

of village houses. For example, Palestinian as well as non-Palestinian readers are invited to learn more about communal traditions that existed within a particular setting, such as *qaws al-ḥawayij* (the arch of clothes), and about collective traditions such as when women gathered before October to patch their roofs. The setting has the power to unify people's memories with shared social experiences, a point I will elaborate on in the section 'Peasantry and Collective Identity'.

Because of displacement and the persistent struggle over land, there is an urge among Palestinians to consciously make an effort to refer to sites of memory prior to 1948, as we shall see in some stories for instance. As memory takes various forms, expressed through different mediums, it becomes evident that collective memory is manifested through symbols or sites which can be understood as a response to and a symptom of a rupture, a lack, an absence and 'a substitute, surrogate, or consolation for something missing' (Zemon Davis and Starn, 1989: 3).[1] In the same way, Palestinians' memory strives to tackle this lack through the idealization of particular sites or symbols, which can shape Palestinian national and collective identity. The compilers, in Tale 31 'The Woman Whose Hands Were Cut Off' (*Muqaṭaʿat al-dayāt*), explained in a footnote the reference in the tale to the 'Gate of the wind' (*Bāb al-hawā*) where the action of the plot takes place:

> *Bab il Hawa* is literally 'Gate of the wind'. In the hilly regions of Palestine, where most villages and towns are located on hilltops (as in the village of Turmushaya, district of Ramallah, where this tale was collected), the approach to the town is always through the valley. The western breeze blows up these valleys from the Mediterranean. (Muhawi and Kanaana, 1989: 241)

The role of this footnote, like the first, is to inform the reader about Palestinian landscapes and geography. The aim is to give a picturesque context to the plot of the folktale, so that readers' visualization and imagination is triggered. The recreation of setting, I think, echoes the role of maps and memorial books discussed by Davis (2007). To a great extent the footnotes help the reader to mark what is important at a particular time or place to a particular population. The geography of the 'Gate of the wind', one could argue, is able to trigger a sense of nostalgia among readers from the first and second Palestinian generations. The reference to place, along with the footnote, transmits to the reader in general and Palestinians in particular the awakening of a site of memory. Evoking a sense of nostalgia, whether in the folktale or in the footnote, has the power to affirm the presence of a past setting, triggering the reader's memories in order to resist a painful present and possibly creating a hope for future return. As I discussed in previous chapters, one of the main functions of nostalgia is that it 'carries existential meaning, serving as a reservoir of memories and experiences that is helpful for coping with existential threat' (Sedikides et al., 2008b: 231).

Mapping out memory in folktales is apparent also in the listing of names of places which no longer exist. In Tale 24 'The Seven Leavenings' (*Im al-sabi' khamāyr*), for instance, the old woman decided to go walking by the sea. In the folktale there is no mention of a specific name, but the compilers added a footnote clarifying where the old lady went:

> The storyteller had the seashore by the city of Acre in mind. For a discussion of the significance of the city of Acre (*A'akka*) عكا in the history of Palestine, see 'Topographical Researches in the Galilee' by Aapeli Saarisalo, which opens thus: 'There is hardly any city in Palestine or in the whole world which has seen more history than Acre, Jerusalem perhaps excepted.' (Muhawi and Kanaana, 1989: 206; inverted commas in original)

In other cultures, a compiler would perhaps be less exhaustive in explaining the setting or even guessing where the hero intends to go. As anthropologists and folklorists, Muhawi and Kanaana chose to explain in order to affirm the historical existence and continuation of a pre-1948 city, basing their footnote on a credible study done during 1929 by Aapeli Saarisalo. Both Palestinian collective and post-memory are embedded within nostalgia and activated through recollection and 'an imaginative investment and creation' (Hirsch, 1997: 22). If we argue that nostalgia is seen as a form of resistance and identity protection, the notion of post-memory could be also seen as tool for activation, particularly in the effort to extend memories and identity to generations who do not have first-hand experience. In Sigmund Freud's essay 'Beyond the Pleasure Principle' (1922), he discusses compulsive repetition by traumatized patients. This manifests itself in the way patients' fantasies and impulses, which were repressed before, are repeated and acted out in the present. The repetition is also seen in 'the form of dreams reliving the original trauma' and 'the symptomatic repetitions of hysterics, who are said to suffer from reminiscences' (Abrahams, 1982: 581). These forms of repetition are all used to circumvent the trauma of loss. Nostalgia, I think can also be read as a form of repeating and idealizing the past. The existence of pre-*Nakba* place references, along with the compilers' framing, can be linked to some extent to Freud's 'repetition compulsion' in its role of actively regenerating the memory of an idealized past.

Likewise, in Tale 26 'Minjal' (*Minjal*), the storyteller felt it necessary to digress during her narration to specify the area she is describing, referring to one of the characters: 'The man, you might say, left his town behind and travelled until he came to a village like *Il-Za'er, Rummane* and *Id-Der*' (Muhawi and Kanaana, 1989: 222; italics added for emphasis). The three villages the storyteller mentions existed before the *Nakba* and were geographically located in upper Galilee north of Nazareth. Reference to those particular villages demonstrates the authority of knowledge among local Palestinians. This confirms Davis's (2007) argument on how imprinting the presence of pre-1948 villages on maps serves as a powerful form of knowledge. Since this authority, she believes,

> maintains Palestinians' ties to pre-1948 Palestinian land by showing their intimate and familiar relationship to as well as their former dependence on the land, the maps help individuals continue to define themselves as Palestinians and as belonging to a particular village. (Davis, 2007: 60)

I argue that through the medium of art and literature, including folktales, knowledge demonstrates the authority of Palestinians in general and Palestinian storytellers in particular over their identity and belonging despite their situation. The storyteller's knowledge is twofold: mentioning the names of old villages is a way of resisting oblivion and an effort to reject Israeli demarcation of land and villages. It also attributes storytellers with authority and knowledge over history and geography, making them credible mediators of Palestinian memory.

Peasantry and collective identity

Peasantry, as depicted in the folktales or in the paratextual materials relating to the folktales, is a sign of unification and a vibrant site of memory work. Peasantry is, as Swedenburg (1990) suggests, 'the symbolic site where intense Palestinian desires for unification for the sake of the struggle against the occupation are expressed, [and] the "peasant" has taken on mythical qualities' (Swedenburg, 1990: 19). The figure of the peasant has been turned into a Palestinian national discourse aimed at remoulding memory to unify Palestinians, particularly the post-memory generation. To a great extent, the figure of the peasant, as seen in the folktales, 'draws much of its emotive force from memories of the peasant as historical agent' (Swedenburg, 1990). In fact, peasantry creates a unifying sense of belonging and promotes collective identity.

Village descriptions and peasantry are important to my discussion in this chapter, particularly when looking at the role of collective identity in shaping collective memory. In this regard, it is worth looking at the way Palestinian cultural identity and memory are evoked by social practices and communal values related to certain locations, such as the fields, wells and springs or natural features of the landscape. Reading folktales, I argue, is like reading a fusion of a memorial book and collective autobiographies. Davis explains how memorial books can be a form of collective autobiography. I go further: the Palestinian folktale is a tool combining shared collective stories, designed in a literary form, with history and collective memory work. In Tale 33 'Im Awwad and the Ghouleh' (*Im 'awād w al-ghūla*), the folktale begins by referring to women going 'to wash their clothes at the spring on the edge of town' (Muhawi and Kanaana, 1989: 253). In the old days, as the compilers explained in a footnote, the women used to go in groups to wash their clothes, then dry them on trees and bushes. The spring was a meeting point for women who performed their daily activities together. The recreation of the image of women together at the spring connects the site of memory, in this case the spring, with a harmonious collective past. The site of memory evokes memories of the past and nostalgia. Poetry in Palestinian literature bears an emotive force, evoking vivid images and memories to names of places, natural landscapes and, as I will analyse later in this chapter, food, create a direct emotional recall.[2]

Tales 20 'Lady Tatar' (*Al-sit tatar*) and 41 'The Louse' (*Al-qamla*) deal with different plots and topics but share a peasant environment and customs, which the compilers thought worth pointing out. Not only does the footnote in Tale

20 explain the practices of raising animals, but more importantly it relates them to their cultural and social significance for Palestinian women:

> In Palestinian villages families ordinarily raised animals in the yard. The mothers would designate a hen or two for each of her marriageable daughters so that they could sell their eggs to buy beads, thread, and other embroidery items in preparation for marriage. (Muhawi and Kanaana, 1989: 178)

Raising hens is not just a means to earn a living or a hobby for Palestinians. Rather, it is a tradition practised, circulated and shared among villagers, mainly women, in preparation for their weddings. The sharing of experience transcends the physicality of description, where the individual's experience is merged into a past tradition that everyone in the village might still relate to:

> Palestinians story the places of their past through verse, personal recollections, collective histories, maps, and artwork. Representations of people's activities transform the physical place – buildings of neighbourhood, the village square, or a tree – into meaningful spaces of village and communal life. (Davis, 2007: 64)

Similarly Tale 41 describes the life of a louse and the chain of communication between different animals or insects, which all metaphorically stand for human interaction, communal life and collectivity, a point I will address in more depth shortly. My main observation here is that the compilers use the word *tasakhamat* in Palestinian Arabic (meaning 'she smeared herself') to refer to the louse who lost her husband, the flea. The louse is very sad upon the loss of her husband, so she smears her face. The smearing of women's faces in death is related to a mourning tradition in Palestinian villages. The act of showing grief in public, as the footnote describes, is meant to show her grief so that she is praised for her devotion. The cultural interpretation alludes to a shared past and tells the non-Palestinian of the existence of a collective history and tradition, while allowing the Palestinian reader to relive an idealized memory of a village life.

The folktale accurately portrays 'a live descriptive movie of peasants' houses, moves, fields, typical food and clothing' (Al-Sarīsī, 2004: 215). The living quality of the folktale, I think, can be linked to the use of photography in recording or even reconstructing a memory. Being a record and an emanation of a real incident, the photograph, as explained by Marianne Hirsch (1996: 669), is 'the medium connecting memory to postmemory'. Similarly, peasant sites, such as farms and valleys, recreate the setting, triggering the emotive memory power of a shared past:

> Wells, caves, valleys, hills, paths, plots of farmland, buildings, mosques, churches, trees, and stores embody this collective knowledge and are recorded, post-1948, as the essential components of the village or neighbourhood or town. (Davis, 2007: 54)

For example, most of the tales in Group IV (Environment) depict vivid images of rural life, agricultural rituals and peasant lifestyle. Apart from the role of language in showing the interconnectedness of plot and characters within the frame of collective identity, which I will elaborate on shortly, the tales symbolize 'acts of memory' (Nora, 1989). The active role of acts of memory comes, as Nora explains, to procreate experienced loss and ruptures, which Palestinians have endured and are still suffering from today. In this case, 'purely material' sites (such as village sites and peasant tools or lifestyle) become 'lieux de mémoire' 'only if the imagination invests [them] with a symbolic aura' (Nora, 1989: 19). The art of storytelling and the folktale itself carry, I believe, the imagination and creativity needed to mobilize a sense of belonging and hence memory work across post-1948 generations.

Another powerful site for activating memory, I would argue, is the use of allegory, as is the case with many tales in *SBSA*. Allegoric tales, such as 'The Louse', play a powerful role in establishing a cultural bridge between older and younger generations. Allegory features as part of the genre of folktales, in which meanings, themes and lessons are transmitted to the reader through symbolism. According to Samuel Taylor Coleridge, 'Allegory always partakes of the reality which it renders intelligible; and while it enunciates the whole, abides itself as a living part in that unity of which it is the representation' (1971: 467–8). Allegory is an implicit form of representation of forms of reality from which one deduces the embedded meaning. In his article 'Crabwalk History: Torture, Allegory, and Memory in Sartre', Debarti Sanyal explains how particular violent historical acts are evoked through allegory: 'The traumatic nature of experiences such as detainment, torture and extermination often prompt the displacements of allegorical inscription in order to become *legible and transmissible*'

(Sanyal, 2010: 52; italics added for emphasis). Allegory can be also seen as a tool of framing cultural and social codes so as to make them more 'legible and transmissible' to children. For instance, in Tale 38 'The Little She-Goat' (*Al-'anza al-'nayzīa*) in Group V (Universe), the story revolves around the adventures of the she-goat. Because the hyena cannot eat the kids of the she-goat, he wants to have her tail cut by the ant, as a form of disguise to trap the kids. The ant, however, says she will not 'chop off [his] tail unless [he] goes to *the threshing floor* and brings a measure of wheat' (Muhawi and Kanaana, 1989: 281; italics for emphasis). The significance of the threshing floor, known as *baydar*[3] in Palestinian society, is allegorically related to what many Palestinians would see as a marker of their peasant status and collective memory. In addition to being an important space for villagers, the *baydar* plays an important social function. Families used to meet there during harvest time and spend the evenings singing, eating and chatting until dawn. It is for Palestinian villagers a folkloric feast where all neighbours get together, help each other and enjoy a collective seasonal celebration. The description of places within an allegorical frame exposes shared experiences and sentiments associated with 'a nationalist idealization of peasant life' (Davis, 2007: 54).

The interconnection between collective memory and cultural identity not only features in nostalgic associations with specific sites but can also be seen in the way Palestinian folktales mobilize the roles of important professions, such as woodcutting, fishing, carpentry and blacksmithing. All of these portray a natural flow of life in the past. In *Speak, Bird, Speak Again*, we find many instances where the stories revolve mainly around the fisherman and barber (Tale 37 'The Fisherman', *Al-samāk*), the woodcutter (Tale 36 'The Woodcutter', *Al-ḥaṭāb*), the merchant (Tale 34 'The Merchant's Daughter' *Bint al-tājir* and Tale 25 'The Golden Rod in the Valley of Vermilion' *qadhīb al-ẓhab bi wadī al-'aqīq*) and the shoemaker (Tale 44 'Maruf the Shoemaker' *ma 'rūf al-iskāfī*). These trades and crafts were even used as titles for the folktales by the tellers, which attribute them, in addition to their knowledge power, as discussed before, with strong interpretive skills. Like village landscapes or landmarks, working and earning a living portray the normality of village life among Palestinians. In fact, each one plays a role in revealing the fabric of society in operation and reinforcing the collectivity of Palestinians. The livelihood of some people in a Palestinian rural setting portrays the dynamics of Palestinian communal life, as each one plays a specific role in the village. For instance, though not as prominent as the fisherman or the woodcutter, the barber seems to have a notable social status with Palestinian villagers. Following the mysterious cleaning that happened in the fisherman's house, the fisherman, in Tale 37 'The Fisherman' went to see the barber to ask him for advice or explanation. The barber in Palestinian popular culture is endowed with wisdom and knowledge, and his opinion is of great importance among people: 'The assumption is that the barber is reputed for his knowledge and wisdom. In the village economy of old the barbers performed several functions, including primitive surgery. They would know what was going on in the village better than anyone else' (Muhawi and Kanaana, 1989: 272).

The reoccurrence of professions in Palestinian folktales is meant to connect work life with landscapes, such as forests and shores, and thence to stable pre-1948 life. In grounding the folktale in a Palestinian setting, the aim is to map the memory like a history book of the main locations, then connect the latter to people's collective knowledge and lifestyles. The purpose is also educational, aiming at raising national and international awareness of the true mapping of places before the *Nakba* as Palestinians carried out their professions, such as woodcutting in non-limited areas across Palestine:

> The occurrence of woodcutting in Palestinian folktales and society is normal, bearing in mind that Palestine contains many mountains across the country [literally 'from north to south']. I have myself witnessed how Palestinian men and women use forests as spaces for woodcutting, such as Ḥarsh Bāb Al-Wād on the Jaffa-Jerusalem road. (Al-Sarīsī, 2004: 216–17)

Likewise, fisherman was a common profession among Palestinians, as Al-Sarīsī explains:

> The fact that the fisherman is frequently mentioned in folktales, more than any other profession, is not surprising if we remember that the length of the Palestinian coast is over 230 km. (Al-Sarīsī, 2004: 217–18)

Mentioning professions, particularly woodcutters, is a common feature of folktales, reinforcing the translatability and the transcultural mobility of folklore across nations. Yet the distinctiveness of Palestinian folktales is twofold. One, to highlight the richness and beauty of Palestinian landscapes, prior to the *Nakba* – as illustrated, for instance, by Al-Sarīsī's mention of the length of the Palestinian coast – helps to raise awareness and reduce identity erasure. Two, through the medium of the folktale, each Palestinian seems to maintain a normal flow of life in a set environment such as where a fisherman used to fish, or in which forest a woodcutter used to work. Establishing a natural environment and plot for the fisherman or the woodcutter shows the importance of integrating such professions into human life in general and Palestinian lands in particular, triggering hope for the future within coming Palestinian generations. Aspects of Palestinian harmonious social life, cultural norms and interaction will become more evident when I discuss the power of Palestinian dialect in revealing the strength of collectivity among families and neighbours. Through the medium of language the reader gains a better picture of how folk religion and official religion are intertwined in Palestinian society.

Language and folk religion in society, environment and universe groups of folktales

As I have discussed, features, symbols and ideals highlighting a communal sense of collectiveness in Palestinian memory are transmitted from one generation to another thanks to efforts made by groups to preserve national memory and identity. In other words, in order to continue to exist, the group maintains its identity, of which memory represents its cornerstone. Thus the sense of continuity is protected by remembering and by letting identity find its position and name among a particular group or nation. While true for every nation, these observations are particularly appropriate for the Palestinians as a partly diasporic people still engaged in a struggle for statehood and an ongoing process of nation building. The notion of 'nationhood' and 'nationalism' in the Palestinian case is an important element in the formation of Palestinian collective memory[4] and narrative identity. The latter is usually about how we make sense of our experiences and how we construct and interpret our realities and lives through narratives. The way we construct our life stories and the way we interpret them will shape the narrative self and thus our identities. Because we are the products of our experiences and social interactions, communication, whether written or oral, lies at the heart of transmitting and interpreting our identities. Communication is represented via language which is a dynamic component in forming narrative identity, and hence memory. In order to revive memory, language is given importance as the bedrock of national language and cultural heritage. And by reviving linguistic heritage in literary, religious and historical texts, memory is strengthened and transmitted from one generation to the next. In such ways, both memory and language are key elements in constructing and maintaining national and cultural identity, and it is useful to consider this 'triangle' of memory, identity and nationhood when dealing with the Palestinian context. So how can the interconnection between language and collective identity reinforce Palestinian cultural identity and aid the preservation of memory?

The folktales under study, particularly Group IV (Environment), demonstrate the role of language in expressing collectivity among Palestinians. Unlike other folktales in *SBSA*, this group of tales is referred to as 'formula tales' (Muhawi and Kanaana, 1989: 290). The compilers explain how, being formulaic, those tales require 'a verbal precision that becomes part of the content, there is little room in them for tellers to show individuality in weaving the narrative' (Muhawi and Kanaana, 1989: 290). Those tales are, in fact, circular in structure with the end contained in the beginning. In Appendix 4, I have given both the Arabic and English versions of one particular folktale, entitled 'The Old Woman and Her Cat' (*Al-'ajūz w al-bis*). The interdependence of language and plot in this tale shows that the cat will be forgiven by the old lady, if he fulfils a different chain of requests. Formulaic language in these tales conveys 'a harmonious interdependence with the environment, both animate and inanimate' (Muhawi and Kanaana, 1989). Both language and plot are structured in such a way as to symbolize the importance of a balanced community, in which everyone has a role to fulfil. As discussed, allegorical tales are effective and more transmittable. The combination of allegory and formulaic language empowers Palestinian dialect, giving rise to the artistic beauty of the folktale. In fact, one can argue that language, plot and allegorical integration reflect the Palestinian's harmonization with his/her environment and society.

The opposite is true if disharmony erupts, as formulaic tales reveal. In 'Dunglet',[5] disharmony is created when one of the links in the chain is disrupted, thereby 'triggering a process of readjustment in all the other links until equilibrium is restored' (Muhawi and Kanaana, 1989). The missing harmony in society calls for stability and equilibrium, and the formulaic tale symbolizes and highlights the importance of maintaining order and unity for Palestinians. Analysing this category of tales reveals that an action may appear inconsequential but can affect the whole chain and damage the entire community. In addition to the fact that Palestinian dialect reinforces national and cultural identity, it is noteworthy how formulaic language is highly structured in order to convey the collectivity of Palestinian social fabric. The formulaic tales are, in other words, tools for portraying ideal pre-1948 society and rituals among neighbours, which rely on cooperation, interdependence and the interconnectedness of human beings with nature. Reinforcing solidarity and cooperation among animate and inanimate creatures has a role in encouraging Palestinians to maintain national and cultural unity. The harmony between content and language in Group III (Society) is not as prominent as the ones in Group IV (Environment), yet the notion of collective identity prevails, in which actions revolve around neighbours' interaction, solidarity and collective responsibility towards each other. The interaction of the fisherman with his society in Tale 37 'The Fisherman' highlights neighbourly cooperation. Being aware that the fisherman lives by himself, one of his neighbours always cooks lunch for him. The spirit of solidarity and care was and still remains in some Palestinian villages, where neighbours may even replace family members. Care for your neighbour is, in Palestinian popular culture, more important than your own home. Neighbours' solidarity and care are empowered by Palestinians' religious beliefs.

As with the embodiment of a national and collective narrative of memory through the symbol of the peasant in Palestinian literature, religious beliefs highlight a sense of collectivity in Palestinian memory. Reflecting human interactions among Palestinians, the supernatural imbues them with an entirely 'other' apprehension of reality 'based on the beliefs and superstitions of the folk' (Muhawi and Kanaana, 1989: 40). While analysing different tales, I found that all share universal themes, such as the supernatural influence of some creatures, the fusion of reality and fiction and the notion of 'fate'. Nonetheless, the folktales under discussion maintain their distinctiveness to Palestinian cultural identity through their depiction of fate and religion. Through the medium of language, I argue, religious beliefs in folktales connect to Palestinian memory, reflecting an embedded cultural identity. Before analysing how specific religious references and narration formulae in the tales in the compilation shape Palestinian identity and memory, it is necessary to explain the difference between official and folk religion in Palestinian society.

Palestine has long been associated with three religions, namely, Judaism, Christianity and Islam. Because religion is predominant in everyday Palestinian life, official religion tends to be practised under the influence of folk culture, particularly among villagers. One can argue that religion has been adapted to culture, social interpretation and folklore, resulting in a blend of official religions with folk beliefs. As the compilers note in their introduction, 'village peasants in Palestine do not distinguish between official religion and its teaching on the one hand, and the beliefs and superstitions of folk religion on the other' (Muhawi and Kanaana, 1989: 41). This means that the distinction between the two spheres in everyday life is not always clear, nor is it between the belief and the cultural interpretation of the belief. These categories shift back and forth in reality and therefore also in folktales, since the teller of the folktale is a peasant of the same society.

For instance, in Tale 19 'The Old Woman Ghouleh' (*Al-ghūla al-'ajūz*) the female Ghoul, Ghouleh, cannot be seen but makes her presence felt. According to the storyteller's description, the Ghouleh can resemble a supernatural being, yet she can also appear in the form of an animal or human being. In Tale 22 'Clever Hassan' (*Al-shāṭir ḥasan*), the merging of folk and official religion is apparent in the storyteller's form of narration. In the tale, the Ghoul appears to be a religious saint who is trying to help clever Hassan to find the treasures in the cave, advising him on where to go and what to do. While narrating how Hassan follows the Ghoul's advice, the storyteller says,

| Going right in, the youth filled a sack with watermelons, taking three extra melons for the aged sheikh. Pulling himself together, he came out of there fast. *A thousand* followed him (*in the name of Allah!*) but they were unable to catch him.
(Muhawi and Kanaana, 1989: 191; italics added for emphasis) | فات دغري, ملّى هالكيس, و أخذ كمان ثلث بطيخات للاختيار. حمل حاله و طلع. لحقوه ألف (اسم الله) ما غدروش يمسكوه.
(Muhawi and Kanaana, 2001: 174; italics added for emphasis) |

The word 'thousand' refers here to 'devils', but the storyteller avoids mentioning the name explicitly because, according to Palestinian folk religion, reference to devils serves to evoke them. Instead, one should allude to them indirectly and mention the name of Allah to drive them away, as she did.

In this regard, Al-Sarīsī observes the interconnectedness between language, religious and folk beliefs in Palestinian culture and how folktales are projected in Palestinians' real life. He develops his argument by referring to a Palestinian folktale entitled *Qurūd Dara ' ma* (The Monkeys of Dara ' ma), in which a group of Muslim men would not have been able to defeat some Jinni had they not pronounced the name of Allah. According to Al-Sarīsī, the folktale refers to reality, as it happened in one of the villages in Palestine; moreover, some Palestinian families bear the surname Dara ' ma. He explains the connection to the fact that Palestinian daily life and beliefs are grounded in social reality and culture. It is common among Palestinian mothers, for instance, to ask their offspring to pronounce the name of Allah before drinking water in a dark place since they believe that Jinni can be in the water, making it harmful to children (Al-Sarīsī, 2004).

The shift between official and folk religion might create a mix in interpreting religious practices or beliefs but I consider that the fusion enriches Palestinian popular culture and empowers Palestinians' cultural identity, collectivity and solidarity. In Tale 34 'The Merchant's Daughter', the neighbour not only comes to the rescue of the merchant's daughter when she is in danger, but he also assumes the father's role in marrying her off (Muhawi and Kanaana, 1989). The way religion is merged into Palestinian popular culture is clear in the following extract and the self-definition of the neighbour reveals this:

'I am not related to her [merchant's daughter]. I am not her paternal or maternal uncle. I am only her neighbour, and her father had entrusted her to my care. And the prophet himself bade us take care of our neighbour, and our neighbour's neighbour, down to the seventh neighbour' (Muhawi and Kanaana, 1989: 258)	'أنا لا قريبها و لا عمها و لا خالها. أنا جارها, و أبوها وصاني و النبي وصّى بالجار و جار الجار لسابع جار.' (Muhawi and Kanaana, 2001: 233–4)

The neighbour's comment is backed up with the compilers' footnote:

> This is a very well-known and often-quoted *hadith* (saying, or tradition) of the prophet. A popular proverb also confirms this concern: 'Ask about the neighbour before you ask about the house' is *'āl 'n al-jār qabl al-dār*. The cultural importance of neighbours is accurately reflected in the tale. Because people tended to live in the same house for generations, they had the same neighbours for *many, many years* [italics added for emphasis]. Hence, neighbours were sometimes closer to a family than their own relatives, sharing sorrowful and joyous occasions. (Muhawi and Kanaana, 1989: 258)

The combination of the neighbour's comment and the compilers' footnote reinforce the interconnection between cultural identity and memory. Based on the argument I put forward in Chapter 3 about the fusion of 'intergenerational memory' and 'trans-generational memory' (Hirsch, 2008), daily beliefs and folk culture are transmitted through social and familial interaction, perpetuating a specific cultural identity. The level of communicative memory is then transformed into cultural memory through the compilers' efforts to document and convey society's self-image to Palestinians and non-Palestinians. As I will elaborate in more depth, the institution of religion is strongly embedded within Palestinian popular culture and society. The overlap of popular culture and religion is productive because helping and caring for neighbours becomes a collective duty undertaken by the whole society in order to maintain harmony.

The repetition of 'many' in Muhawi and Kanaana's footnote is only available in the English compilation. This is, in my opinion, meant to emphasize the concordance of time and identity with collective memory. Reference to time is linked to narrative alluding to human thought, intention and positioning because, as Ricoeur (1984) argues in *Time and Narrative*, 'our being-in-the-world' and our very 'within timeness' is achieved or completed in the narrative experience of time (Ricoeur, 1984: 35). In other words, the narrative is realized through a process of telling or reading, through which our relation to time is marked. In this example, the compilers situate Palestinians' long-established social structure within a rooted past, affirming the narrative of collective memory. Raising awareness among Western readers about the longevity of Palestinian culture is deemed important by the compilers. The folklorists' voice in this case rectifies, reconstructs and frames memory in line with reinforcing collectivity and cultural identity.

The overlap between folk religion and official religion is also seen in the way protagonists concretize the spiritual, including different forms of the supernatural, even the divine. For instance, childless women, in four different tales, namely, Tale 1 'Tunjur, Tunjur', Tale 8 'Sumac! You Son of a Whore Sumac!' (*Sumāq yā ibn (...), sumāq*), Tale 13 'Sackcloth' and Tale 40 'Dunglet', address God directly asking for a baby, and their wishes are fulfilled. In Palestinian folk religion, God can be imagined as a physical being, who can be seen in the brilliance of the light shining from 'the gates of heaven' (Canaan, 1927). At the moment of childbirth, for instance, it is believed that 'the gates of heaven' (*bawābat al-samā '*) are supposed to open and all wishes come true; moreover, all the bad deeds of the mother are forgiven. It is also believed, according to the compilers, that at midnight on the twenty-seventh of Ramadan, or what Muslims refer to as the 'night of destiny' (*laylat al-qadr*), people stay up late and villagers claimed to see a 'door in heaven open and a strong light emanate from it' (Muhawi and Kanaana, 1989: 42).

In addition to the overlap between folk religion and official religion in folktales and real life, the events and development of characters' actions in the tales find their source in Palestinian social reality. Despite being controlled by supernatural forces,[6] action is rooted in Palestinian approach to, for instance, rewards and punishments and the doctrine of predestination in Islam. Language, once more, plays a major role in unfolding the action in the tales, which follow a blend of folk and official religious beliefs. Here, my discussion will focus mainly on language as a shaper of Palestinian cultural identity and memory, as studied, among other examples, in the last category of folktales: Group V, Universe. The tales in this group share one central theme, namely, God's wisdom and the acceptance of His will as manifested on a day-to-day basis. The heroes and heroines in this particular group exhibit a continual trust in God no matter how onerous their life becomes.

In Tale 43 'The Rich Man and the Poor Man',[7] the wife of a rich man was greedy and not contented with her wealth but consumed by envy of her poor sister when she also became rich. The envy or wickedness of the rich man's wife led to her end, and her metaphorical punishment was to be eaten by scorpions and serpents. The opposite happened to the wife of the poor man, whose acceptance of her lot in life and good relationship with her husband led to her being rewarded with wealth. Wisdom of character and advice can be seen when the rich husband advises his wife not to be greedy and imitate her sister, upon the latter's sudden wealth:

'Listen wife!' said the husband, 'Allah has blessed us with more than we need. We are content in our life, and we don't need anything more. Your sister was a poor woman, may God help her! Why don't you just forget about this?' (Muhawi and Kanaana, 1989: 305)	'يا مرة الله منعم علينا و مفظل علينا و قاعدين و مبسوطين و مش معتازين. هذيك أختك كانت فقيرة, الله يساعدها. شو بدك بهالشغلة؟' (Muhawi and Kanaana, 2001: 274)

Contentment with one's lot and satisfaction is expressed through religious phrases in Palestinian dialect, which are culturally embedded in everyday language. The weight of meaning of *Allah mina 'am a 'alyinā w mfaẓil/mufaḍil* (literally 'Allah has blessed us and is very generous with us') is part of people's beliefs and is used on a daily basis to express satisfaction with one's destiny no matter what. In my opinion, not only does Palestinian dialect relate to Palestinian communicative memory on a day-to-day basis, but its power is also imbued with the presence of religious expressions, highlighting the religiosity of Palestinian folk culture. The role of language creates bridges between communicative memory and cultural memory. Assmann (1995, 2006) allows, as I explained in Chapter 3, for a transitional memory work between intergenerational memory and intra-generational memory (Hirsch, 2008).

Another prominent example showing the power of language is seen in Tale 41 'The Woman Who Fell into the Well'.[8] Both the man and the woman who fell into the well accept God's will and welcome what befalls them. Fate in this tale is in full control of the plot and sequence of actions. The concordance between time and fate is harmonious since events unfold in a meaningful and chronological order. In fact, one action inevitably leads to another, until the woman is reunited with her brothers. Before and upon falling into the well, both the woman and the man express wisdom, strength and equanimity through language. It was a common practice for merchant-salesman travelling in remote villages in Palestine to stop by and ask for food at private homes (Muhawi and Kanaana, 1989), and the tale starts with this:

'Of course,' she said, and reached for the bread, *giving him what Allah put within her means to give* – a loaf, maybe two.

And, *by Allah*, on his way out of the house, he stumbled over a dog tied to a tree. Startled, the man fell backward, and behold! He ended up in a well that happened to be there. It was a dry well and held no water at all.

'There is no power and no strength except in Allah!' exclaimed the woman.

'O sister,' the man cried out, 'lower the rope and pull me out!'

Throwing him the rope, the woman started to pull him out but when he almost reached the mouth of the well her strength failed her. His weight grew too heavy for her, and she fell into the well with him.

'There is no power and no strength except in Allah!' exclaimed the man. 'But don't worry sister. *By Allah's book*, you are my sister!'

(Muhawi and Kanaana, 1989: 297; italics added for emphasis)

قالتله: 'طيب' تناولت اللي الله قدّرها عليه, رغيف, رغيفين, و أعطتهم لهالزلمة

و الله و هو طالع من هالدار و قام في هالكلب عرق الشجرة و قام يقع فيه. نقز الزلمة و رجع لورا, الّا في هالبير _بير ناشف ما في ميّ_ و قام هالزلمة يندبّ في هالبير.

قالت المره: 'لا حول و لا'

قالها: 'ياختي دلّي الحبل و انشليني'

دبّت الحبل عليه و دارت تنشل فيه. لمّن صار بده يصل باب البير ما قدرتش, غلب عليها, اندبت هي و اياه.

قال الزلمة: 'لا حول و لا. أقعدي يا ختي, إنتِ أختي في كتاب الله'

(Muhawi and Kanaana, 2001: 267)

For a translator, the most difficult aspect of working with the Arabic language is how to translate religious expressions into the target language. One solution, according to James Dickens et al., in *Thinking Arabic Translation*, is either to omit the expression or explain it in a footnote (Dickens et al., 2002). One of the problems with this approach, however, is a loss of the spirit and identity of the language, especially when translating folktales in colloquial Arabic. The compilers, being folklorists as well as translators, opted deliberately for a literal translation. 'In rendering colloquial Arabic into English, the translator must decide on the linguistic level, or tone, that best conveys the spirit of the original' (Muhawi and Kanaana, 1989: 51).

Opting for a literal translation could be the safest option if faithfulness to the language protects its cultural identity. When the woman offered some bread, *giving him what Allah put within her means to give* (for *tanāwlat alī allah qadarhā 'alīh*, the translation could have been avoided, and it would not have affected the flow of the plot or meaning; however, the compilers deemed it important since it reflects the way Palestinian religious beliefs are fundamental to cultural identity and ways of thinking. The same is observed with the abbreviated expression *lā ḥwlā w lā* which stands for *lā ḥwlā w lā qūwata ilā biallah* meaning literally 'there is no strength or power but with God's help'. The expression, used frequently in situations that are beyond individual control, is popular in other Arab Islamic countries. The distinctiveness of the religious expression, I think, lies in the way it is embedded by the storyteller in Palestinian dialect and context to convey the way Palestinians perceive and should perceive hardship. Finally, the man promises to respect the woman's honour, which in an Islamic and conservative context is interpreted so as to disclaim any sexual intentions. He even makes a binding declaration of honourable intent, saying *intī ukhtī fī kitāb allah*. The expression carries the weight of an oath and it means literally 'you are my sister by/according to the book of Allah'. Because Palestinian villagers are quite conservative, it is very unusual to find a woman and a man alone in the same place, hence the man feels it important to reassure the woman.

Language plays a very important role in shaping the plot of this tale, connecting the actions with fate. When the woman marries the man, she bears three children, named Maktūb, Kutba and Muqaddar. The names' meanings are variations on the theme of fate. The first name means 'that which is written'; the second refers to the writing itself (fate) and the third means 'that which is decreed'. The names allude to the unfolding of actions according to fate. Language is used in the form of puns which anticipate the fate of the woman, who is reunited with her brothers at the end. The fusion of folk religion and official religion in this particular case is apparent. It is a common belief among Muslims that one's fate 'is written on the forehead' (*maktūb a 'l jibīn*) or 'what is written on the forehead will be seen/lived' (*alī maktūb a 'l jibīn mā tishūfo ilā al-' ayn*). Both sayings express the notion of a pre-existing order, in which human life from birth till death is traced by God. This belief is embedded in Palestinians' interpretation of daily actions and therefore becomes indispensable in their communicative memory. The compilers, in this regard, explain in their introduction:

> As we study plot structure and the meaning of action, we observe a congruence of the traditional, predominantly Islamic Palestinian worldview and the significance of action in the tales. The equation we make between the concept of plot in art and the doctrine of predestination in life may be verified from the metaphor alluded to, 'It is written on the forehead,' that is used to express the notion of a pre-existing order. Life from birth to death is like a story authored by God, who breathes life into the soul at conception and sends the angel of death at the end. (Muhawi and Kanaana, 1989: 48)

The abovementioned tales share universal themes of reward and punishment or predestination found in many other folktales; yet the specificity, distinctiveness and power of actions in relation to fate lie in the language. The power of language, as mentioned, empowers the notion of 'national' and 'cultural' identity, giving prominence to Palestinian cultural memory. In this regard, cultural memory has the capacity to formalize communicative memory, turning the latter into a cultural system or 'a system of values' (Assmann, 1995: 131). The latter represents a form of knowledge that cultural memory tries to safeguard. Cultural memory is, according to Assmann, '*formative* in its educative, civilising and humanising functions and *normative* in its function of providing rules of conduct' (Assmann, 1995: 132; italics in original). Thus religious beliefs, via the medium of language, maintain a sense of continuity, knowledge and affirmation, giving voice to the heritage of a nation.

Woven with fictional images and supernatural forces, the plot, characters, themes and actions of folktales translate Palestinians' reality, constituting a unitary whole of the moral outlook of the community (Muhawi and Kanaana, 1989). A good example which shows the way language controls folktales and community outlook features also in the storytellers' opening statements. The opening formulas, used by the majority of storytellers in *SBSA*, reflect a unified and collective vision of God. Here are some common expressions adopted by the tellers:

Teller: Testify that God is One!
Audience: There is no God but God.
(Muhawi and Kanaana, 1989: 55)

الراوية: وحّدوا الله
الحضور: لا إله إلا الله
(Muhawi and Kanaana, 2001: 65)

Teller: Allah has spoken, and His word is a blessing.
Audience: Blessings abound, Allah willing!
(Muhawi and Kanaana, 1989: 148)

الراوية: قال الله و قال خير
الحضور: خير إن شاء الله
(Muhawi and Kanaana, 2001: 139)

Teller: Once upon a time but first a prayer of peace for the Virgin.
Audience: Peace be to her!
(Muhawi and Kanaana, 1989: 188)

الراوية: كان يا مكان عالعذرا صلاة السلام
الحضور: عليها السلام
(Muhawi and Kanaana, 2001: 171)

Teller: Once upon a time ... O my listeners, let him who loves the Virgin hail with blessings of peace!
Audience: Peace be with her.
(Muhawi and Kanaana, 1989: 255)

الراوية: كان يا مكان يا مستمعين الكلام, اللي يحب العذرا يرمي عليها إشارات السلام
الحضور: عليها السلام
(Muhawi and Kanaana, 2001: 230)

Teller: Once upon a time, O my listeners ... but not until you bear witness that God is One.
Audience: There is no god but God!
(Muhawi and Kanaana, 1989: 230)

الراوية: كان يا مكان يا مستمعين الكلام, حتى توحدوا الله
الحضور: لا إله إلا الله
(Muhawi and Kanaana, 2001: 208)

Teller: May Allah bless the prophet!
Audience: Allah bless him!
(Muhawi and Kanaana, 1989: 241)

الراوية: صلّوا عالنبي
الحضور: اللهم صلي عليه
(Muhawi and Kanaana, 2001: 218)

The six opening formulas contextualize the folktale in two monotheisms: Christianity and Islam. The importance of the opening formulas, in my opinion, consists in creating a collective sense of agreement of God's blessings and oneness. The opening formulas invite the listeners to look at the folktale as one of God's blessings to unify people upon believing in his greatness. The second formula in particular, according to the compilers, carries profound significance:

> First it glorifies the power of speech by attributing it to a divine source; second, it equates material blessings (*kher*) خير with the Logos, the divine word; and third, it demonstrates the importance of folktales to the community, since the formula implies that telling them is a blessing. (Muhawi and Kanaana, 1989: 148)

In my opinion, the blend of official and folk religion can empower collective belief and wisdom. The belief in God's strength and will reunites the community under the context of folk telling. In addition, the combination of Christian and Islamic formulas, in the third and fourth examples, emphasizes the diversity and tolerance of a harmonized community. The constant reference to the three monotheistic religions in Palestinian folktales is aimed at relating the religious history of Palestine, as the sacred land and the cradle of religions to Palestinian memory and to the richness of their cultural identity across time and space.

Folktales not only articulate desires, wishes and/or social reality, but also consolidate underlying attitudes which people hold about the meaning of life, about being predestined and about the acceptance of one's fate. One of the roles of the folktale, I argue, is to reveal the religious beliefs and practices which represent a shared system among the majority of Palestinians. Whether folk or official religion, superstitious or simplistic, Palestinian folktales, via the medium of language, are reflexive of 'the self-image of the group' (Assmann, 1995: 132). Reflexivity characteristic of cultural memory, discussed by Assmann, is not optional in the Palestinian case but a necessity in order to preserve Palestinian heritage and to strengthen communal bonds in the midst of increasing denial. The existence of Palestinian memory, whether collective or cultural, depends mainly on nurturing the specificity of Palestinian national identity. In fact, 'national identity requires both having a heritage and believing it to be unique' (Gillis, 1994: 4). In the same vein, the following section highlights the cultural significance of food in relation to memory, which, like religious expressions, symbolizes versatile cultural and social realities and a long-established heritage.

Food and memory

In its predominantly rural setting, Palestinian society used to rely heavily on labour-intensive agriculture on limited land, 'in which the size of an individual household could be thirty or more' (Muhawi and Kanaana, 1989: 37). Food was the main resource at the family's disposal. It is clear that Palestinian village life before 1948 revolved around the cultivation, consumption, storage, sale and distribution of food. As the compilers explain in their introduction, food

> is the family's primary concern and it takes up the greatest portion of their time. It is therefore not surprising that food assumes such an important role in the tales, and not merely as nourishment but as motivator for the action in some and a source of metaphor and symbol in others. (Muhawi and Kanaana, 1989)

The question raised, in this case, is how food can be linked to memory. If so, how can the former reinforce the latter? The folktales, as discussed so far, connect the Palestinian peasant to his/her land and rural setting, revealing how connected and collective the notion of 'identity' among villagers is. The peasant and the agricultural setting described can be considered as national signifiers (Swedenburg, 1990) and sites of memory (Nora, 1989). Along these lines, I will look at the way food and related rituals can present vivid sites of memory in Palestinian popular and oral literature in general and in *SBSA* and *Qul Ya Tayer* in particular. My aim in this section is to shed light on the way food features as an essential component of Palestinian cultural identity, mainly in the way it nourishes the preservation of collective memory. In order to do so, I will base my discussion on notions such as prospective memory (Sutton, 2008) and sensuous and sensory memory (Holtzman, 2006).

The development of food studies and journals such as *Food, Culture and Society* and *Food and Foodways* reveal a heightened awareness concerning the role of food and its connection to memory and identity. The question, according to Sutton, is 'to what extent can food be a key mediator of social relationships, a symbol of identity and a marker of difference' (Sutton, 2008: 159). In his works, mainly *Remembrance of Repasts* (2001), Sutton built on his analysis of food in relation to memory following his observations on the Greek Island of Kalymnos. Sutton noticed, for example, how the seasonal food cycle shapes 'prospective memory' (Sutton, 2008: 159) as people look forward to pears in August. In other words, memory appears through the nostalgia of performing particular rituals related to food. More significantly, people develop an active sense of nostalgia realized in looking forward to the next ritual practice. Sutton explains how outdoor ovens in Kalymnos are created by Kalymnians during Easter in particular in order to make 'prospective memory or active planning to make Easter celebrations memorable in the future' (Sutton, 2008: 164).

Through prospective memory people actively plan to remember meals, their taste and most importantly project the habit and desire onwards over future generations. Prospective memory, I argue, has the power not only to reinforce the memory of a particular food ritual or food experience but to also regenerate the desire to recreate past occurrences. Not only is the folktale an artistic and literary tool, it is the most comprehensive, precise, self-contained 'chunk of the culture' (Kanaana, 2012, see Appendix 1), which portrays Palestinian life, social interaction and daily routines. References to food and food rituals, as I will show, are prominent in the majority of tales. Once more, my analysis of food references will look at the way they feature in the folktales and in the paratextual elements.

Prospective memory

David Sutton's analysis of the way the people of Kalymnos engage during Easter time in cooking a traditional dish of lamb (Sutton, 2008) involved looking at people's discussions, rituals and expectations prior to and during the cooking process. The effort and 'active planning' of people to make the experience memorable also connects people to past, present and future. According to Sutton, this is seen when 'people complained of their hunger in the present while *reminiscing* about previous Easters and *looking forward* to the upcoming celebration' (Sutton, 2008: 164; italics for emphasis). 'Reminiscing' and 'looking forward' are key phrases which I would like to reflect on when looking at the way food features in the folktale collection under investigation. My aim is to discuss particular food references in specific tales as I believe that they are active agents and sites of Palestinian cultural identity and the essence of collectivity among Palestinians.

Food is very much present throughout the folktales. According to Muhawi and Kanaana, it is 'the basic motivator of action in all the *Environment* tales and it figures prominently in several others as well (e.g. Tales 1, 9, 14, 15, 27, 29, 34, 36, 45)' (Muhawi and Kanaana, 1989: 37). References to food are seen in different ways: in some cases food is the focus of social gatherings and celebrations; in other cases food takes the form of symbols and metaphors, whether in the story titles or in the actual tale. In all these cases, as I will discuss in more detail, food and food rituals enlighten the reader as to various cultural, religious and national elements of Palestinian identity. Memory, as I have analysed, is mainly collective and sustains its presence within social contexts (Halbwachs, 1992). Connerton (1989), however, sees social memory as 'an implicit rule that participants in any social order must presuppose a shared memory' (Connerton, 1989: 65). Although it is true in the sense of memory as an establishing social system in a well-settled society, Connerton's argument could be questioned in the case of Palestinians, for whom social memories are the product of interactions with the humans, objects, religion, history and institutions. Palestinian memory is intertwined within communicative and cultural memories (Assmann, 1995). The paradoxicality of Palestinian social collective memory lies in the bittersweet sense of nostalgia, which at one end fixates on the past and creates a narrative of escapism from the present; at the other end, however, it can be a form of reminiscence, and hope in a better future.

To understand how nostalgia and aspiration can consolidate Palestinian cultural identity, I will look at food in the folktales as sites of memory in the same way I looked at rural imagery. Food space within Palestinian society is versatile and culturally nurtured. Because food is important to the confines of the extended family, traditions related to food express values of Arab culture, hospitality and generosity. For instance, there is a constant reference to the concept of the *maḍāfa* or 'guesthouse', where Palestinians expressed their hospitality, mainly towards strangers. The guest would stay for at least three days, during which he/she was well fed and looked after by the host family. The guesthouse 'was a feature of Palestinian villages and towns well into the period of the British Mandate' (Muhawi and Kanaana, 1989: 39). Reference to the origin of the guesthouse concept by the compilers in their introduction merges history with memory and nostalgia on one hand. On the other, it extends the knowledge, more specifically the culture, related to hospitality to Palestinians in the diaspora or post-memory generations, who had not had first-hand experience of such settings and traditions.

Along the same lines, food is used to express many cultural and social aspects of Palestinian society. It is shared among Palestinians in birth, circumcision, death and 'possibilities of *nasab* (in-laws) and *ṣulḥa* (reconciliation) between two families' (Muhawi and Kanaana, 1989: 40). Food can also entail less noble motives as it can be used among villagers to compete for recognition and wealth. In other words, the more you spend on food the wealthier and more prestigious your social class. Like other societies, Palestinian families prepare huge feasts of food in order to 'seek for recognition of their generosity' (Muhawi and Kanaana, 1989: 39). The folktale and its framing by the compilers reveal society as it was, and still is, projecting the consequences of such beliefs on the disturbance of the harmony of the society. Even when food was not plentiful, favouritism is criticized in the society, and hence in the folktales. It leads 'to envy, jealousy, and conflict. Those who conspire in this favouritism are considered traitors to the collective interests of the family and thieves' (Muhawi and Kanaana, 1989: 38–9). Food representation in *SBSA* and its Arabic version, whether within the tales or in the framing, emphasizes the bond between food, memory and ethnic identity. I base my observation on the works of Brown and Mussell (1984) and Comito (2001) among others, who discussed the way ethnic identities, American in particular, are preserved and performed through food, for instance to validate ethnic identities during festivals and celebrations.

One of the main characteristics of popular culture, as I discussed in previous chapters, is 'resilience' against a particular regime, ideology or institution. Popular art and literature express in this way the voice of the masses in fighting or opposing oppression. In the case of the present folktales, I argue that food, in all its forms, is used as a means for resilience against the melting pot of other identities or cultures. Palestinians, both the masses and the intellectuals (in our case the compilers), use food not only as a memory site or platform for affirming their past but also to resist amnesia and Israeli's denial of Palestinian nationhood. Moreover, the power of reminiscence or nostalgia in Palestinian popular culture is a form of activating memory in the present and future, as I will elaborate shortly. The following quote by Muhawi and Kanaana lies at the heart of my discussion of the interconnectedness of social and collective memory with ethnic identity and food:

> The sharing of food, in short, is a *regular* and very important feature of Palestinian social life, forming an important link in the bonds that give the society its *coherence* and its *distinctive* character. (Muhawi and Kanaana, 1989: 39; italics for emphasis)

The words 'regular', 'coherence' and 'distinctive' convey the main characteristics of Palestinian memory, in my opinion. Regularity alludes to continuation and existence throughout time and space. In fact, sharing food, as I will discuss, is not confined to festivals or celebrations in Palestinian society but is seen as a transition from the individual to the collective, creating a coherent social harmony. Sharing food is also seen as symbol of a distinctive identity or even used explicitly in the creation of a national identity (Bellasco and Scranton, 2002; Anderson, 1983; Hobsbawm, 1983). As a cultural marker and symbol of identity, food features in the folktales not just within gatherings or solemn social occasions. Food and its processes – from growing and storing it, to eating and then defecating – are meant to generate metaphor and symbolism that reflect specific social and cultural attitudes within Palestinian society. The way food is referred to in some of the tales in the present folktale compilation draws attention to how food is connected to notions such as 'prospective memory', triggering the individual's particular food-related memory or sensation to be reproduced again in the future. In other words, the desire for the experience is projected onto the future. For instance, food is used in Palestinian culture and society as sign of love. In Tale 14 'Sackcloth' (*A 'bū al-lababīd*) and Tale 15 'Shahin' (*Shāhīn*),⁹ female characters interact with male characters over sharing food together. In 'Sackcloth', the lady disguised in sackcloth is being asked to take dinner to her master, the prince. Suspecting her disguise he says:

'Come sit here with me,' said the prince, closing the door. Let's eat the dinner together.'
'Please, master!' she protested, 'Just look at my condition. Surely it will disgust you.'
'No. Do sit down! I would like to have dinner with you.'
(Muhawi and Kanaana, 1989: 130)

قالها: تعالي أقعدي أتغذى انا و إياكِ
قالتله: يا سيدي إطّلَع كيف حالتي, بتقرف مني
قالها: لأ, أقعدي بدي أتغذى أنا و إياكِ
(Muhawi and Kanaana, 2001: 124)

In 'Shahin', the king's daughter, along with the daughters of the ministers and dignitaries of state, wanders about until they found the house of a young man. The latter usually prepares food for his forty brothers, who go out to hunt every day. The king's daughter is attracted by the young man and the following conversation starts:

'What's your name?'	شو اسمك ؟
'Shahin,' he answered.	قالها : شاهين
'Welcome, Shahin.'	قالتله: أهلا و سهلا شاهين
He went and fetched a chair, and set it in front of her. She sat next to him, and they started chatting. He roasted some meat, gave it to her, and she ate. She kept him busy until the food he was cooking was ready. 'Shahin,' she said when the food was ready, 'you don't happen to have some seeds and nuts in the house, do you?' (Muhawi and Kanaana, 1989: 131–2)	راح جابلها كرسي و حطها قدامها. قعدت حدّه و صاروا هذولا يتعرفوا و صار يشويلها لحم و يطعميها, و هي توكل. ظلت تعاقب بيه تخلّص الأكل. لمن خلص الأكل قالتله: شاهين كنّه فش عندكو نقل؟ (Muhawi and Kanaana, 2001: 125-6)

The king's daughter steals all the food he has prepared for his brothers. The young man seems vulnerable to her attraction so the same trick happens to him three consecutive times. According to the compilers, the young man is naive to the extent that he cannot resist the wit and charm of the princess, who fools him three times. My point of interest here is to look at how rituals of love within Palestinian culture, though seen within an imaginative plot, are often associated with food. Not only does reading the folktales foster the reader's literary pleasure and imagination but essentially it invites the reader to project their memory of 'the grilled meat' or 'the eating of seeds and nuts' onto the desire to relive the same experience of sharing food with their loved ones. Hence, one can see that prospective memory in relation to food rituals is often associated with particular feelings and emotions, such as love. These feelings are vividly entwined with a past that is longed for and looked forward to experience again.

Prospective memory, like post-memory (Hirsch, 1996, 1997, 2008), gives room for the future existence of past memories, past food-related rituals and even social and religious beliefs. Although consumed collectively, food remains the property of the patriarch (Muhawi and Kanaana, 1989). His permission is even sought before distributing food among the extended family. The patriarch's authority, according to Muhawi and Kanaana, can extend to controlling the mother's milk. In this regard they explain in their introduction:

> The wife may not nurse another woman's baby without his [the husband's] permission. (Actually, the concern here may be less over the loss of the milk than over the fact that milk siblings, who will likely be first cousins, are forbidden by religious law from marrying each other). (Muhawi and Kanaana, 1989: 37–8)

From a religious and cultural point of view, this belief not only existed in the past but persists still in many villages in the West Bank and among Palestinians living in Israel. The fact that breastfeeding can be problematic is also related to the traditional family structure in villages, being patrilineal, polygynous and endogamous. Even food distribution follows particular structures and social hierarchy to which many Palestinian families relate to today. For example, the patriarch tends to be given the best slice of meat or biggest portion of food (Muhawi and Kanaana, 1989); the family may wish also to honour its head by serving him first. Those cultural traditions related to food distribution may be interpreted as favouritism or even discrimination among members of the family. The folktale, in its educational and cultural mission, has to be faithful to the social system it is reflecting, in this case the Palestinian one. I am not in a position to disagree with a whole social system at this stage; however, I argue that the folktale is a vehicle for expectations to be fulfilled in the present and activated to persist in the future – through the concept of 'prospective memory' – or for future generations to be raised and educated to follow the same pattern – through post-memory.

As I have discussed previous chapters, I aim to show how Palestinian memory is dependent on collectivity and social interaction. Within the arena of food studies and memory, one can argue the fusion of individual and social memory; otherwise referred to as 'intimate' and 'public' memories. It is not my intention to go over the differences between individual and social memory at this stage. However, I agree with Holtzman that we need to look at the power of food for memory by 'intrinsically traversing the public and the intimate' (Holtzman, 2006: 373). In other words, the joy of eating and tasting has deeply private characteristics, but at the same time it is transacted through collective ways of sharing or social ritual. As he argues, 'One might consider the significance of this rather unique movement between the most intimate and the most public in fostering food's symbolic power, in general, and in relation to memory, in particular' (Holtzman, 2006). Thus there is an overlap or criss-crossing between the 'public' and the 'intimate'.

I find the interaction between the intimate and public spheres apparent in most folktales in this collection, particularly tales in Group IV (Environment). As discussed at the beginning of this chapter, the tales in this group are also known as 'formula' tales since they require a verbal precision that becomes part of the content (Muhawi and Kanaana, 1989). I have argued that language and content in this particular category of tales, such as 'Dunglet' or 'The Old Woman and Her Cat', complement each other, showing interdependence between the animate and inanimate worlds. The tales, in fact, symbolize the interconnectedness of Palestinian society and how that equilibrium can only be achieved if a communal effort is maintained among people. Food within these tales is also a major marker, showing people's dependence on nutritious elements which are associated with Palestinian villagers in particular. In Tale 40 'Dunglet' (Ba'irūn), the woman, who is unable to bear children, prays one day to God, wishing even for a 'piece of dung!'(Muhawi and Kanaana, 1989: 285). Her wish is fulfilled, and Dunglet helps his father, the ploughman, by taking lunch to him. Dunglet is, however, very greedy so devours everything he finds, even his father, mother and aunts. Apart from the fantastical element in the tale, the repetition of yogurt and bread as part of the formulaic language of the tale gives the reader, particularly the Westerner, an idea of the main food elements in Palestinian villages. The compilers chose to add a footnote in the English compilation (but not in the Arabic one) on the significance of yogurt and bread, saying,

> Yogurt is a major item in the peasant diet. With bread it makes a whole meal, and village families rely on the combination, together with olives and fresh vegetables, for sustenance, especially during the summer months. (Muhawi and Kanaana, 1989: 286)

The fact that the ploughman's lunch consists of yogurt and bread, among other elements such as olives, introduces the reader to ethnic and national food markers for Palestinians in the past and present. Like rural imagery, food can be a marker for collectivity among Palestinians. The village turns 'peasant-ness' and related food consumption into national dishes (Swedenburg, 1990). Furthermore, the folktale, in both English and Arabic versions, reflects normality within the daily life of people, who go to work while their wives prepare lunch for them. The children, who play the role of facilitators and support for Palestinian families, carry food to their fathers in the field, then help other members of the family with the washing. The cycle of order and normality is related to the harmonious sharing of food or help in food-making and delivery. Based on this example, it becomes clearer how the folktale and the compilers' framing turn the intimate sites of food's relation with the individual into a wider and more public sphere, reflecting the interaction, order and collective roles of family members among each other.

When disharmony arises, there is also an observable translation into the public sphere. This happens, as we saw at the beginning of the chapter, in this particular group of tales, 'when one of the links in the chain of relationships is upset, thereby triggering a process of readjustment in all the other links until equilibrium is restored' (Muhawi and Kanaana, 1989: 290). The 'readjustment' the compilers refer to symbolizes accordance and harmonization within all members of the society. In 'Dunglet', the disorder came when the dunglet started devouring everyone, and the only way to destroy him is to pierce his belly. The images related to the big belly and devouring are common beliefs in Palestinian folklore, symbolizing greed and dissatisfaction with one's lot. In fact, this tale has an educational function, according to the compilers, used by Palestinian mothers 'to teach lessons about the metaphorical significance of "devouring"' (Muhawi and Kanaana, 1989: 292). Thus, greedy people cause harm to social integration and damage the collective union each individual strives for.

Likewise, in Tale 39 'The Old Woman and Her Cat' (*Al- ' ajūz w al-bis*), the old woman's milk has been taken by the cat. Being angry, the old woman cuts off his tail, as a result the cat has to find milk in order to get his tail back. To restore order, the cat has to go through a chain of conditions made by the tree, the ploughman, the baker and the cobbler, among others. From the above examples, one notices the integration of the intimate and public in order to show the distinctiveness of food in relation to Palestinian peasant identity. Moreover, food-related symbols and actions are used in the folktales to reveal how social harmony is dependent on respecting fair shares and through asking for help to achieve social balance.

Sensuous memory

Similar to Paul Connerton's (1989) notion of bodily memory and Paul Stoller's (1995) emphasis on embodied memories, David Sutton (2001) discusses the sensuality of food, which causes it to be a powerful medium of memory. Because eating involves both physical and emotional experiences, provoked by the smell or the taste, the experience of food, according to Sutton, evokes recollection. For example, Luce Giard (1998) interprets the everyday practice of eating as making 'concrete one of the specific modes of relation between a person and the world, thus forming one of the fundamental landmarks in space-time' (Giard, 1998: 183). In the same manner, Julia Powles (2002) argues how the collective memory of displacement for refugees in Zambia is constructed through their common experience of the absence of fish. Thus, references to food, food practices and even absence can generate strong bodily memories and nostalgia, and foster prospective memory.

Based on Sutton's useful discussion of food, I argue that food is perceived as the engine or motivator of not only bodily memories but also collective memory. At the beginning of the chapter, I discussed how the relations of peasantry to imagery in the folktales reinforce the sense of collectivity and highlight the distinctiveness of Palestinian rural identity. The reference to particular peasant items and rural landscapes helps, as I explained, to instigate a sense of active remembering. Along the same lines, reference to food in some of the folktales in *SBSA* and *Qul Ya Tayer* serves to inform the Western reader of Palestinian food markers, which relate culture to identity and memory. In addition, food references for the Palestinian reader are meant to activate his/her bodily memory and thus nurture his/her nostalgia.

If we take Tale 8 'Sumac! You Son of a Whore, Sumac' (*Sumāq yā ibn (...), sumāq*), the story revolves around a complex plot, but the main element needed for the hero to regain his lions and caravans is to guess the content of one of the loads, which is sumac. Because Sumac is a popular spice used in Palestinian cuisine, the compilers deemed it necessary to explain it:

> *Summaq*, the crushed red fruit of a non-poisonous plant of the cashew family (genus Rhus), is used extensively in Palestinian cuisine; the leaves, fruit, and bark are also used in tanning and dyeing. (Muhawi and Kanaana, 1989: 98)

This spice is commonly used in making a very popular dish named *musakhan* in the countryside. For the majority of Palestinians, this spice is connected to the making of *musakhan*. The storyteller could have replaced the spice with other kinds of spices; however, the integration of specifically *sumac* into the folktale provides a more authentic, ethnic and national level to the understanding of Palestinian cuisine, and hence its relevance to Palestinian cultural identity. Moreover, reference to the spice stimulates the Palestinian reader to recollect memories related to eating *musakhan* and the pleasure of sharing it with others, since it is always eaten in a group. Like Tale 8, Tale 12 'Jummez Bin Yazur, Chief of the Birds', has reference to food in the title. 'The fruit Jummez, is a type of fig (Ficus sycamorous) that hangs down in bunches more like cherries than figs' (Muhawi and Kanaana, 1989: 117). According to the compilers, the use of fruit and other foods symbolizes sexuality. However, I am more interested in the combination of this particular fruit with a village called *Ya'zūr*. *Ya'zūr*[10] is the name of a Palestinian village which, prior to 1948, was located on the coastal plain close to Jaffa. The fact that the title combines a fruit with the name of a historic village from pre-1948 Palestine has the power to trigger the sensuousness of old memories, which carries a sentimental weight for first and second generation Palestinians. In this particular example, sensuous memory and collective memory are combined, inviting the Palestinian reader to associate the name and existence of this type of figs to a pre-*Nakba* land.

In fact, the bond between the land, the trees and fruits and Palestinians is strong and vivid. As Bardenstein (1999) describes in her article on the link between trees and forests in the shaping of Israeli and Palestinian collective memory, Palestinian literature, such as the works of Fadwa Tukan, Mahmoud Darwish and many more, rely on vivid descriptions of land, fig trees, olive trees and orange blossoms in order to express and transmit the power of their collective memory to coming generations:

> When this bond is recalled or imagined as intact, as 'the good old days' before its disruption, or the glorious days to come with its restoration, it is portrayed as a state of almost cosmic harmony; trees thrive and flourish in affirmation of Palestine peopled by Palestinians as the natural order of things. (Bardenstein, 1999: 150)

The way nature is portrayed in Palestinian literature gives the impression that nature is in sympathy with the Palestinians. In a more particular sense, fig trees, for example, stand for an idealized time and state. The sensuousness of tasting a fig or having a fig tree encapsulates for Palestinians a lost paradise, which is reactivated continuously, as sites of memory, due to loss and dislocation.

A similar example is seen in Tale 13 'Jbene' (*Jbīna*). Jbene, a very beautiful girl, goes one day with her friends to collect some fruit from *shajarat al-dūm* (the dom tree). The compilers feel the need to explain the dom tree in a footnote in both Arabic and English collections. Based on the study of Crowfoot and Baldensperger (1932) on folklore of plants in Palestine, the compilers quote the following:

> *Dom*, or Christ-thorn (Zizyphus spina-christi), is a wild tree bearing edible fruit. Tradition has it that Christ's crown of thorns was made from the branches of this tree. Some specimens are centuries old and have attained considerable size. (Crowfoot and Baldensperger in Muhawi and Kanaana, 1989: 122)

The dom tree is renown among Palestinians for being similar to the palm tree in terms of strength and longevity of life. The dom tree can also survive in very dry conditions but maintain a shiny green colour throughout the year. As I have discussed in previous chapters and this chapter, the storytellers were able to ground the tales within Palestinian society and culture as well as landscapes and food. The choice of this particular tree rather than others, in my opinion, raises questions on the symbolism of this tree in Palestinian culture. Being a national symbol in Palestinian culture, related images and metaphors to fig trees and olive trees are prevalent in written and oral literature. Trees are not only used to call upon a longing for a homeland but are also used to assert Palestinians' *ṣumūd* (steadfastness) in the face of adversity (Swedenburg, 1990). Trees such as *jumīz* and *dūm* are immortalized, standing for Palestinians' rootedness and heritage, which in spite of the odds will not vanish.

Oral literature, in this case folktales, address the whole society, both young and old, which, I argue, means that it can deliver a stronger message than written literature. Oral or popular culture discourse is not confined to particular social classes or linguistic registers; on the contrary, the speech is earthy, direct and potentially more powerful. Being a source of pleasure, particularly if experienced collectively, storytelling and folktales can be more effective in reinforcing Palestinian collective memory among younger generations. Palestinian children, both in diaspora or in occupied Palestinian territories, can become familiar with the significance of particular trees or fruit in the construction of their belonging and cultural identity. Trees such as the olive tree or fig tree become 'the repository for Palestinian collective memory, which will live on to bear witness to the details of Palestinian suffering long after the human beings who experienced it are gone' (Bardenstein, 1999: 155–6). Hence the occurrence of trees or fruit in Palestinian oral and written literature is seen as a powerful spiritual metaphor, serving to symbolize the strength of Palestinian collective memory as well as encouraging future generations to outlive the present unnatural order of things.

Food references, as we have seen, represent a marker for national identity and collective memory. They can also trigger gustatory nostalgia (Sutton 2001). In Tale 28 'Chick Eggs' (*Bayẓ faqāqīs*), the father is ashamed of his daughter, who became pregnant from eating eggs, and wants to get rid of her. Fearing disgrace among the others in the village, he decides to leave her somewhere remote and not come back for her. The pregnant daughter, unaware of her father's intention, waits for him to come back and get her, saying,

'Father, you're taking so long to crap	'يا بوي ما أطول خراك \ نبّت الزعتر'
The thyme has started to sprout!'	'وراك'
(Muhawi and Kanaana, 1989: 231)	(Muhawi and Kanaana, 2001: 209)

The Palestinian reader would find the Arabic funny since Palestinian folkloric humour tends to use body parts or defecation in jokes or old sayings. Sounding like a proverb in the Palestinian vernacular, the statement means idiomatically that 'her father is taking ages/a long time to come back'. The deliberate mixing of humour and food reference, namely, *za'tar* (thyme) is explained in a footnote by the compilers:

> Thyme is a component of *za'tar* زعتر, which may be considered the Palestinian national dish. The herb, together with other herbs as well as solid ingredients such as roasted wheat and garbanzo beans, is ground into a fine powder. Bread is dipped into oil and then into the *za'tar* زعتر, all being accompanied by fresh green vegetables. Although this meal is usually eaten for breakfast, it forms part of the staple diet in the Palestinian household. (Muhawi and Kanaana, 1989: 231)

If read separately, one would think that this footnote or description is taken from a cookbook. The information given by the compilers aims at introducing this particular dish as unique to Palestinians. In fact, *za'tar* marks their national identity and is perceived as crucial in any Palestinian house. The purpose of the footnote is twofold. If read by Westerners, the information will highlight the importance of *za'tar* in Palestinian cuisine, in general, and its national characteristic, in particular. But when Palestinians, particularly of the diaspora generations, read it, either in the Arabic or the English version, what Sutton (2001) refers to as 'gustatory nostalgia' will be triggered. Humorous language is also perceived as a medium for relating laughter with food in order to recreate a pleasant memory.

Nostalgia in this sense is seen as a form of memory, in food-centered nostalgia studies. In this regard Sutton, for example, has analysed the longing evoked among diasporic communities by particular smells or tastes of a lost homeland. The power of nostalgia, in his opinion, is central to the creation of memory since sentiments of longing foster diasporic communities' sense of belonging to a specific nation. In other cases, gustatory nostalgia relies also on 'a lay notion of sentimentality for a lost past, viewing food as a vehicle for recollections of childhood and family' (Holtzman, 2006: 367). Because nostalgia usually emerges after displacement, individuals, including Palestinians, make continuous efforts to establish a shared past they can relate to and nurture. Loss, according to Fred Davis, results in identity discontinuity, 'which nostalgia can repair by creating a shared generational identity to mend the lost one' (Davis quoted in Milligan, 2003: 384). Echoing Davis's argument, the sensuousness of food in oral literature, as I explained, is a site for memory activation and memory work in the Palestinian case; the power of food can be construed as a vehicle for Palestinian memory in the past and today.

Food and women: Agents of memory

Food references not only represent sites of memory in the folktales of *SBSA* but can also allude to the role of agents of memory, namely, Palestinian female storytellers. Palestinian women, as I discussed in Chapter 3, play a vibrant role in the transmission of collective memory, both as storytellers and as main characters in folktales. I extend my argument in this chapter to suggest that Palestinian female storytellers have gendered the tales through the medium of food to give rise to a feminine form of memory. In this regard, a number of studies have discussed the existing interconnection and relationship between women, food and memory. Miriam Meyers (2001), for example, sees 'food heritage' as a gift transmitted from mother to daughter; it can, in her opinion, help in reinforcing or correcting dysfunctional relationships between mother and daughter. Benay Blend (2001) interprets tortilla making, a ritualized act, as reinforcing the role of Latina women in creating a gendered cultural identity, seeing: 'Tortilla making as a woman-centred, role-affirming communal ritual that empowers women as the carriers of tradition' (Blend, 2001: 47). Some even consider the kitchen as a repository for memory, in which the woman exercises her power. Paul Christensen (2001), for instance, describes his mother's experience: 'To open the skin of a garlic and dice its contents into grains allowed her to become a daughter again, to re-enter the female world of her childhood' (Christensen, 2001: 26). I am therefore interested in looking at the way Palestinian women, both as storytellers and principal characters in the folktales, mediate collective memory at the social and cultural level through food.

In the realms of individuality versus collectivity, the way in which women transfer individual memories into a broader sphere of collective memory is significant. Each Palestinian female storyteller in the collection under study has a mature approach to life, society and narration and hence has earned her credibility and power. In studies conducted on oral history, David Middleton and Derek Edwards (1990) noted that 'the study of remembering in conversation affords unique opportunities for understanding remembering as organised social action' (Middleton and Edwards, 1990: 43). Based on this, Graham Smith (2007) analysed how talking in groups allows experiences to be shared and the emotional context of remembering to be transmitted. The force of communication, he argues, lies in the concept of 'transactive memory', as defined by Daniel Wegner:

> Transactive memory can be defined in terms of two components: (1) an organised store of knowledge that is contained entirely in the individual memory systems of the group members, and (2) a set of knowledge-relevant transactive processes that occur among group members. Stated more colloquially, we envision transactive memory to be a combination of individual minds and the communication among them. (Wegner quoted in Smith, 2007: 79)

In his study, Smith showed how women in groups shared individual experiences, safe in the knowledge that the others will relate to them. Hence, the process instigates a communal ground of shared emotions and experiences, which they enjoy reminiscing about together. The notion of 'transactive memory' is relevant to my discussion on the way Palestinian female storytellers, endowed with experience and knowledge, transfer Palestinian cultural values, traditions and beliefs to another group of people: a young male and female audience, who all share the aftermath of *Nakba* and quest for identity affirmation. Through references to food, one can understand social and cultural aspects of Palestinians through the 'feminine' lens.

As seen in Chapter 3, the role of women is central to every folktale, as the motivators of actions and as main characters. At this stage, I am interested in analysing how references to food are used by women or about women in *SBSA* to portray the Palestinian culture, hence also engendering a feminine form of memory, both cultural and collective. One of the first elements that caught my attention is the title of some folktales in *SBSA* and *Qul Ya Tayer*: Tale 1 'Tunjur, Tunjur', Tale 12 'Jummez Bin Yazur, Chief of the Birds', Tale 13 'Jbene', Tale 28 'Chick Eggs' and Tale 35 'Pomegranate Seeds'. These tales express in one way or another Palestinian women's desire, roles and wishes in a culture which would not usually allow women to express their sexuality and other aspects of their experience.

In the case of Tale 1 'Tunjur, Tunjur', *Ṭunjur*, the title is the name of the heroine:

> The name of the tale is an onomatopoeic derivation for the sound of a rolling cooking pot (*tunjara*). The feminine ending of this word helps to establish the equation of 'pot' with 'girl'. In the translation the neuter 'it' is used when the pot is perceived as an object. (Muhawi and Kanaana, 1989: 55)

The tale, as discussed above, revolves around the wish of a woman to become pregnant after a long wait. Her desperate desire for offspring made her pray to have a female child, even if she were a cooking pot. As we saw, her wish comes true and she has a cooking pot called *Ṭunjur*, who helps her mother by providing food and goods for the household. The importance of having children in Palestinian society is a recurrent theme in the tales. According to the compilers, 'The tale demonstrates the economic value children have in Palestinian society' (Muhawi and Kanaana, 1989: 82), particularly females.

Conversely, food is used as metaphoric symbols to make women conceive, such as in Tale 6 'Half-a-Halfling' (*Nuṣ nṣīṣ*), when the sheikh advises the husband to get his wife pomegranate seeds, as these are believed to increase women's fertility in Palestinian culture and folklore. (See below for the symbolism of pomegranates in Palestinian society.) Similarly, Tale 28 'Chick Eggs' (*Bayẓ faqāqīs*), the young lady buys eggs – believed to help women conceive – from the market. Being unmarried, she starts craving things till the father realizes that his daughter is pregnant and, as explained previously, decides to get rid of her. In this case, pregnancy is not favoured at all and is even strictly prohibited socially and religiously in the conservative Palestinian society. In fact, Palestinian society considers unmarried pregnant woman a disgrace to the family's honour. In both 'Chick Eggs' and 'Tunjur, Tunjur', food symbolizes the metaphoric desire to become pregnant or bear children. In spite of the importance of offspring in Palestinian society, shared in both tales, there are social, religious and cultural constraints which prevent unmarried Palestinian women conceiving a child. Women's memory is transmitted through a formative and educational role to younger generations, signposting the difference between acceptable and non-acceptable conduct.

Along similar lines, the cultural weight of pregnancy is also seen in the way Palestinian society perceives the cravings of pregnant women. In Tale 43 'The Rich Man and the Poor Man' (*Al-ghanī w al-faqīr*), there are two sisters, one married to a poor man and the other to a rich man. One day, the wife of the poor man visits her sister. Being pregnant, the wife of the poor man had cravings for a Palestinian popular dish her sister was making, called *malfūf* (stuffed cabbage), but her sister did not offer her any. The storyteller says,

Now the wife of the poor brother had recently become pregnant and she craved the food. When she smelled the cabbage, she sighed, 'Alas!' she thought in her heart. "Would that I had even one of those cabbage ribs to eat!" (Muhawi and Kanaana, 1989: 302)	هذيك مرة الأخو الفقير فيّتها جديد و بتتوحم. شمّت ريحة هالملفوف و صارت تتنهد و تقول بقلبها: 'علوّاه يصبولي و لو إنه ضلع ملفوف آكله!' (Muhawi and Kanaana, 2001: 271)

In this particular tale, I believe that different notions of memory and food are combined. Firstly, the reference to *malfūf* ('stuffed cabbage') triggers the reader's sensuous memory of the dish and gustatory nostalgia among Palestinians;

furthermore, it invites the Western reader to discover more about the Palestinian cuisine and culture, particularly following the compilers' footnote:

> Stuffed cabbage (*malfuf*) is one of the most popular of Palestinian dishes. The description of its preparation is abbreviated in the tale. The cabbages are first boiled and then separated into leaves from which the ribs are removed. The boiled ribs are popular as snacks for the children while the meal is being cooked, or they may be inserted under or among the rolled leaves in the saucepan. The stuffing consists of minced lamb, rice, ghee, and condiments (salt, black pepper, and turmeric and/or cumin), and whole cloves of peeled garlic are added among the stuffed leaves. Stuffed cabbage, when cooking, has a characteristic aroma. (Muhawi and Kanaana, 1989: 302)

The detailed footnote draws also on prospective memory as it activates what I would call 'productive nostalgia', generating the desire to relive and look forward to the experience in the future. The compilers even describe the 'in-between' process, in which children eat the boiled ribs as snacks before the meal is ready. Hence, the joy of eating is the joy of sharing collectively the traditions related to it, which affirm social and cultural 'Palestinian-hood'. The feminine discourse of memory exemplified in the medium of food finds its main force from memories of pre-*Nakba* lifestyle and customs. Referring to food can be seen as a nostalgic technique used to 'foster affiliation or stronger social bonds' (Sedikides et al., 2008b: 231). As I discussed throughout this chapter and the second chapter, nostalgia, though complex and ambivalent, can act as a social mobilizer, unifying people who shared the same experience. Food's role, representation and symbolism, I argue, are twofold: It reinforces women's discourse of memory within the private sphere, empowering women's cultural and national voice as storytellers and protagonists. Moreover, food is a tool for activating collective memory through the medium of nostalgia; the latter helps in reinforcing social bonds within the public sphere. The compilers do not content themselves with the abovementioned footnote but explain further the importance of cravings in Palestinian society. Consolidating their argument through Hilma Granqvist's insight on craving in Palestine, they quote from her work *Birth and Childhood among the Arabs* (1947:

> Regarding smell, she says, 'The same woman had once cooked something which gave a very strong smell and then a woman relative said to her, "Do not forget! In the next house dwells such and such a woman and she is in

a certain condition thou must give her some of the food!" She at once took some down to her.' In general, says Granqvist, 'if a person cannot satisfy his desire for a special food this harms him. If he can see the food, it is also harmed and in that way they who eat of it. People are afraid to eat food which another has longed for. They say that his soul is in it.' (Granqvist quoted in Muhawi and Kanaana, 1989: 302)

Craving in Palestinian society thus transcends the physical or bodily desire for food. There is, I think, a craving culture among Palestinians, whether among pregnant women or in simple longing for food. The belief might look superstitious or simplistic; however, I regard such cultural beliefs as essential in establishing a distinctive cultural identity for Palestinians. More importantly, it encourages solidarity, compassion and collectivity by emphasizing the social role of sharing and helping. The collective sense of responsibility towards craving pregnant women is also seen in Tale 2 'The Woman Who Married Her Son' (*Ilī tzawajat ibinhā*), in which the mother, who is disguised as the wife of her son, gets pregnant. She starts craving sour grapes, so asks her servant to get some from the neighbours, saying,

'O mistress of our mistress,' said the servant, 'you whose palace is next to ours, give me a bunch of sour grapes to satisfy the craving on our side!' (Muhawi and Kanaana, 1989: 61)	يا ست ستّنا ياللي قصرك بجنبقصرنا أعطيني قطف حصرم للوحام اللي عندنا (Muhawi and Kanaana, 2001: 70)

Craving can be considered a powerful tool to draw the attention of neighbours, family and husband. Everyone in Palestinian society is expected to fulfil the cravings of a pregnant woman, no matter how hard to realize. Since the storytellers are women, the tales are told and construed through their lens. Through storytelling Palestinian women not only communicate their embedded cultural values, but most importantly they seem to regulate or veto specific social practices thanks to their endowed authority and wisdom. As a result, the Palestinian reader of, or listener to, the folktale would relate to the collective duty towards pregnant women and subconsciously inherit the cultural perception. Thus the folktale gains its strength through women's transmittable desire to share their individual experiences, rooted cultural customs and memories across generations.

Food references are also used by women in the folktales to symbolize sexuality and beauty. In Tale 12 'Jummez Bin Yazur, Chief of the Birds', Tale 13 'Jbene' and Tale 35 'Pomegranate Seeds', the titles of the tales refer to the hero (Tale 12) and heroines (Tales 13 and 35). In 'Jummez Bin Yazur, Chief of the Birds', the bird, explain the compilers, connotes male sexuality (Muhawi and Kanaana, 1989:117). As mentioned before, the first part of the title refers to a particular type of fig in the village of Yazur. This tale is one of those in *SBSA* addressing women and men's sexual awakening and desires, as classified by the compilers, among Group I (Individuals), in the third sub-group, Sexual Awakening and Courtship. The young lady in the tale is looking for the best man to marry so asks her father to bring her from pilgrimage the chief of birds, Jummez Bin Yazur, who is symbolized by the bird.

In the same sub-group of tales, we find Tale 13 'Jbene' *jbīna*. Jbene, which is the diminutive of 'Jibne' (cheese), is the name of the heroine. It is unusual to name a girl 'Jbene' but because the mother had wished to conceive a beautiful girl with a fair complexion, her wish was fulfilled:

One day, when a cheese vendor passed through, she gathered herself and cried out, 'You who ask, your wish be granted!' May Allah grant me a daughter with a face as white as this piece of cheese!' (Muhawi and Kanaana, 1989: 122).	يوم مرّ بيّاع هالجبنة. قامت قالت: 'يا طالبة يا غالبة, تطعمني بنت يكون وجهها ابيظ مثل قرص هالجبنة.' (Muhawi and Kanaana, 2001: 119)

The mother as a result gave birth to a girl with a fair complexion and a face as round as the cheese she was craving. The compilers sought to explain the connection between food and culture, as follows:

> The cheese referred to here is made from sheep's milk. It is white and comes in slabs (*qraas*, sing: *qurs*) of about three inches square by half an inch, with rounded corners, that are stacked in brine. Thus, the mother is asking for a daughter with fair complexion and a round face. (Muhawi and Kanaana, 1989: 122)

As in Tale 43 'The Rich Man and the Poor Man', the compilers evoke the readers' sensuous and transactive memory, explaining beauty culture, particularly in Palestinian villages, where food, animals and landscapes shape people's standards of beauty. The heroine, Jbene, turns out to attract the attention of many neighbours, who are captivated by her beauty. Cheese, hence, is culturally construed among Palestinian villagers to symbolize beauty and later sexuality, being very attractive. Once again themes of conceiving and craving are raised in this tale, which highlights the importance of having children in Palestinian society. As I discussed in Chapter 3, a woman who does not conceive in rural conservative Palestinian community usually loses her authority at home and would expect to become a co-wife or even a divorcee.

In addition to the sexual connotation of fruits in the folktales, naming girls with fruit names can have a religious interpretation, such as in Tale 35 'Pomegranate Seeds' (*Ḥab al-rumān*). It is not usual to name a girl 'Pomegranate Seeds', but for the sake of conveying a particular message, it is used as a symbol. The image of pomegranate seeds is associated with deep redness and ripeness and hence refers to health and beauty (Muhawi and Kanaana, 1989). Grace Crowfoot and Louise Baldensperger (1932: 111) describe in an account of Palestinian lore about the pomegranate that 'brides are often compared to pomegranate for beauty'. Taufik Canaan (1927), as the compilers quote in a footnote, says that 'every pomegranate has one seed which has come from heaven' (Canaan, 1927: 166). In the same vein, he adds that city Muslims 'take great care not to drop or lose any of the seeds, since that might be just the one which came from paradise' (Canaan cited in Muhawi and Kanaana, 1989: 261). In Palestinian folklore, there is even a proverb that goes 'Pomegranates fill the heart with faith' (*al-rumān bīmlī al-qalb īmān*). Similarly, in the fusion of folk and official religion discussed at the beginning of the chapter, the imagery of pomegranates stands for highly respected beliefs in Palestinian culture and religion. Pomegranates represent beauty and holiness and thus have positive connotations.[11] Transactive memory does not confine itself to the transmission of personal or social memories but more importantly reinforces community beliefs about beauty, for example, which in Palestinian society is mixed with folk religion.

Food references also bear various cultural, religious, folkloric and social layers of meaning, which would have vanished if the tradition of storytelling among Palestinian women had not existed. The voice of women as storytellers and heroines in the folktales, seen in the themes or titles, plays an essential role in framing, transmitting and preserving Palestinian memory, engendering a feminine form of Palestinian memory. The tales and footnotes discussed above, among others, reinforce my argument of the successful integration of paratextual elements within and around the tales. The consistency and harmony of cultural elements, storytelling, Palestinian dialect and compilers' elaboration, not only render *SBSA* and its Arabic version a scholarly and comprehensive work on Palestinian oral literature but also give readers a solid image of Palestinian national and cultural identity.

Final Reflections

The preceding chapters analyse an essential constituent of Palestinian literature, namely oral and folkloric literature, giving special focus to Muhawi and Kanaana's compilation *Speak Bird, Speak, Again* (1989) and *Qul Ya Tayer* (2001). Given the very useful cultural, anthropological and folkloric insights offered by the compilers, and which many other compilations failed to match, in these chapters I analysed all of the compilers' roles, the storytellers' narratives and the folktales from the point of view of cultural and memory studies. While some answers have been given to some questions, a great many more have been raised, awaiting future study. Not only the compilation under discussion but the many other folktales as well lend themselves to analysis from a variety of disciplinary angles, not only in folklore but also in the sphere of comparative literature, literary theory, gender studies and many more cultural, political and historical approaches. My aim in this book has been to give academic scrutiny to, and to contextualize Palestinian folktales and storytellers, offering the reader a mix of description, analysis and theory in order to understand how this particular genre in Palestinian oral literature can frame Palestinian memory and identity.

What these chapters have made clear is that although collective memory and post-memory work can manifest itself in the arts, there is still more work needed to analyse the agents of memory transfer. In this book I tried to shed some light on the female storyteller in gendering and engendering Palestinian cultural identity and memory through the folktale genre in Palestine from the perspective of social, cultural and memory studies. It is however worth taking this further and analysing her agency as a storyteller within the political arena. Although a lot of research has been carried out on Palestinian women's historical narratives in refugee camps, the diaspora and Palestine, and its association with politics and nationalism (Kassem, 2011; Abdel Haddi, 2018, there are hardly any studies that analyse the political and national impact of folktale telling among Palestinian women. The focus has always been on epic or legendary tales narrated by men at the *diwan*, or on Intifada tales (see below, Appendix 1). It would be also very interesting to look at the fusion of the public and private spheres in folk telling. As I discussed in this book, the domestic sphere is the main setting for women to tell folktales; it is private and familial. Nowadays, however, according to a number of women storytellers I spoke to in the West Bank, there is a shift from the private/domestic setting to the public. More and more women storytellers are performing in public and on stage, an area usually dominated by men telling epic stories. There is in fact a growing interest among young women in learning storytelling in order to perform in public, which also means that there is a growing interest in performance studies and theatre among young educated Palestinian women. For future studies, the merge between the domestic and public, the private and the national, the familial and social within cultural, drama and gender studies could bring valuable insights to the development of storytelling in Palestine.

Within the recent development in storytelling, there is also much talk among Palestinian folklorists about rewriting the folktale, which is different from documenting it. Sharif Kanaana (2017)[1] in this regard thinks that the folktale could be rewritten and adapted to a specific time and for a particular purpose. This means that the folktale can be a written product as well as oral; moreover, the storyteller has some freedom to modify or change the plot of the folktale. Kanaana believes that by rewriting the folktale we secure its transmission giving room for the storyteller to be creative. This is definitely another way for documenting orality, which in the Palestinian case has a significant urgency. It, however, leads us to question the extent of which either the folklorist or the storyteller has to change, adapt or manipulate the reception of the final product. In this book I discussed the distinctive scholarly paratextual materials surrounding the tales that have explained and contextualized some of the most popular Palestinian folktales from anthropological, social and folkloric perspectives. This scholarly effort on the part of Muhawi and Kanaana is, as I have said, unique in Palestinian folktale compilations either in English or Arabic. The framing nonetheless made the reader see the interpretation of the tales through the compilers' lens, which in some cases could be questioned. The question here is to what extent can the authorial voice of the folklorist interfere in presenting or explaining the tale? Although the tales were kept as authentic as possible in their Palestinian Arabic dialect of origin, whether rural or urban, the reader does not have first-hand experience of the tale. The process has gone through many filters. On the one hand, we have the compilers who first choose the storytellers; they then choose the folktales they want to present in their compilation. This is not to mention that the storyteller might have made some changes to the original folktale while narrating. On the other hand, the compilers' voice and interpretation of the tale or characters could be different from the storytellers' interpretation, or might only overlap to a certain extent, particularly if the compiler is male and the storyteller is female. Having said that, both Muhawi and Kanaana have highlighted the pioneering role of Palestinian women in mastering this particular genre of folk telling and in passing it on to coming generations. Another niche for study in the future could be though to focus only on the voice of storytellers and tales, minimizing authorial manipulation or filters.

Within the public sphere, and particularly in Gaza and the West Bank, *Qul Ya Tayer* (2001) ceased to be part of the Palestinian school curriculum following claims from some Palestinian Islamic parties and the Palestinian Authority that the book contains inappropriate expressions and taboo words, which in their opinion should not be taught to children. In 2007 the Palestinian Ministry of Education ordered the withdrawal of all copies from the libraries and schools. This move sparked much controversy among Palestinian politicians, folklorists and ordinary people. Voices were raised protesting against the change or supporting it; the majority, however, defended the idea of maintaining the book in Palestinian schools, for its cultural value and as part and parcel of Palestinian heritage and identity. This incident raises some questions about the role of public institutions in safeguarding Palestinian cultural memory. The latter, as I discussed before, is manifested through traditional archiving of memories seen 'through monuments, days of remembrance and other structures or institutions that together form a shared identity for a group' (Hirsch, 2008: 111). Since 2010, however, there has been a growing interest among cultural institutions, theatres and in the Ministry of Culture in teaching the importance of storytelling by encouraging young people to become storytellers. For instance, there are a number of workshops run to train young people to become storytellers, whether in epic stories or folktales (or both).[2] The shift is encouraging and very much needed in the current political context, but it leaves us wondering about the positioning once again of the public/official role of documenting and perpetuating the tradition of storytelling within the parameters of political powers, as opposed to the personal, familial/private and more social/collective effort of gathering, telling and spreading epic or folktales.

Finally, the folktales under discussion in *SBSA* and *Qul Ya Tayer* are, as I discussed, not political in nature, but feature the familial and social structures of Palestine before 1948. This category of folktales is still widespread in the domestic sphere, although less than before due to a number of factors, such as displacement, current political instability and the dominance of technology and internet communication. Another factor is the surge of other types of oral narratives, mainly contemporary legend tales and Intifada tales. According to Kanaana (2017) these two genres evolved after the First and Second Intifada, and both adults and children have contributed to the narration and creation of the plot. The stories find their source in traditional folktales but are adapted to a more contemporary setting, featuring Palestinian children as heroes against Israeli occupation. Their bravery in resisting and throwing stones at the soldiers and their heroic acts in saving others from the soldiers consist the main plots of these two genres. Looking at the development of these contemporary tales from the perspective of memory and cultural studies, as well as children's literature, will be in my opinion a valuable field of future study so as to understand the various types of tales and their development and impact socially and politically today.

Appendix 1: Interview with Dr Sharif Kanaana

Interview with Dr Sharif Kanaana, co-compiler of *Speak, Bird, Speak Again* (1989) and *Qul Ya Tayer* (2001)[1]

Date: 4 July 2012

Context, motives and choice of literary type

Farah: To start with, could I ask what motivated you and Ibrahim Muhawi to embark on this project?

Sharif: Actually, the project was my project. Ibrahim was not at Birzeit when I started collecting the folktales. I am an anthropologist, a folklorist by training. When I came back to the Palestinian University of Birzeit, back home, I started to go more towards folklore rather than anthropology (maybe we could talk about it later). I had been gone to the States for fifteen years and I would say it was a combination of guilt and nostalgia. Upon my return, I wanted in a sense to make up for what I missed and what I did not do. The fifteen years of absence made me very nostalgic; fifteen years made the whole difference. When I left, I just wanted to run away, I revolted against society, the culture and the occupation. In my mind, I wanted to make up for the fifteen years I was away as well as to revive the old days.[2] I started working on two projects in 1967, which to a great extent I am still working on. Both projects reveal both trends of guilt and nostalgia. One of the projects is about folklore in general and folktales in particular. Having been the head of the research centre at Birzeit University for five years, I started working on my second project, entitled 'The Palestinian Destroyed Villages'. The product of the project is seen in Walid Khalidi's book, entitled *All That Remains* (2006).[3] The project was both funded and edited by Khalidi. Both projects are related in the sense that both go back to the root: one is about physical/material danger and the second is on reviving cultural heritage.

Farah: In much of your work you seem to favour the folktale as opposed to other literary and popular genres, such as short stories or novels. Can you explain the rationale for this preference? What attracts you to the genre of folktale?

Sharif: I would not compare the folktale with the short story or the novel because they are invented or written by an individual, and that I do not care about. It is true that they reflect something about the society but for me as an anthropologist, I would have to collect all the short stories and glean something from them. The folktale represents the whole society which participated in forming it. Therefore, I think that the folktale reflects the whole society, a whole system and not the viewpoint of one or a few individuals, this is why I prefer it. Maybe the comparison can be made with relation to other types of folkloric elements, such as the folk song, the legend or the fairy tale. My favourite among these types is the folktale. Now why the folktale? The answer is that the folktale is a coherent and distinctive chunk of the culture; it gives a setting and what takes place within that setting. It is more comprehensive; it gives a more complete picture than a folk song or other folkloric types. You have to collect a pot of folksongs to have something equal to one folktale. What made me lean towards the folktale more than other genres of folklore is my affiliation as an anthropologist rather than a folklorist.[4] I was instead looking for chunks of that culture, and since I understand culture, all I needed is that picture which I could convey to others. I did not feel that I needed to collect.

I wanted pieces of the culture that bring these things together in order to acquaint others with this culture, with this society. The folktale, as I said, to me is the most comprehensive, precise, self-contained chunk of the culture that I could transmit. I would say explain or translate to other people in other cultures.

Farah: I agree with you. Folktales, as you said, are vivid pictures of a society like the one we have.

Sharif: It gives you a picture, which is complete, of one setting that you can carry and show to the rest of the world.

Speak, Bird, Speak Again[5] and *Qul Ya Tayer*: Publications/editions

Farah: I agree. Reading the folktales in the Arabic compilation *Qul Ya Tayer* gives the reader a sense of cultural unity also because the tales are kept in the Palestinian dialect. I noticed that the new Arabic edition of *SBSA*, the one published in 2010 and addressed to children, contains less Palestinian colloquial and more standardized Arabic. Is there a reason for that?

Sharif: To be honest, I was not happy with the new Arabic edition. The agreement with the Institute of Palestine Studies was that one page should be in the original Palestinian slang/colloquial, facing or opposite a simplified version in Modern Standard Arabic. However, the new edition has only one page with simplified MSA. I was very disappointed since the whole point was to reinforce the cultural bond Palestinians have through the Palestinian dialect. My aim was to keep the spirit of Palestinian culture and its identity through the telling of Palestinian folktales in Palestinian dialect! Another problem I have with this new edition is related to the way characters and trees are portrayed. For example, the Ghouls' representation was alien or different from the one we, Arabs and Palestinians, are familiar with. Since pre-Islamic history, Ghouls, both in Palestine and the Arab world, are portrayed as ugly human beings with the body of a monkey. In the new Arabic edition of *SBSA*, the Ghouls' illustration was completely different. Moreover, some fruits and trees were not portrayed in the same way Palestinians know. Our audience for this edition are children, Palestinian children, so I wanted them to learn about their culture through authentic representations and illustrations.

Farah: Back to the main activators of your project, namely, guilt and nostalgia. How are they linked to the appearance of the English publication in 1989 before the Arabic one in 2001? In other words, why did the English translation precede the Arabic version? In fact, the Arabic collection appeared over ten years later. Could you tell me the reasons for this delay?

Sharif: I connect this with what I said before, related mainly to the guilt part, not the nostalgia. It was my national desire, which was trying to emerge. I was trying to pay back to the culture, to the society, to the people and to the village I am from. The feeling I had was not addressed to Arabs, but the message and the way we presented the folktales were for non-Arabs. The message is for those who do not know Arabs, don't know Palestinians. The purpose is to give others a picture and image of the culture and of the society. It is in a way meant to advocate for the Palestinian cause, not by complaining about the Palestinian cause, but by saying indirectly: here is Palestinian society. *SBSA* does not have anything political; the only political statement, maybe, is found in Alan Dundes's[6] preface to the collection.

Farah: Was the publication of *SBSA* in 1989 timed with the first Palestinian Intifada in 1987?

Sharif: Actually, it is not connected to the Intifada or to any specific incident. The project reflects the Palestinian cause altogether because, as I said,

I started collecting the data in 1977–8. The project took longer than expected in order to turn it into a book. It might have been a conscious decision by the publisher to publish it around that time but as far as we are concerned, the project is the fruit of ten years of work.

Palestinian folktales: Past and present

Farah: To what extent do you think that Palestinian folktales are able to represent Palestinian society and aspirations, both in the past and today?

Sharif: As I said the book does not include anything political, there are no political statements. The political statement is in producing the book, writing this book for the Palestinian cause and in order to acquaint the world with Palestinian culture. This is the political statement of this book! But as you know the book is mainly cultural and folkloric in nature.

Farah: In the middle of Palestinian hardships and political upheavals, how would you describe the state of Palestinian folktales and storytelling today?

Sharif: Folklore of course never stops, it evolves and changes. Some of its aspects are more responsive to sociopolitical changes as well as economic. Folk songs in weddings reflect the moment, the joke and humour, all of which are very responsive. For example, I have been working on Palestinian political humour since the beginning of the Intifada, and I can confirm the direct connection between political humour and rising conflicts. Folktales, however, are not responsive types of folklore since it takes a long time to concretize them. As a matter of fact, folktales lag in time about sixty to seventy years behind present reality. Folktales in *SBSA*, in fact, definitely lag fifty to sixty years in time. For example, the story of the old woman and the cat, where the woman, while sweeping the floor of her room, found a *bishlīk* or *mesīdīa* in Arabic. The word *bishlīk* is originally a Turkish word used to refer to particular currency coin during the Ottoman Empire and in the transition period to the British Mandate. In fact, some of those folktales are two to three thousand years old, and some of them can be traced back to the Egyptians or other cultures, with modifications of course. The folktales are expected to represent the spirit of the culture not temporary or passing events; the folktales are the essence of the culture, flavour not incidents.

Back to the situation of folktales, it is a worldwide phenomenon that folktales have been committed to books. People stopped telling them orally because of media influence, which is the case for Palestinian society as well. The existent part of the storytelling tradition goes back to pre-1948 where Palestinians made the effort to collect, tell stories and listen to them. But at the present time, I don't think there is any Palestinian family gathering in the evenings to tell folktales, which is sad.

Farah: Some Palestinians in the diaspora, however, use the collections as a cultural reference, a resource for reviving Palestinian collective memory. The second and third generations – our parents and parents of my generation – try to maintain this link with the homeland by telling stories.

Sharif: As I said the message is for non-Palestinians; it is for the outsiders. I did not think that Palestinians needed a book like our project. However, I found out afterwards that Palestinians and Arabs need them too. When I started my project in the seventies, there were still storytellers and the tradition was more popular at the time and more circulated. But since then, I noticed that Palestinians, in particular Palestinians in the diaspora, again are the ones who are happy to tell them. Telling and reading Palestinian folktales are like a compensation for what Palestinians lost; it is a form of retrieving some of what they lost. I was myself surprised that the book was very well received in Arabic and that many people told me that they read the stories to their children mainly because they have forgotten them! Second- and third-generation Palestinian parents do not know them by heart. In my role, I was urging them not to read those stories from the book but to make the effort and learn them by heart hence tell them orally (without reading).

Farah: In comparison to other Palestinian folk narratives, how would you situate your work?

Sharif: The answer to this question is found in Alan Dundes's foreword to our book. He says that the book introduces Palestinian folktales and culture to the rest of the world. The Arabic works on Palestinian folk narratives which don't include the social message we have in our project, mainly because our book is directed to the West. Had I written the book for Arabs, I would not have written it that way because I would have assumed that Arabs know and understand but would have just added more stories.

Farah: While reviewing other works on Palestinian folk narratives, I noticed that some works rely on analysis more or others had more space for tales than their explanation. Your work, however, establishes a balance between both. This leads me to ask you about the criteria for selecting these tales? What is distinctive about the forty-five folktales chosen? Is it anything to do with how old they are thought to be? Is the age of the tales important? What about the storytellers? Content? Setting?

Sharif: At the time I didn't pay much attention to the criteria. I just selected the ones I liked more, the ones I thought would get my message across more. I cannot really say there was a hidden criterion, with the exception that stories present a coherent picture of individual, familial and cultural aspects of the society. The question I was trying to answer was how much a foreigner can understand and appreciate the collection on its own terms. How can I invite, in other words, the foreigner to the culture through the folktale? I did not want to translate the culture but wanted to allow the tales to be a gateway for the foreigners to see the culture.

The role/power of the folklorist

Farah: Do you think that the folklorist has the power to change the role of folktales in society?

Sharif: Yes, of course the compiler or editor is an author at the end of the day. The folktales do not speak for themselves. They do but they need elaboration, explanation and translation, making a huge difference to the way they get received by the audience.

Farah: You, Muhawi and Patai[7] have combined different roles ranging from the compiler, or anthropologist to the folklorist and translator. Would you agree that the compiler has the power to construct the real in the name of the fantastic or vice versa?

Sharif: Stories have some fantastic elements but they are very real. Quite often, the picture drawn of reality contains some fantastic elements only to portray something real but not necessarily described. For example, *al-ghūl* (the Ghoul) can represent inner feelings which are real and existent in us. The stories do not have the quality of describing feelings or emotions; there is no use of descriptive adjectives for instance. The folktales tend rather to show actions that make you understand how the person feels and the fantastic is quite often simply a representation of the intangible emotions or feelings that are real in the human nature.

Farah: Would you see yourself as a 'cultural translator'?

Sharif: I do not really like the word 'translator'. I try to invite foreigners, as I said, into the world of these stories. I do not really translate. Ibrahim Muhawi is better positioned than me in this regard. He has lived in both cultures so his linguistic capacities in working towards coherent and well-described tales were more evident. I did discuss this issue, I remember, with him. I did not want to beautify or change anything. I did not want to assimilate to the other culture. On the contrary, I wanted other people to see elements of my culture as they are. I was against giving the tales an American/European flavour.

Farah: I meant cultural translation or mediation, which is not necessarily linguistic.

Sharif: Maybe I am a mediator but I consider myself more as an anthropologist whose role is to unveil facts, not translate.

Farah: Prior to 1948, Palestine was a unified nation with stable social structures. After the *Nakba*, however, Palestinians were scattered around the world, carrying with them their pain, history and folktales. Did the established tradition and stock of folktales undergo any changes as a result of these developments? If so, do these new versions of folktales, in spite of diasporic existence and displacement, authentically represent Palestinian national identity?

Sharif: The collection of folktales I collected belonged to a pre-1948 society, a normal and harmonious society. One of the reasons why Palestinians stopped telling those stories is because these stories stopped being relevant, stopped conveying the situation of Palestinians today. Palestinians have become preoccupied with other stories. Refugees and Palestinians started telling a lot of stories about the 1948 *Nakba*, about what happened in that period and how they were forced to leave Palestine. Women told the stories through the style of a folktale. Other stories were told again by men, following men's traditional form of telling usually about themes of war, heroism and epic adventures. I found that the legend is taking over from the folktale. Palestinians living in Ramallah, for example, hear daily contemporary legends. The legends contain many fantastic elements, told with an exaggerated style. Those stories are popular now. Moreover, we find that in the West Bank and Gaza, the political joke and humour is becoming very popular, whether in defence of Palestinians, or criticism of and/or attack of others. People will never stop telling political jokes since they are suitable in particular situations and subject to time change.

Framing folktales in *SBSA*

Farah: In presenting the folktales to the reader, you have framed them by using an extensive amount of paratextual elements (material around the text/folktale) such as footnotes, introduction, afterwords, etc. Can you explain why and how these elements allow you to fulfil the objectives of your project?

Sharif: I would define those materials in three groups: The fifty- to sixty-page introduction, comments on folktales and folktale motif type. Starting with the third category, the folktale motif type connects the folktales to the world, making them used and accessed by all scholars. Our aim was to render the collection a scholarly and international piece of work similar to the Grimm Brothers' collection. With regard to the introduction, I am an anthropologist and my aim is to acquaint the rest of the world with our culture. I did not make any political publicity; my aim was to present the Palestinians' culture to the whole world. I did dictate the introduction on a tape and Ibrahim Muhawi gave it the final shape in terms of writing and editing the English. The introduction is used to help the reader interpret the folktales accordingly.

Farah: So you are saying that the paratextual elements helped you fulfil your project.

Sharif: The aim is to appreciate the folktales. The comments and footnotes are connected to the cultural aspect of the introduction, which is mainly to provide a ground for the tales to be interpreted.

Farah: After selecting the forty-five tales, you organized them or classified them according to Individuals, Family, Society, Environment and Universe. Is there a reason for this specific classification? With hindsight, would you do it differently now?

Sharif: To start with we needed a frame or a structure; we couldn't just pile them up. Since the tales follow by themselves the formation of a family, from the individual to the family and society, we thought it was suitable to classify them in that order as the tales are about the lives of families. Being also a feminine art, the tales revolved around the lives of women in the family. Women were the main actors, and their lives were centred on *bayt al-'aylā* known as 'the extended family house', where the daily affairs of a family happened. So I assumed it was natural to follow the natural stages of the formation of the family, then gradually merge with society and the outside world.

Farah: I agree with you. The family is considered as the cornerstone of the society or the principal unit of its formation and development.

Sharif: Especially women as they represent the core of the family and society.

Framing in *SBSA* in relation to national identity and collective memory

Farah: Among other purposes, apart from introducing the culture and the folktales, do you see the framing of the tales as relating to contemporary issues of national identity and collective memory in the Palestinian context today?

Sharif: At the back of my mind, I thought that by preserving and interpreting those folktales, I could give a picture of the culture at one particular stage.

That stage, the pre-*Nakba* time, is connected to, what I referred to earlier, as notions of 'guilt' and 'nostalgia'. That period was the moment we left the country hence the trunk of culture was cut off!

Farah: In other words, you tried to revive the tradition of folktales as well as safeguard it.

Sharif: I do not think I was interested in reviving the folktales per se. I wanted to use the folktale as a tool for the preservation of culture, like keeping a set of pictures from an occasion or a wedding. To me those folktales were the pictures taken from the wedding at that particular stage (pre-1948).

Farah: For years, there have been attempts to falsify Palestinian history and to question the existence of a distinct Palestinian culture. This extends to undermining the authenticity and relevance of folktales, given their intimate link with Palestinian national identity and culture. Driven by a strong political agenda, the objective behind such attempts is to present a manipulated and distorted version of Palestinian reality. In your opinion, what role does cultural production, including the kind of work you and Muhawi have been doing, play in challenging such attempts and asserting Palestinian nationhood?

Sharif: Prevent! – I do not think we will be able to prevent the Israelis from falsifying the culture. For example, the existing archive at the University of Haifa has several thousand folktales, not just Palestinian ones but others from all over the Arab world. Arab folktales were carried around by Arab Jews from different Arab countries, and then ended up being called 'Israeli folktales'. I have personally received several complaints from some Israeli scholars because I was mentioning the original name of the place or the village where the folktales in my collection were narrated. Most of the names of those places happened to be part of what is known nowadays as 'historical Palestine' or the 'pre-1948 lands' and now have different names since the establishment of Israel. We can't stop them, but the presence of an authentic picture or representation may at least make other people from other societies know about the specificity of our culture. If there were no stories preserved or documented then there is nothing to compare with, nothing to declare or authenticate from one side or the other.

Farah: You would agree that efforts by Palestinian intellectuals are needed mainly today in order to document, preserve and authenticate oral materials.

Sharif: Definitely true. I will put more emphasis on Palestinian scholars educated in Israeli universities. These people can, not intentionally but by training, fight the Israeli intention of falsifying some of the cultural aspects. I personally noticed that some Palestinian graduates with Israeli passports from Haifa University or Tel Aviv University tend to reproduce the same academic research or path of their Israeli lecturers, which is more harmful. I think they should be proactive and alert about the risks facing their original culture. Responding to Israeli scholars, at the end of the day, is not my priority.

Farah: Your project is a very good response, I believe. The message can come across through authentication, documentation and honest representation, as you mentioned before.

Back to framing, which can also involve the choice of pictures, colours and titles in a text, can you explain the layers of meanings embedded in the title of your collection, *Speak, Bird, Speak Again*?

Sharif: Yes – it is symbolic of course. The title comes from a tale in the collection entitled 'The Green Bird' (*Al-ṭayr al-akhḍar*). It is the story of a boy who was killed by his stepmother then fed to the father. The sister managed to save the bones which made the boy come back in the shape of a green bird. The bird represents Palestinians and *Speak Again* refers to revival, regeneration and also to hope.

The representation of women in *SBSA*

Farah: Finally, how do women feature in the Palestinian national struggle, beyond the question of taking up arms or speaking in public to promote the national cause? What role do they play in private rather than public spaces? Is this connected to the roles they play in the genre of the folktale?

Sharif: Women are the carriers of the culture and the tradition of storytelling; they are the ones to transmit from one generation to the other, especially in our society. Women have the power to perpetuate the whole cultural system more than men. In the Palestinian traditional society, men have less influence on the upbringing of children since most Palestinian men spend their time at the *diwan*, which is a social gathering place for men only. That explains why Palestinian folktales are about women and children mainly. The folktales have two levels, in fact, one for children under the age of twelve to thirteen who grow up exposed to the telling of the stories. The second level is about Palestinian women and their role in transferring/transmitting the culture to next generations. I would say that women play a much bigger role in Palestinian society; they are the core of our society.

Farah: Women are also expert storytellers, as you mentioned in the introduction of your collection. Do you think women tell stories for wish-fulfilment?

Sharif: I think it is true to some extent, especially when it is related to sexual references which are considered taboo in our society. Older women usually feel more comfortable in telling stories with many sexual references as they seem to become asexual. There is also a projection of their inner feelings and desires to the world of fantasy and imagination, which can represent real feelings as we mentioned earlier.

Appendix 2: List of the Tales

I. *Individuals*	**Children and Parents**	
	1. Tunjur, Tunjur	1. ṭunjur, ṭunjur
	2. The Woman Who Married Her Son	2. īlī tjawazat ibnha
	3. Precious One and Worn-Out One	3. al-ghalīa wa al-balīa
	4. Shwesh, Shwesh!	4. shwīsh, shwīsh
	5. The Golden Pail	5. mnashil al-dhahab
	Siblings	
	6. Half-a-Halfling	6. nuṣ nṣīṣ
	7. The Orphan's Cow	7. baqarat al-īatāmā
	8. Sumac! You Son of a Whore, Sumac!	8. sumāq īā ibn […],sumāq
	9. The Green Bird	9. al-ṭīr al-akhẓr
	10. Little Nightingale the Crier	10. blībl al-ṣaīāḥ
	Sexual Awakening and Courtship	
	11. The Little Bird	11. al-ʿṣfūra al-zghīra
	12. Jummez Bin Yazur, Chief of the Birds	12. jmaīz bin īāzūr, shikh il-ṭuīūr
	13. Jbene	13. jbīna
	14. Sackcloth	14. bū al-labābīd
	15. Shahin	15. shāhīn
	The Quest for the Spouse	
	16. The Brave Lad	16. al-shāb al-shujāʿ
	17. Gazelle	17. ghazāla
	18. Lolabe	18. laūlba

II. *Family*	**Brides and Bridegrooms**	
	19. The Old Woman Ghouleh	19. al-ghūla al-ʿjūz
	20. Lady Tatar	20. al-sit tatar
	21. Shoqak Boqak!	21. shūqak būqak
	22. Clever Hassan	22. al-shaṭir ḥasan
	23. The Cricket	23. al-khunufsa
	Husbands and Wives	
	24. The Seven Leavenings	24. ʾim al-sabʿ khamāïr
	25. The Golden Road in the Valley of Vermilion	25. qaẓīb al-dhahab biwadī al-ʿqīq
	26. Minjal	26. minjal
	27. Im Eshe	27. ʾim ʿisha
	Family Life	
	28. Chick Eggs	28. baīẓ faqāqīs
	29. The Ghouleh of Trans-Jordan	29. ghūlat sharq al-ʾurdun
	30. Bear-Cub of the Kitchen	30. dubat al-maṭbakh
	31. The Woman Whose Hands Were Cut Off	31. mqaṭʿat al-daīāt
	32. Nayyis (Little Sleepy One)	32. nʿaīs
III. *Society*	33. Im Awwad and the Ghouleh	33. ʾim ʿawād w al-ghūla
	34. The Merchant's Daughter	34. bint al-tājir
	35. Pomegranate Seeds	35. ḥab rumān
	36. The Woodcutter	36. al-ḥaṭāb
	37. The Fisherman	37. al-samāk
IV. *Environment*	38. The Little She-Goat	38. al-ʿanza al-ʿanīzīa
	39. The Old Woman and Her Cat	39. al-ʿajūz w al-bis
	40. Dunglet	40. baʿīrūn
	41. The Louse	41. al-qamla
V. *Universe*	42. The Woman Who Fell into the Well	42. ilī wqʿat fī al-bīr
	43. The Rich Man and The Poor Man	43. al-ghanī w al-faqīr
	44. Maruf the Shoemaker	44. maʿrūf al-ʾiskāfī
	45. Im Ali and Abu Ali	45. ʾim ʿali w abū ʿali

Appendix 3: Summaries of Tales in Chapter 3

1 Group I (*Individuals*) – Tale 2 'The Woman Who Married Her Son'

While the son was performing pilgrimage rites, his mother threw her son's wife out of the house. The mother then buried a sheep in a grave that she dug in the palace garden. She dyed her hair and changed her appearance so that she looked like her son's wife. When the son came back, the disguised mother/fake wife told him that his mother was dead and that she was buried in the palace garden. He believed her, thinking that she was his real wife, until he made her pregnant. The disguised wife, or mother, started craving grapes so servants were sent to ask for some from the neighbours. The unhappy real wife was living at the neighbours' house so whenever a servant would come asking for grapes, she would ask for scissors to cut the servants' tongues, until one day the son went himself to ask for grapes and found out the truth.

2 Group I (*Individuals*) – Tale 7 'The Orphan's Cow'

This is the story of a father of two children (a girl and a boy) from his first wife, who passed away. The father remarried and got another two children from the new wife. The two children from the first wife had a cow and wandered about with it every day. The cow, a supernatural creature, would feed them, as the stepmother wasn't feeding them properly. One day the stepmother noticed that the boy and the girl had rosy cheeks while her own children were pale. She asked her son to follow them in order to find out the secret. The brother and sister fed her son from the cow and asked him to keep it a secret, which he did. The stepmother then sent her daughter, who revealed the secret to her mother. The stepmother decided to get rid of the cow with the excuse that its presence was making her ill. The father fulfilled her wish by slaughtering the cow.

Angry and sad, the brother and sister from the first wife decided to run away. During their journey, the brother was thirsty so the sister asked a shepherd for water. He told her to drink from the lower spring but not from the upper one, because if he drank from the latter, he would turn into a gazelle. The brother, however, drank from the upper spring and turned into a gazelle. The sister was very upset because of what had happened to her brother; at this point she was found by the sultan's servants, who took her to see their master. The latter welcomed her, liked her and asked her to marry him. Once married, she became pregnant, which coincided with his setting out on the hajj. The sultan asked his sisters and mother to look after his wife and slaughter a lamb once she gave birth. They decided to get rid of the wife as she would be the centre of attention on his return. They dropped her into the well and slaughtered the lamb and ate it. The gazelle (the brother) fed her whenever they fed him by throwing the mouthful of bread to his sister. Upon his return, the sultan found out what happened and followed the gazelle, which was very skinny. He then found out the truth and got her out of the well. Finally, he punished his mother, sister and servant by burning them.

3 Group I (*Individuals*) – Tale 9 'The Green Bird'

This is the story of a man whose wife died leaving him with a son and daughter. The father had a neighbour who was using his children in order to convince him to marry her. The father was trying to postpone the marriage until his daughter could bake, cook and clean. In the end, he married the neighbour who started treating the children very badly. One day the father asked his wife to make stuffed tripe (a traditional Palestinian dish), but the woman ate it all before her husband got back from work. She then decided to kill the son and cook him instead. Once back, the wife and the unknowing father ate the son. The sister was very upset and sad but could not say a word as the stepmother threatened to do the same to her. The sister hid the bones of her brother and buried them. One day there was a wedding, and everyone left except for the daughter. She decided to have a look at the bones since no one was around. While digging she found a marble urn full of jewellery and suddenly a green bird flew out of it. The daughter put on a very nice dress and all the jewellery she had found. Everyone at the wedding was impressed but no one recognized her even when the green bird started singing sadly about what happened to him and how much he loved his sister. People were puzzled and were saying 'Speak, Bird, Speak Again!' He said, only if his stepmother opens her mouth, and he dropped nails and needles into it so she died. They asked him again to speak, but he said, only if his father opens his mouth, and the same thing happened to him, and he died. They asked him to speak again; he said only if this girl (the sister) opens her lap. The bird landed on it, and he returned to his previous form.

4 Group I (*Individuals*) – Tale 6 'Half-a-Halfling'

This is the story of a man who is married to two women, one his cousin, the other wife not a relative. Both wives were unable to bear children so the man went to the sheikh, looking for a solution. The latter advised him to see the *ghūla* (wife of Ghoul) and gave him pomegranates to feed the wives with to become pregnant afterwards. Going through many adventures, he managed at the end to get two pomegranates, but ate half of one of them as he was hungry. He decided to give the remaining half pomegranate to his cousin and the full one to his other wife. As a result, the wives got pregnant: the unrelated wife got Hassan and Hussain, and the cousin got half a human being. Half-Halfling was more courageous and had better luck with hunting than his two brothers. One day, they went hunting and Half-Halfling managed to catch a deer, so Hassan and Hussain asked him to give them the deer; he accepted on one condition, which was to heat a brand and brand each of them on the backside. Hassan and Hussain went back home with the deer and the mother cooked it and then threw the bones at doorstep of the first wife. The latter started crying, asking Half-Halfling 'Why can you not do the same?' He told her it was him and asked her to see the brand on the backsides of Hussain and Hassan. The following day they went hunting again, and saw the *ghūla*, who fed them and treated them kindly. Half-Halfling heard her sing, saying she wanted to eat the brothers while they were asleep. He started playing tricks on her until the sun had risen, and then woke his brothers up and told them to escape. The father was very pleased and to prove he was cleverer than the two brothers, he asked Half-Halfling to kill the *ghūla*, which he did.

5   Group I (*Individuals*) – Tale 12
'Jummez Bin Yazur, Chief of the Birds'

This is the story of a father, who, on his way to hajj, asked his three daughters what they wished for. Each one asked for a particular thing, except for the third daughter, Sit al-ḥusun (which literally means 'Miss Beauty' in Arabic), who was the most beautiful among her sisters and whose mother was different from the others. Sit Al-husun asked her father to bring her Jummez Bin Yazur, chief of the birds. Being an enchanted bird, Jummez Bin Yazur would turn into a handsome man at night during which Sit al-ḥusun enjoyed his company without her father's knowledge. Jealous of Sit al-ḥusun, the sisters tried to hurt Jummez Bin Yazur by injuring him as a bird, during the day, with the glass of a broken window. The enchanted bird was very ill, and no one could heal him. Sit al-ḥusun found out what her sisters tried to do against her, and he went looking for the bird in order to heal him. His sisters, however, imposed on her very difficult tasks to prove her love and devotion to him first. She managed at the end to fulfil all their tasks and was thus allowed to marry Jummez Bin Yazur.

6   Group I (*Individuals*) – Tale 16 'The Brave Lad'

This story revolves around a lad's desire to marry the king's daughter; however, he is too poor to propose. The only condition to marry the daughter of the king is to be able to kill the Ghoul in their town. The lad's quest is motivated by the Ghoul's wife, who wanted to marry her first cousin, but could not as the Ghoul took her against her will. The Ghoul's wife offered to help the lad get rid of the Ghoul by plucking three hairs from him, and as a result, he died. After the Ghoul's death, the lad managed to marry the king's daughter and the Ghoul's wife married her first cousin.

7   Group II (*Family*) – Tale 22 'Clever Hassan'

The first part of the tale concerns Hassan's relationship with his mother, who married a servant without Hassan knowing. The mother, in agreement with the servant, was trying to get rid of her son. She would ask her son Hassan to bring her edible fruit from very dangerous places where no human being survived before, but her plan failed as he was exceptionally courageous and strong. One day, she asked him to bring her the water of life, which he managed. However, on his way the daughter of the king took the water of life and replaced it with another type. The mother then found out the secret of his strength, which lay in seven specific hairs. She plucked them all, killed him, cut him up and threw the pieces of his body into the river. The daughter of the king found out what had happened to him and saved him with the water of life she took from him before. Brought back to life, he went back and killed his mother and the servant. One day the king asked his daughter if she wanted to get married, to which she assented. The day came for her to choose a husband. She wanted Hassan, who was disguised, wearing very old and dirty clothes. The father, as a result, was not happy and decided to reject him. When the king was at war with some enemies, Hassan disguised himself and killed all the enemies (three times over) until the king found out who the warrior was in reality. He finally reconciled with his daughter and thought her decision was ideal.

8 Group II (*Family*) – Tale 23 'The Cricket'

This is the story of a cricket who wanted to get married. She asked her mother to give her advice on whether to marry a camel or a bull, which the mother declined to do. The third suggestion was a mouse, to which the mother agreed as he was the right one in terms of size. One day, both the cricket and the mouse wanted to wash their clothes. Having found the right spot, the mouse went to get some soap while the cricket fell in a small hole. The cricket pleaded for help and asked a man to look for her husband the mouse. The mouse, hence, was told by the man and hurried to rescue her.

9 Group II (*Family*) – Tale 25 'The Golden Rod in the Valley of Vermilion'

This is the story of a man who had three previous marriages, in which the wives cheated on him. As a result, by the time of the fourth marriage he had lost his trust. One day, the fourth wife made an innocent comment on how her black bag matched her white skin. He, however, interpreted it to mean that she wanted to be with a black man. Being angry, the husband asked his wife if there was any other man more handsome or stronger than him, she said there wasn't. He then kept on beating her, until one day her female friends found out what the husband was doing to her. They advised her to say 'yes' if he asked her again, presuming that the husband would go away for few days, leaving her to look for the man who was more handsome and stronger than him in the Valley of Vermilion. On his way, the husband saw the Ghoul, who asked him about what happened to his first three wives and on what basis he was accusing the fourth one. Only later, did the husband realize his mistake and he went back and apologized to her, but the Ghoul had already taken her away from him as a punishment.

10 Group II (*Family*) – Tale 24 'The Seven Leavenings'

This is the story of an old lady who successfully managed to help a woman who was beaten up by her husband because she could not bear children. The old lady made the husband stop beating his wife by telling him that she was pregnant. She lied and replaced the supposedly newborn baby with a toy. The old woman also helped another couple in Aleppo in Syria, as the husband was suspicious of his wife's behaviour, thinking she preferred a black man over him. Likewise, thanks to the old lady's wisdom, she helped the poor woman who was also being beaten by her husband.

11 Group II (*Family*) – Tale 27 'Im Eshe'

This is the story of Im ʿAysha who went to visit her daughter ʿAysha with her husband, Abū ʿAysha, when their daughter gave birth. One day, Im ʿAysha was washing the baby's head but without realizing killed the baby with hot water. So Im ʿAysha ran back to her house, asking her husband to open the door for her. He did not open the door for her, afraid of her angry reaction for slaughtering the chickens. She did not mind and asked him again to open the door, but he refused. She did not mind again but he told her that he had also asked the cow to feed him but when it did not he had killed it. Im'Aysha reassured him that she would not hurt him or be angry with him; she just wanted him to open the door. Convinced she would be very upset, he told her that the camel ate his penis. She said she could accept the loss of everything except the loss of his balls.

12 Group II (*Family*) – Tale 31
'The Woman Whose Hands Were Cut Off'

This is the story of a sister and her brother whose parents passed away, leaving them with only a chicken. Both brother and sister were relying on the eggs laid by the chicken. One day the girl found money under the chicken so asked her brother what would he do if they found money, he said that he would buy a cow and a camel. Then she waited a few years and asked him again, and he said that he would get married. She then told him the story and started to look for a bride for him. Having found a wife, she helped him to get married, using the money their parents left. The wife, however, turned out to be a Ghoul who was eating the brother's offspring and then accusing the sister of doing so. Being naive, the husband believed her and cut his sister's legs and hands off. Sad and very disappointed, the sister wished that a needle would go into his foot and never come out. The wish came true and the brother was in pain, and no one could take the needle out of his foot. Years later, he discovered the truth and found out about the wife's identity. While still looking for someone to take the needle out, he came across his sister's house, knocked on her door and apologized. She in her turn forgave him and took the needle out.

Appendix 4: 'The Old Woman and Her Cat' (Al-ʿjūz w al-bis) and 'Dunglet' (Baʿīrūn)

Tale 39 'The Old Woman and Her Cat'

Once there was an old woman who had a cat. One day she brought some milk home, and the cat came and lapped it up. Feeling angry, she cut off his tail.

'Meow! Meow!', he cried. 'Give me back my tail.'

'Give me back my milk,' demanded the old woman.

'And how am I going to bring back the milk for you?', he asked.

'Go bring it from that ewe over there,' she answered.

Going to the ewe, the cat said, 'Ewe, give me some milk, and the milk is for the old woman, and the old woman will then sew my tail back on.'

'Bring me a branch from that tree over there', said the ewe, 'and I'll give you the milk.'

So to the tree he went and said, 'O tree, give me a branch, and the branch is for the ewe, and the ewe will give me some milk, and the milk is for the old woman, and the old woman will then sew my tail back on.'

'Go tell that plowman over there to come plow under me,' replied the tree.

To the plowman then he went and said, 'O plowman, come plow under the tree, and the tree will give me a branch, and the branch is for the ewe, and the ewe will give me some milk, and the milk is for the old woman, and the old woman will then sew my tail back on.'

'Bring me a pair of shoes from the cobbler,' said the plowman.

He went to the cobbler and said, 'O cobbler, give me some shoes, and the shoes are for the plowman, and the plowman will plow under the tree, and the tree will give me a branch, and the branch is for the ewe, and the ewe will give me some milk, and the milk is for the old woman, and the old woman will then sew my tail back on.'

'Bring me two loaves of bread from that bakerwoman over there,' answered the cobbler.

The cat then went to the bakerwoman.

'Bakerwoman', he said, 'give me two loaves of bread for the cobbler, and the cobbler will give me some shoes, and the shoes are for the plowman, and the plowman will plow under the tree, and the tree will give me a branch, and the branch is for the ewe, and the ewe will give me some milk, and the milk is for the old woman, and the old woman will then sew my tail back on.'

'Bring me a bucketful of manure from that pile over there,' said the bakerwoman.

So, bringing a bucket full of manure, the cat gave it to the bakerwoman, and she gave him two loaves of bread. Taking the bread, he gave it to the cobbler, and the cobbler gave him the shoes, which he gave to the plowman, who plowed under the tree. The tree then gave him a branch, which he gave to the ewe, who gave him the milk. Taking the milk with him, he went running back to the old woman.

'Meow! Meow!', he cried. 'Why don't you sew my tail back on?'

The old woman took the milk and sewed the cat's tail back on, and they became friends again.

The bird of this tale has flown; are you ready for the next one?

قصة 39 _ العجوز و البس

هاظا في هالعجوز, عندها هالبس. رايحة هالعجوز جايبة هالحليبات. اجا هالبس لقهّن اجت هذيك من الحراق قطمت ذنبته.

قالها: 'مو مو أعطيني ذنبتي'

قالتله: 'أعطيني حلبياتي'

قالها: 'منين بدي أجيبلك حلبياتك؟'

قالتله: 'روح جيب من الشاه هذيك'

راح, قالها:' يا شاة, أعطيني حليب, و الحليب للعجوز و العجوز تقطبلي ذيلي'

قالتله:'روح جيبلي قصفة من هذيك الشجرة بعطيك حليب'

راح قال للشجرة :'أعطيني قصفة و القصفة للشاة و الشاة تعطيني حليبات, و الحليبات للعجوز, و العجوز تقطبلي ذنبتي'

قالتله:'روح للحرّاث هاظاك يحرث تحتي'

راح للحارث: ' يا حارث, احرث تحت الشجرة و الشجرة تعطيني قصفة و القصفة للشاة و الشاة تعطيني حليبات, و الحليبات للعجوز, و العجوز تقطبلي ذنبتي'

قاله: ' روح جيبلي مداس من عند الإسكافي'

راح للسكافي قاله: ' ياسكافي أعطيني مداس, المداس للحرّاث و الحرّاث يحرث تحت الشجرة و الشجرة تعطيني قصفة و القصفة للشاة و الشاة تعطيني حليبات, و الحليبات للعجوز, و العجوز تقطبلي ذنبتي'

قاله:' روح جيبلي رغيفين خبز من الخبازة هذيك'

راح للخبازة:' أعطيني رغيفين , و الرغيفين للسكافي, و السكافي يعطيني مداس, و المداس للحرّاث و الحرّاث يحرث تحت الشجرة و الشجرة تعطيني قصفة و القصفة للشاة و الشاة تعطيني حليبات, و الحليبات للعجوز, و العجوز تقطبلي ذنبتي'

قالتله: 'روح جيبلي قفة زبل من هالمزبلة هذيك'

راح جاب قفة هالزّبل و أعطاها للخبازة تزّبل فيه الطابون , و الخبازة أعطته رغيفين خبز, أخذ الرغيفين الخبز للسكافي و السكافي أعطاه مداس, و المداس أعطاه للحرّاث و الحرّاث حرث تحت الشجرة و الشجرة أعطته قصفة , و القصفة أخذها للشاة, و الشاة أعطته حليبات, أخذ الحليبات و راح يركظ للعجوز: 'مو مو أقطبيلي ذيلي'

قطبتلو ذيله و رجعوا أصحاب.

و طار طيرها و عليكو غيرها.

Tale 40 'Dunglet'

Once there was a woman who had no children. Her husband was a plowman, and every day they had a hard time finding someone to take food out to him. They had a few sheep, and one day, as the wife was sweeping out their pen, she cried out, 'O seeker, your wish be granted! May I become pregnant and have a boy, even if it is a piece of dung!'

It was as if Allah Himself had spoken with her tongue. When she gave birth, she delivered a pile of dung. All those present at the birth gathered up the dung and threw it outside, but lo! a piece of it rolled under the wardrobe. The woman became very, very sad.

One day, while kneading the dough, the wife called out, 'O Lord, if only you had given me a son, he would have taken the food out to his father!' And behold! the piece of dung jumped out from under the wardrobe and said, 'Mother, I'll take the food to my father.'

The woman set to preparing the food, bringing together some yogurt and seven loaves of bread, and she gave it to Dunglet, who carried it to his father.

'Welcome!', said the father when he saw him in the distance. 'Welcome, Dunglet, and the path that led Dunglet, who's bringing his father the yogurt and the seven loaves!' And behold! Dunglet answered, 'Death to Dunglet and the path that brought Dunglet, who ate the yogurt and the seven loaves and has come to follow them up with his father and the yoked oxen!' He then devoured his father and the oxen.

Going back home, he found his mother kneading dough.

'Welcome!', she said. 'Welcome, Dunglet, and the path that led Dunglet, who's coming to help his mother with the kneading!'

'Death to Dunglet', he answered, 'and the path that brought Dunglet, who ate the yogurt and the seven loaves, finished off his father and the oxen, and has now come to follow them up with his mother and her dough!' He then devoured his mother.

The next day he went to visit his father's sister, and found her patching her roof.

'Welcome!', she said. 'Welcome, Dunglet, and the path that brought Dunglet, who's coming to help his aunt with the patching.'

'Death to Dunglet', he answered, 'and the path that brought Dunglet, who ate the yogurt and the seven loaves, finished off his father and the oxen, his mother and her dough, and has now come to follow them up with his aunt and her clay.' He then devoured his aunt.

The following day he went to visit his mother's sister, and found her doing the laundry.

'Welcome!', she said. 'Welcome, Dunglet, and the path that led Dunglet, who's coming to help his aunt with the washing.'

'Death to Dunglet', he answered, 'and the path that brought Dunglet, who ate the yogurt and the seven loaves, finished off his father and the oxen, his mother and her dough, his aunt and her day, and has now come to follow them up with his second aunt and her laundry!' He then devoured his second aunt.

The next day he went to visit his grandmother, and found her spinning.

'Welcome!', she said. 'Welcome, Dunglet, and the path that led Dunglet, who's coming to help his grandmother with the spinning!'

'Death to Dunglet', he answered, 'and the path that brought Dunglet, who ate the yogurt and the seven loaves, finished off his father and the oxen, his mother and her dough, his aunt and her day, his second aunt and her laundry, and has now come to follow them up with his grandmother and her spinning!' He then devoured his grandmother.

On his way home he ran into a wedding procession.

'Welcome!', people said. 'Welcome, Dunglet, and the path that led Dunglet, who's coming to help us celebrate the wedding!'

'Death to Dunglet', he answered, 'and the path that brought Dunglet, who ate the yogurt and the seven loaves, finished off his father and the oxen, his mother and her dough, his aunt and her day, his second aunt and her laundry, his grandmother and her spinning, and has now come to follow them up with the bride and groom!' He then devoured the bride and groom.

As he was walking down the street, he met two blind men who were trying to cross it.

'Welcome!', they said. 'Welcome, Dunglet, and the path that led Dunglet, who's coming to help us with the crossing!'

'Death to Dunglet', he answered, 'and the path that brought Dunglet, who ate the yogurt and the seven loaves, finished off his father and the oxen, his mother and her dough, his aunt and her clay, his second aunt and her laundry, his grandmother and her spinning, the bride and the groom, and has now come to follow them up with the blind men!'

One of them pulled a little knife out of his pocket and gashed Dunglet's belly. All the people he had devoured came tumbling out, and everything went back to normal.

قصة 40- بعيرون

في هالمرة, مالهاش اولاد. جوزها حرّاث, و كل يوم بتتغلب مين بيعثّله أكل. في عندهم هالغنمات . يوم قاعدة بتكنّس تحتهن , قامت صارت تدعي لربها:' يا غالبة يا طالبة , إني أحمل و أجيب ولد ولو كان بعره'

قام الله نطق علسانها. لما ولدت, جابت كوم هالبعر. صاروا هالحاضرين يلموا في هالبعر و يكبوا فيه. وإلا هالبعرة دخلت تحت الخزانة.

حزنت هالمرة كثير كثير. يوم و هي قاعدة بتعجن , صارت تقول:' يا ربي لو إنك أعطيتني ولد , كان أخذ الأكل لأبوه'

وإلا هي هالبعرة نطّت من تحت الخزانة و قالت:' أنا يمّا باخذ الأكل لابوي'

قامت المره حضّرت الأكل و حطّت مخمر اللبان و سبعة الرّغفان و حملتهن لبعيرون.

راح بعيرون تيودي الأكل لأبوه, شافه أبوه من بعيد.

صار يقول:'أهلًا أهلًا بعيرون , ودرب جابت بعيرون , اللي جاب أبوه مخمّر اللبان و سبعة الرّغفان'

وإلا هو بعيرون قاله: 'قِطعن بعيرون و دربِ جابت بعيرون , اللي أكل مخمّر اللبان و سبعة الرّغفان, و جاي يلحقه على أبوه و الفدان' قام أكل أبوه و الفدّان.

روّح لقي إمه بتعجن, صارت تقول: 'أهلًا أهلًا بعيرون, ودربٍ جابت بعيرون, اللي اجا يساعد إمه عالعجين'

قالها:' قطعن بعيرون, ودربٍ جابت بعيرون, اللي أكل مخمّر اللبان و سبعة الرغفان, و أبو و الفدّان, وجاي يلحقه على إمه و الاعجان' قام أكلها.

ثاني يوم, راح عند عمته, لقيها بتطيّن قامت قالتله:' أهلًا أهلًا بعيرون, ودربٍ جابت بعيرون, اللي اجا يعاون عمته عالطين'

قام قالها:'قطعن بعيرون , ودربٍ جابت بعيرون , اللي أكل مخمّر الرّغفان, و أبوه و الفدان, و إمه و الإعجان , وجاي يلحق على عمته و الطيّان ' قام أكلها.

في اليوم الثاني راح عند خالته, لقاها بتغسل. قالت: 'أهلًا أهلًا بعيرون, ودربٍ جابت بعيرون, اللي جاي يعاون خالته عالغسيل'.

قام قالها:' قطعن بعيرون , ودربٍ جابت بعيرون , اللي أكل مخمّر اللبان و سبعة الرّغفان, و أبوه و الفدان, و إمه و الإعجان, و عمته و الطيّان, و جاي يلحّق على خالته و الغسلان' قام أكلها.

ثاني يوم راح عند ستّه, لاقاها بتغزل صوف. لمّا شافته, صارت تقول: 'أهلًا أهلًا بعيرون, ودربٍ جابت بعيرون, اللي جاي يساعدني عالغزل'.

قام قالها:' قطعن بعيرون , ودربٍ جابت بعيرون , اللي أكل مخمّر اللبان و سبعة الرّغفان, و أبوه و الفدان, و إمه و الإعجان, و عمته و الطيّان, و خالته و الغسلان, و جاي يلحق على ستّه و الغزلان' قام أكلها.

و هو مروحٍ, لاقى هالعرس. صاروا الناس يقولوا: 'أهلًا أهلًا بعيرون, ودربٍ جابت بعيرون , اللي جاي يغني معنا في العرس'.

قالهن:' قطعن بعيرون , ودربٍ جابت بعيرون , للي أكل مخمّر اللبان و سبعة الرّغفان, و أبوه و الفدان, و إمه و الإعجان, و عمته و الطيّان, و خالته و الغسلان, وسته و الغزلان , وجاي يلحّق عالعرس و العرسان' أكلهن.

و هو ماشي في الشارع , لقي اثنين عميان , بدهن يقطعوا الشارع , قالوله: "أهلًا أهلًا بعيرون, ودربٍ جابت بعيرون , اللي جاي يقطعنا الشارع'.

قالهن :' قطعن بعيرون , ودربٍ جابت بعيرون, للي أكل مخمّر اللبان و سبعة الرّغفان, و أبوه و الفدان, و إمه و الإعجان, و عمته و الطيّان, و خالته و الغسلان, وسته و الغزلان , و العرس و العرسان , و جاي يلحق على العميان'.

قام واحد منهن طال هالموس من جيبته, و بطّ بعيرون, وطلعوا كل هالناس من بطنه, و رجع كل شي زي ما كان.

Appendix 5: Summaries of Tales in Chapter 4

1 Group V (*Universe*) – Tale 42 'The Woman Who Fell into the Well'

This is the story of a group of salesmen who stopped for food, following their custom of knocking on people's doors asking for sustenance during their travels. One of the salesmen called at a house and was given two loaves of bread by a young woman. A dog barked at him on his way out, and this caused him to fall into a well. When he asked to be rescued, the young girl extended a rope into the well to help him out. She, however, also fell into the well. The young lady's brothers were all out harvesting, and no one was available to help them. They waited until one harvester passed by the well and heard them shouting. Once he got them out, the young lady asked the harvester to keep the incident a secret because if her brothers knew what had occurred they would question her reputation and honour. She even offered to give him extra money, as a form of compensation, once the harvest was complete.

The man promised to do so and received the money. His wife, however, did not believe what happened. She insisted on knowing until he told her. She then spread the news among other neighbours until the brothers of the young lady found out what happened. Being very angry, they wanted to kill her. She escaped and found refuge at the salesman's house where his mother looked after her. As result, the young lady married the salesman and left the village. She eventually had three children with him, called Maktūb, Kutba and Muqaddar. One day, the brothers happened to be walking by her house so they knocked at her door seeking a place to sleep. The husband welcomed them, offered them food and told them the story of the well. The brothers did not know who he was nor did he know about the brothers, until the wife came out of her room.

2 Group V (*Universe*) – Tale 43 'The Rich Man and the Poor Man'

This is the story of two sisters married to two brothers, one very poor and the other very rich. One day the poor one went to visit her sister who was making *malfūf* (a traditional Palestinian dish). The poor woman was craving this kind of food as she was pregnant, but the sister did not offer her any. When she returned home she told her husband about her craving. Being very poor, the husband told her that he would save money for a whole week so he could buy the ingredients. He then bought them and decided to invite the minister to eat with them. They invited the minister, and while the wife was serving the food, she farted. In complete embarrassment, she wished that the earth would open up for her to hide. The wish came true, and the poor woman found herself in a big market. She was looking for the fart, as were all the people. Everyone laughed at her until they found him (the fart) well dressed in a cafe. People asked why the fart had embarrassed the poor woman in front of the minister. The fart said that he was not happy where he was so he went out and made himself clean. People however asked him to go back to make it up to the woman. To redeem himself, he made the woman drop golden coins every time she opened her mouth. Once she was back and telling the story to her husband, these coins kept on dropping out of her mouth. The couple hence became extremely rich and bought a castle with servants.

The rich sister, two days later, went to visit her sister after realizing that she had not offered her any of the *malfūf* she cooked last time. She could not find her, however, and was told by the neighbours that the poor sister was living in a castle. In disbelief, the rich sister insisted on knowing what happened. Being greedy, the rich sister wanted to do the same thing, but the husband discouraged her as they were already rich. Nevertheless, she copied the poor sister and farted deliberately in front of the minister. The rich sister ended in the same situation looking for the fart. However, the fart, unlike the one before, was not happy to be forced to leave its new abode. Her punishment was thus to have scorpions and snakes come out of her mouth.

3 Group I (*Individuals*) – Tale 14 'Sackcloth'

This is the story of a king who wanted to marry his own daughter after the death of his wife. Being scared, she escaped. To protect herself, she disguised herself in a sackcloth and left the king's castle. No one knew her and everyone thought she was a poor man who could not do much. One day there was a wedding so the woman waited until everyone left and took her sackcloth off and put on her jewellery and nice clothes. She went to the wedding and danced with the prince. The same incident happened three more times until the son followed her one day and discovered her true identity. It is, according to the compilers, the Palestinian version of Cinderella.

4 Group I (*Individuals*) – Tale 15 'Shahin'

This story is about women's playfulness and intelligence in dominating men. It starts with a girl's adventure as she wanders about with her friends, until she happened to knock on Shahin's door. The girl made Shahin cook for her, and then stole all the food he was cooking for his forty brothers. The young lady, who was taking the food to her forty friends, managed to trick Shahin more than twice; she even tricked his brother. Women's desire in this tale is to initiate marriage and seduce males. As a result, the solution to all these tricks was for the forty brothers to marry the forty women. At the end, women's desire is fulfilled no matter what. The tale shows the juxtaposition between the social status granted to men by society and their weakness in facing women's cunning.

Notes

Introduction

1 Khunfse (meaning a small cricket) and Tunjur (meaning a cooking pot) are very popular characters in Palestinian folk literature. Reference to these characters and others are discussed in more depth in the coming chapters.
2 See Zu'bi (2014: 3): 'The theft of the shari'a court registries in Acre to the ransacking of the Palestinian Research Center archive in Beirut in 1982 and the archive of the Arab Studies Society in Orient House in Jerusalem in 2001 – have a significant role in the marginalization of the Palestinian historical narrative and in putting in place numerous obstacles to the documentation and writing of Palestinian history.'
3 In every Palestinian extended family there is *Al-dīwān*, which is a place for social gatherings, usually for men only.

Chapter 1

1 For further readings see Nora (1989); Halbwachs (1992); Erll and Nunning (2008).
2 Many scholars have contested the binary opposition between history and memory. For instance, Yael Zerubavel (1995) sees that history and memory do not operate in totally detached opposite directions; rather, their relationships are underlined by conflict as well as interdependence. The past cannot be literally construed; it can only be selectively exploited, as collective memory continuously negotiates between available historical records and current social and political agendas. Another opponent of the binary opposition between history and memory is the French historian Jacques Le Goff, for whom collective memory is mythical and distorted. He considers collective memory to be a tool used in order to mix the past with the present in a confusing way; nonetheless, it is the living connection between both periods (Le Goff [as discussed in] in Kwathrānī, 2000). Le Goff questions the credibility of collective memory as the only source for knowing the past, but at the same time he gives more importance to history written by 'expert historians', as he likes to refer to them.

3 The French sociologist Maurice Halbwachs developed the notion of 'collective memory' as part of a discourse within a cultural framework rather than a simple physical process of remembering information. In *Les cadres sociaux de la mémoire* (1925), translated into English in 1992 under the title of *Collective Memory*, Halbwachs argued that 'the individual calls recollections to mind by relying on the frameworks of social memory' (Halbwachs, 1992: 182). The contribution made by Halbwachs was to show that collective memory is socially constructed rather than a given reality; moreover, memory can only be collective if it is marked by the remembrance of particular groups or individuals. In *On Collective Memory* (1992), he explains, 'While the collective memory endures and draws strength from its base in a coherent body of people, it is individuals as group members who remember' (Halbwachs, 1992: 84). Rejecting the Freudian belief which stresses the role of the individual's unconscious in retrieving or repressing past experiences, Halbwachs argues that the act of remembering can happen coherently within the groups to which individuals belong. 'There is [thus] no point,' he argues, 'in seeking where ... [memories] are preserved in my brain or in some nook of my mind to which I alone have access: for they are recalled by me externally, and the groups of which I am a part at any time give me the means to reconstruct them' (Halbwachs, 1992: 38).

4 Litvak (2009: 2) explains this as follows: 'The breakdown of the Ottoman Empire, the failure of an indigenous successor-state to unite ex-Ottoman Syria, the escalating Zionist challenge, the establishment of British rule over a territorially distinct Palestine, and the corresponding politicization of Palestinians due to unsettled conditions between 1914 and 1923.'

5 For example, Benedict Anderson (1991) has explained the importance of language in nation formation. In his opinion, modern nations have worked on the construction of their culture, history and memory by reviving their languages using the collective imagination of people. In this regard, Anderson highlights the role of intellectuals, dictionary editors and writers, using local languages, in the formation of European nations in the nineteenth century (Anderson, 1991). Anderson also focuses on the dynamic modes of identity construction and emphasizes the creative and contingent character of national identity, as well as its adaptability to different political and social contexts in the modern world. He perceives the diffusion of the written word, in Anderson's terms 'print capitalism', as mobilizing and facilitating collective political action. Newspapers and novels are the tools of print capitalism, helping to generate a new sense of community. Thus there is an interconnection between memory, language and nation formation.

6   Mahmud Darwish (1942–2008): 'Poet and journalist, an interpreter of the exile and hopes of the Palestinian people. Darwish's major theme in his poems is the fate of his homeland. Darwish has described the conflict between Palestinians and Israelis as "a struggle between two memories".' Ibrahim Muhawi, his translator, has written that 'his is poetry of witnessing'. Cited in http://www.kirjasto.sci.fi/darwish.htm [accessed on 24 March 2012].

Ghassan Kanafani (1936–72): Palestinian novelist, short-story writer and dramatist. The main themes in his writings are uprootedness, exile and national struggle. In his stories he often uses the desert and its heat as a symbol for the plight of the Palestinian people. 'Ghassan Kanafani's life and career as a writer was closely connected to the situation of the Palestinians, and his intense involvement in Palestinian affairs gave him a unique vantage point. Kanafani's first two novels, which experimented with language and form, rank among the most complex in all of Arabic fiction of that time.' Cited in http://www.kirjasto.sci.fi/kanaf.htm [accessed on 24 March 2012].

Chapter 2

1   Adolf Bach (1937) *Deutsche Volkskunde,* Leipzig: S. Hirzel.
2   André Jolles (1929) *Einfache Formen,* Halle: Max Niemeyer Verlag.
3   All translations of Arabic quotations are my own unless otherwise indicated.
4   Wilhelm Maximilian Wundt (1832–1920) was a German medical doctor, psychologist, physiologist and professor, known today as one of the founding figures of modern psychology. He is widely regarded as the father of experimental psychology.
5   Juha is a folk character of arguable origin, most likely Persian, from around the eighth century; he has since been claimed by both the Arabs and the Turks. His stories – which number in the hundreds – are a mainstay of Arab popular humour and are widespread all over the Middle East. He also has cousins in other folk traditions, including the seemingly naive but sly peasant whose predicaments have an entertaining logic. (Nice, 2001: 57).
6   By 'carrier' or 'active carrier', I refer to those who 'show an intense personal interest in preserving and transmitting the practice' (Muhawi and Kanaana, 1989: 9–10).
7   Based on the actual migration of the eponymous Hilal tribe from the Arabian peninsula to Tunis between the tenth and twelfth centuries, the epic narrative has

been transmitted by oral poets since the fourteenth century (Reynolds, 1995: 1–2, 9; Slyomovics, 1997: 1).

8. For more discussion on the role of women in Arabic and Egyptian tales see El-Shamy, 1980, 1999.

9. '*Canaan* was a Semitic-speaking region in the Ancient Near East during the late 2nd millennium BC. The name *Canaan* occurs commonly in the Bible, where it corresponds to the Levant, in particular to the areas of the Southern Levant that provide the main setting of the narrative of the Bible' (Drews, 1998: 43).

10. Starting from Goffman's notion of frames, realized in 'schemata of interpretation' that allow communicators 'to locate, perceive, identify, and label events and occurrences' (1974: 21) and Tannen and Wallat's understanding of frames as being 'knowledge structures' (Tannen and Wallat, 1993: 59), I would define framing as the lens through which we establish the meaningfulness of structured events. For more discussion on framing see Goffman (1974); Tannen and Wallat (1993); Benford and Snow (2000); Gamson and Modigliani (1987).

11. The work of the French critic Gérard Genette, *Paratexts: Thresholds of Interpretation* (1997), offers a detailed and comprehensive model for the examination of paratexts. For further reading on the typology of paratexts, use in media and translation, see Collins and Skover (1992), Gürçağlar (2002), Koş (2007), Watts (2000) and Dòmine (2002).

12. A paratext is above all the responsibility of the author, but this is not necessarily the case. Paratexts are not simply the outcome of an author's choices but instead are the end product of a series of decisions made by other agents involved in the process of text production, such as editors or publishers, who may control the choice of paratextual input according to their ideological or commercial interests, and of course translators, who often add paratextual material of their own, such as footnotes and glossaries.

13. The concept of 'paratext' includes elements which are outside the immediate text in question, such as reviews, interviews and correspondence, referred to as 'epitext'. The latter are not materially appended to the text but presented independently to comment on the work and its author and/or translator (Genette, 1997). Given the wide range of elements that fall under the category of *paratexts* and *epitexts*, it is clear that both categories inevitably play an important part in shaping the reader's attitude towards the main text and help him or her to reach certain understandings as well as conclusions about the text in question. In fact, paratexts provide links between the text and everything else that surrounds it, constituting what Genette (1991: 261) calls 'a zone not just of transition, but of *transaction*' (emphasis in original).

14 Given the significance of paratexts in framing the source or the target text, paratextual tools appear in different places around the text, performing specific functions. By defining the elements of paratexts, Genette focuses on determining each element's 'position (the question *where?*), its date of appearance, and eventually of disappearance (*when?*), its mode of existence, verbal or other (*how?*), the characteristics of its communicating instance, addresser and addressee (*from whom? to whom?*), and the functions which give purpose to its message (*what is it good for?*)' (Genette, 1991: 261). In order to answer these questions, Genette divides paratexts into two major categories, related to their positioning around or within the text. The first category referred to as 'peritext' consists of layout and the format of the book, type of front cover, title, preface and sometimes notes. This category of paratexts is considered *informative, commercial* and *illustrative* (Kovala, 1996); informative in the sense of describing the work itself and contextualizing it, realized in prefaces, blurbs and note sections. Moreover, it is commercial since the central aim of some agents, such as the publisher, is to advertise the book, using the back cover and the blurb. Finally, the illustrative paratext employs striking illustrations/images on the front and back covers, and sometimes illustrations within the text itself (Kovala, 1996). The second category of paratexts is 'epitexts' (Genette, 1997), usually produced during or after the publication of the book. They are all messages which are situated, at least originally, outside the book and 'generally with the backing of the media (interviews, conversations), or under the cover of private communication (correspondence and private journals)' (Genette, 1997: 55). In other words, epitextual paratexts are not found within the covers of an individual work in book form. In most cases, peritexts tend to be the responsibility of the publisher, what Genette refers to also as 'editorial paratexts', especially when dealing with the choice of cover, blurb and sometimes the title. The author, however, can be in control of some peritextual elements, known also as 'authorial paratexts', such as the introduction, dedication and notes, in addition to all kinds of epitexts. For the purposes of my analysis, I will focus on peritexts since they are physically part of the data under analysis, namely, foreword, preface, footnotes and introduction.
15 More elaboration on the differences between preface, foreword and introduction can be found at http://www.writersandeditors.com/preface__foreword__or_introduction__57375.htm [last accessed 5 August 2018].
16 Gürçağlar shows that the translations of a number of Western canonical works of literature by the Translation Bureau, which was set up by the Ministry of Education in Turkey during the 1940s to 1960s had 'an educational function and were intended to transfer the ideas contained in the principal literary works of the

West to Turkish readers and especially the young' (2002: 48). These translations were preceded by prefaces written by significant political Turkish figures of the time or by translators working for the Translation Bureau (not in this case the original authors or translators). As explained by Gürçağlar, these prefaces went beyond the aim of informing or presenting the text they accompanied since they were introducing 'an ideological angle, placing the text within the general project of modernization. ... They (prefaces) guided the reader's perception of the text and were intended to create an emotive effect on the reader, making him/her feel a part of the cultural modernization of the country' (2002: 52).

17 'Brothers Jacob (1785–1863) and Wilhelm Grimm (1786–1859) were German academics and linguists who spent years collecting popular fairy tales and folktales. Their resulting compilation of over 200 stories, *Kinder- und Hausmärchen* (Children's and Household Tales) is one of the most famous collections of tales in the world, influencing generations of writers, artists, academics, composers, filmmakers, and animators.' https://www.taschen.com/pages/en/search/brothers-grimm [last accessed 5 August 2018].

18 I conducted an interview with Sharif Kanaana (in English) in summer 2012 via audiovisual communication (Skype). I recorded the interview then transcribed it into a written script. With Kanaana's permission, I have made slight editing to the language and structure of the interview. The written script of the interview is used in my analysis and appears as Appendix 1 below.

19 The notion of 'post-memory' is a mediation between present and past; it 'defines the present in relation to a troubled past rather than initiating new paradigms. ... It is a structure of inter- and trans-generational transmission of traumatic knowledge and experience. It is a consequence of traumatic recall but (unlike post-traumatic stress disorder) at a generational remove' (Hirsch, 2008: 111). I will discuss the notion of post-memory in more detail in Chapters 3 and 4.

20 'The Institute for Palestine Studies (IPS) is the oldest institute in the world devoted exclusively to documentation, research, analysis, and publication on Palestinian affairs and the Arab-Israeli conflict. It was established in Beirut in 1963 and incorporated there as a private, independent, non-profit Arab institute unaffiliated with any political organization or government. It is led by a Board of Trustees composed of scholars, businessmen and public figures from across the Arab world, and by a volunteer Executive Committee elected by the Board.' Cited in http://www.palestine-studies.org/content/history [accessed on 4 November 2018]. IPS is generally 'looked upon as the major source of accurate information and analysis on Palestinian affairs and the Arab-Israeli conflict, and as a model of institutional organization and independence' (Hirsch, 2008).

21 Founded in 1994, The A M Qattan Foundation is a UK-registered charity with offices in London, Ramallah and Gaza City. It is named after its founder Abdel Mohsin Qattan, who is a Palestinian business man deeply involved in Palestinian charitable and developmental projects. Through its work in Palestine and elsewhere, the foundation seeks to invest in people and to provide a fertile cultural soil upon which they can build their lives. 'Al-Qattan began his active involvement in social, charitable and developmental work. He was one of the founders of the Institute for Palestine Studies and Taawon – Welfare Association, served as Palestine's governor at the Arab Fund for Social and Economic Development, and member of the Board of Trustees of the American University of Beirut. Al-Qattan supported many Palestinian and Arab students and many other organizations including the Centre for Arab Unity Studies, the Ahmad Bahaa Edin Foundation, Birzeit University, The Palestinian Center for Policy Research & Strategic Studies – Masarat, and many others' cited in http://qattanfoundation.org/en/qattan/about/abdel-mohsin-al-qattan [accessed on 4 November 2018]

22 Jābir Sulaymān is credited with 'translating and revising' (Muhawi and Kanaana, 2001: xix). His starting point of reference is *SBSA* and the original tapes made of the tales being told. He is the translator and language editor for the Modern Standard Arabic and Palestinian regional dialects for *Qul Ya Tayer* (2001). Sulaymān was born in Al-Tarmas in Palestine in 1945. He studied in Egypt and Poland, where he obtained his master's degree. Sulayman worked for the Palestinian Planning Centre, run by the Palestinian Liberation Organization (PLO), from 1973 to 1979. From 1979 to 1982, he worked for the Palestine Information and Documentation Centre, and in 1982 he became the head of the documentation department at the Institute for Palestine Studies. He was also the editor in chief of the 'Wafa' Palestinian news agency. Sulayman continues to write for various magazines and newspapers, such as *Shu'ūn Falasṭīnīa* (Palestinian Affairs) and *Al-kātib al-Falasṭīnī* (the Palestinian Writer). Information from http://www.falestiny.com/word.php?did=166 [accessed on 10 May 2009; page no longer extant].

23 See the section 'Storytelling and Language' in Chapter 1.

24 *Qul Ya Tayer* (2010) is a selection of twelve out of the forty-five folktales in *Qul Ya Tayer* (2001).The newer collection is full of illustrations designed for a young audience with very few paratextual elements. The present study will not focus on the content or presentation of *Qul Ya Tayer* (2010) but will refer to it when needed.

25 Aarne and Thompson's Motif and Tale type index is the most widely accepted standard method to catalogue and classify folktales and fairy tales, constituting

'two of the most valuable tools in the professional folklorist's arsenal of aids for analysis' (Dundes, 1997: 195).

Chapter 3

1. The names, following the same order, are 'Precious One and Worn-out One', 'Jbene', 'Gazelle', 'Lolabe', 'Lady Tatar', 'Minjal', 'Im Eshe', 'The Woman Whose Hands Were Cut Off', 'Im Awwad and the Ghouleh', 'The Woman Who Fell in the Well', 'Im Ali and Abu Ali'.
2. The interconnection between rural setting and pre-*Nakba* setting is a theme I will discuss in more depth below.
3. See the summary of the tale in Appendix 3 (number 1).
4. One of the processes or devices of transfer between one generation and another is developed in Marianne Hirsch's concept of 'post-memory' (Hirsch, 1996, 1997, 1999). Traumatic experiences are lived and experienced once within a specific frame of time and generation; however, their effect can persist, be transmitted and documented, as part of a nation's collective memorial experience, thanks to joint efforts between past and present generations. Within memory studies, this particular relation to a parental past has been analysed and seen as a 'syndrome' of belatedness or 'post-ness' and has been variously termed 'absent memory' (Fine, 1988), 'inherited memory', 'belated memory' and 'prosthetic memory' (Lury, 1998; Landsberg, 2004). These terms refer in one way or another to the existing connection between the descendants of survivors of massive traumatic events with the previous generation's remembrance of the past. The transmission of memory thus involves those who were not actually there to live an event (Hirsch, 2008).
5. In an interview published in an arts and media journal (Ben-Zvi, 1999: 80), Hassan says,

   > My clearest meeting with Palestinian history as a story, a narrative, and not a collage of isolated incidents, I owe to my mother. I was six or seven years old and my mother took us to our bedroom. She sat on the bed and we three sat in a circle around her (which is what gave me the idea for the central scene in *Ustura*, in which Umm Salim tells her story). I only remember her telling the story without any tragic note, without victimhood, but with a dramatic sense of survival. She was full of anger, a strong will, and much hope. We went to bed, and for the first time in my life I felt grown up, not

just 'a big boy,' but grown up, like kids think about grown ups. I understood that I live in my homeland, Palestine that I belong; I am Palestinian, and no one can take that away from me.

6 The existence and importance of history in the Palestinian case is unavoidable. History, in effect, as argued by Landsberg (2004: 24), 'must become like memory in order to inform subjectivity, in order to change and alter consciousness, which is the basis for any kind of political alliance or action'. The mass media can give people an experience and taste of history, giving the same impact and feel of memory and hence help in raising the mediated collective identification across existing social divisions.

7 Gramsci's notion of hegemony highlights the control of one social class over the other, whether socially, politically or economically. For him hegemony features over two levels: '"civil society", that is the ensemble of organisms commonly called "private", and that of "political society" or "the State". These two levels correspond on the one hand to the function of "hegemony" which the dominant group exercises throughout society' (Inverted commas in original; Gramsci, 1992: 67).

8 People are invited 'to take on memories of a past through which they did not live' (Landsberg, 2004: 8). Since remembering is initially physically experienced by human beings, it can derive much of its power through effect. The same idea is developed in Alison Landsberg's (2004) notion of prosthetic memory, in which a mimic reproduction of the effect can be achieved through the use of mass culture. 'Mass culture makes particular memories more widely available, so that people who have no "natural" claim to them might nevertheless incorporate them into their own archive of experience' (Landsberg, 2004: 8–9).

9 According to Landsberg (2004):

> Prosthetic memory emerges at the interface between a person and a historical narrative about the past, at an experiential site such as a movie theatre or museum. In this moment of contact, an experience occurs through which the person sutures himself or herself into a larger history [...] In the process that I am describing the person does not simply apprehend a historical narrative but takes on a more personal, deeply felt memory of a past event through which he or she did not live. The resulting prosthetic memory has the ability to shape that person's subjectivity and politics (Landsberg, 2004: 2).

10 In her article 'The Generation of Postmemory', Marianne Hirsch elaborates on the work of Jan and Aleida Assmann, originally written in German: *Das kulturelle*

Gedächtnis: Schrift, Erinnerung und politische Identität in früheren Hochkulturen (1997) and *Der lange Schatten der Vergangenheit: Erinnerungskultur und Geschichtspolitik* (2006).

11 'The pleasure principle' and 'the reality principle' are concepts initially discussed by Sigmund Freud (1914).
12 See the summary of the tale in Appendix 3 (number 2).
13 The 'Brother–Sister Syndrome', according to El-Shamy, is described as follows:

> Within the nuclear family the Brother–Sister Syndrome is manifested through brother–sister love, brother–brother hostility, sister–sister hostility, parents–children hostility, and husband–wife unaffectionate relations. The structure of sentiments in the larger kinship group is congruent with that found in the nuclear family; these sentiments include brother–sister's husband hostility; sister–brother's wife hostility, and child–mother's brother affectionate ties. The child's positive relationship with the maternal uncle is a product of the love a mother has for her brother, and the strong bonds of affection between a child and his or her mother (but not father). (El-Shamy, 1999: 3).

14 See the summary of the tale in Appendix 3 (number 3).
15 For more details see the Stephan, 1928 on the symbolism of birds in Palestinian proverbs.
16 See the summary of the tale in Appendix 3 (number 4).
17 The interview was conducted by Robin Myers and Shadi Rohana in 2011 on http://electronicintifada.net/content/interview-sharif-kanaana-palestinian-folklore-and-identity/9825 [last accessed 2 August 2018].
18 It is worth mentioning that both Muhawi and Kanaana rely heavily on the seminal work by Granqvist, *Marriage in Palestine*, Vols I and II: 'The Night of Henna' and 'Marriage Customs', constantly referring to her works in their footnotes. The reason why she seems to be a credible eye witness is because, and unlike her orientalist colleagues at the time, she worked at getting a view from within, making sure not simply to observe customs or ceremonies, but also 'to investigate local explanations, views and motives' (Granqvist, 1931: 19).
19 Hilma Granqvist conducted studies of the village of Artas in the 1920s and 1930s. The results showed how Palestinian women were responsible for owning, preserving and transmitting songs and dances that celebrated the central peasant institution of marriage (Granqvist, 1935; Sayigh, 2007).
20 See the summary of the tale in Appendix 3 (number 5).
21 See the summary of the tale in Appendix 3 (number 6).
22 See the summary of the tale in Appendix 3 (number 7).

23 See the summary of the tale in Appendix 3 (number 8).
24 Quote taken from an online article entitled 'Stories Told by and for Palestinian Children' by Sharif Kanaana on 11/03/2008 on https://www.ihs-humanities.com/stories-told-by-and-for-palestinian-children [accessed 4 November 2018]; [accessed 17 November 2013; page no longer extant].
25 As Granqvist noted, 'children have little freedom in their own marriages. … Children must bow to the father's authority and choice of mate' (Granqvist, 1931: 54).
26 See the summary of the tale in Appendix 3 (number 9).
27 See the summary of the tale in Appendix 3 (number 10).
28 See the summary of the tale in Appendix 3 (number 11).
29 Further folktales in the present compilation treat the problems arising between wives and husbands within a polygynous situation, such as 'Chick Eggs' (*Bīẓ faqāqīs*) and 'Bear-Cub of the Kitchen' (*Dabit al-maṭbakh*). In 'Chick Eggs', 'the man must attend both to his present wife and to his daughter, who represents her own mother in the household' (Muhawi and Kanaana, 1989: 249). In 'Bear-Cub of the Kitchen', the prince is struggling to balance his emotional dedication to the older wives and the new wife. In both tales, the husband appears to be manipulated emotionally by the wife.
30 See the summary of the tale in Appendix 3 (number 12).

Chapter 4

1 The characteristics of the missing 'thing' in the past and how it is regenerated in the present resemble Lacan's idea of 'the mirror stage' and 'object petit a' (2011), the latter known as 'the unattainable object of desire'. Lacan's idea is that the child identifies with the image of selfhood through a desire for the ideal other. 'It is an expression of the lack inherent in human beings, whose incompleteness and early helplessness produce a quest for fulfilment beyond the satisfaction of biological needs' (Krishner, 2005: 83).
2 See, for example, Mustafa Khalil al-Sayfi's (1993) poem, ' Trip in the ruins of Al-Walja'; a selection is quoted in Sa'di and Abu-Lughod, 2007: 65:

> *I am thirsty … where are the springs and wells?*
> *Nothing only wasteland and desert,*
> *Nothing but murky wilderness*
> *The earth of the fields covered in stones.*

3 Claude Reignier Conder (1879: 259) describes the *baydar* in his work *Tent Work in Palestine*: 'It is a broad flat space, an open ground, generally high; sometimes the floor is on a flat rocky hill-top, and occasionally it is an open valley, down which there is a current of air. ... The size of the floor varies, from a few yards to an area of perhaps fifty yards square, and rich villages have sometimes two such floors.'

4 The work of scholars such as Benedict Anderson and Antony Smith provide insights when discussing Palestinian nationalism. As discussed in Chapter 1, language and its manifestation, in the press and novels, or what we can call 'print capitalism', constitute the cornerstone for the growth of any nation, according to Anderson. Being part of Arab culture and history, Palestinians used the development of the modern Arab press during the Ottoman era to develop their own national and local newspapers. The move was meant to create a foundation for a distinct Palestinian identity. A second important aspect that Anderson describes as 'shaping modern national consciousness' (Anderson, 1991: 19) is the role of colonial boundaries. Following the First World War, new borders and territorial entities were created under different foreign administrations, and governed by different political systems in the Middle East. The presence of the British Mandate on the one hand consolidated the idea that Palestine was part of historical Syria (*Bilād Al-Shām*), and on the other hand encouraged Palestinians to react by making efforts towards shaping their own national identity. In his discussion of nationalism, Anthony Smith considers that there is an important ethnic essence to all modern nations (Smith, 1999). To understand modern political nationalisms, reference to these earlier ethnic ties and memories, in some cases to pre-modern ethnic identities and communities are needed (Smith, 1999). His idea is very useful in understanding Arab nationalism but may be of less help in understanding Palestinian nationalism. Palestinian nationalism has evolved, in fact, following conflict between two groups over territory; in Smith's words, 'The frequency, intensity and duration of wars between rival polities is itself a significant factor in crystallizing ethnic sentiments among an affected population' (Smith, 1986: 38). When we look at the Palestinian case, we find that the threat of loss or disappearance, mainly triggered by the Zionist challenge, has created a strong sense of community among Palestinians. In a similar vein, the political geographer Oren Yiftachel explains how, due to the constant struggle with Zionism over the land, Palestinian nationalism grew as 'ethnonational in character' in which territory became part and parcel of the nation (Yiftachel,

2002). Smith has also discussed how every national movement's quest is to establish and even reinforce a common historical past. Despite the fact that some nationalisms are based on fabrications or flawed interpretations, the belief of having a shared historical ground is necessary for the survival of communities and their national identity. Nationalism could be considered as the most powerful agent and activator in the construction and reconstruction of Palestinian collective memory. In fact, 'nationalism identifies the available repositories of the past and selects fragments or elements of past periods, events, symbols, or heroes from which it creates a new unified collective past' (Litvak, 2009: 19). The national past becomes memory rather than historical past. This memory is materialized by sites, rituals and representations, which end up being part of a collective identity. For further discussion, see Sa'di, 2002; Khalidi, 1982, 1997; Doumani, 1992.

5 See Appendix 4.
6 Muhawi and Kanaana (1989: 40) expand on this point, saying, 'Sometimes the supernatural takes specific shape in the form of jinn, ghouls, giants, or other supernatural beings (e.g., Tales 5, 6, 8, 16, 17, 18, 19, 22, 29, 30, 32, 34, 35, 36, 37, 40); at other times it remains an abstract force, such as chance or predestination (e.g., Tales 13, 14, 28, 32, 42, 43, 44, 45). In some tales the supernatural helps the action along, whereas in others it presents obstacles to be overcome so that the desired result, such as the completion of a quest or the ridding of an evil influence from the community, may be achieved.'
7 See the summary of the tale in Appendix 5 (number 2).
8 See summary of the tale in Appendix 5 (number 1).
9 See the summary of tales 14 and 15 in Appendix 5 (numbers 3 and 4).
10 The village or the land belongs now to Israel. According to the Palestinian historian Walid Khalidi, 'Two village shrines remain standing. One is made of stone and its roof is topped with a dozen domes clustered around a more prominent dome at the center. A number of other structures and houses also are still intact; some are utilized for various purposes' (Khalidi, 1992: 234).
11 As another example of the proverbs, idiomatic expressions and cultural set phrases used in this compilation, the metaphor 'mouthful of happiness' (*luqmat al-sa'āda*) has been commonly used in a number of folktales. The set phrase alludes to the food newly-weds eat in wedding feasts or their first breakfast together, as we see at the end of many folktales.

Final reflections

1. Sharif Kanaana explains the following in his article entitled 'Stories Told by and for Palestinian Children' (2017):

   Had our societies continued to be illiterate, tradition oriented, village societies, where tales are transmitted and told to children orally, then I would have advocated that traditional folktales should not be modified intentionally and consciously because oral stories would evolve automatically to suit new circumstances. But since now we read to our children from books rather than tell the stories from memory, which prevents tales from evolving, then I agree that they should be modified and updated.

2. There have been a number of workshops that are run across the West Bank since 2011 organized by some universities, such as Hebron and Birzeit universities as well as the Ministry of Culture. Most recently in 2017 the Palestinian National Theatre run a workshop called 'Hakawati', meaning 'the storyteller' aimed at training those interested in learning the skill of storytelling; it is mainly addressed to young Palestinians.

Appendix 1

1. The interview with Sharif Kanaana was conducted in English. It was realized through the use of audiovisual communication (Skype). With Kanaana's permission, I have taken slight liberties in correcting grammatical mistakes when needed. I have also structured the interview according to thematic sub-headings.
2. He elaborates,

   I am from the Galilee, which is in Israel, and not the West Bank. I graduated from school in 1954 which means 4/5 years after the 1948 catastrophe. I worked then as a school teacher till 1961. The situation was so bad that I could not take the work at school. At the time, things were even worse for Arabs inside Israel. I had actually run away! I was not keen on studying, getting degrees or studying Anthropology. So I wanted to escape from that situation and gradually I started to feel guilty about doing that. Escaping meant leaving the situation and of course leaving behind a big family and relatives etc. As a matter of fact, I learnt that there was a short course of

Anthropology. So I started to look for a way to connect again, to go back to the situation. I saw an advertisement by Birzeit University that they were changing from a two-year college course to a four-year degree-granting university. I wrote to them and the first thing I mentioned was that 'I had never the chance to serve my people and my country, thus I would like to make up for that by working in the Palestinian University'. This is how I sincerely felt.

3   For more about the project see http://palestine-studies.org/books/all-remains-palestinian-villages-occupied-and-depopulated-israel-1948-hardcover (last accessed 9 August 2018).
4   Kanaana elaborates, 'I am by training an anthropologist; I never took a course on folklore but went towards it as a result of nostalgia. Moreover, I am an anthropologist and I didn't want to do what anthropologists do in foreign cultures.'
5   Hereafter *Speak, Bird, Speak Again* will be referred to as *SBSA*.
6   Alan Dundes, a Jewish anthropologist at the University of Berkeley in California, wrote the foreword of *SBSA* (1989), also translated into Arabic in *Qul Ya Tayer* (2001).
7   The current study started by comparing and analysing *SBSA* and *Qul Ya Tayer* with Raphael Patai's compilation, *Arab Folktales from Palestine and Israel* (1998); however, the focus changed throughout the research, ultimately excluding Patai's compilation.

Bibliography

Primary texts

Muhawi, Ibrahim, and Sharif Kanaana (1989) *Speak, Bird, Speak Again: Palestinian Arab Folktales*, Berkeley and Los Angeles: University of California Press.

Muhawī, Ibrahīm, and Sharīf Kanā'na (2001) *Qul Ya Tayer: Qūl yā ṭayr*, Beirut: The Institute of Palestine Studies.

Secondary texts

Abdel Haddi, Faiha (2018) 'Gender Representation of Oral History : Palestinian Women Narrating the Stories of Their Displacement', in Nahla Abdo and Nur Masalha (eds), *An Oral History of the Palestinian Nakba*, London: Zed Books, 159–81.

Abrahams, Roger D. (1982) 'Storytelling Events: Wake Amusements and the Structure of Nonsense on St. Vincent', *Journal of American Folklore*, 95: 389–414.

Abrams, M. H. (1981) *A Glossary of Literary Terms*, New York and London: Holt Rinehart & Wilson.

Al-Herthani, Mahmoud (2009) 'Edward Said in Arabic: Narrativity and Paratextual Framing', PhD Thesis, Manchester, CTIS: University of Manchester.

Anderson, Benedict (1983) *Imagined Communities*, London: Verso.

Anderson, Benedict (1991) *Imagined Communities: Reflections on the Origin and Spread of Nationalism*, revised edn, London: Verso.

Asaad, Talal (1986) 'The Concept of Cultural Translation in British Social Anthropology', in James Clifford and George E. Marcus (eds), *Writing Culture: The Poetics and Politics of Ethnography*, Berkeley, CA: The University of California Press, 141–64.

Ashliman, D. L. (2004) *Folk and Fairy Tales: A Handbook*, Westport, CT, New York and London: Greenwood Press.

Assmann, Jan (1995) 'Collective Memory and Cultural Identity', trans. John Czaplicka, *New German Critique*, 65: 123–33.

Assmann, Jan (2006) *Religion and Cultural Memory*, Stanford: Stanford University Press.
Augé, Marc (2004) *Oblivion*, trans. Marjolijn De Jager, Minneapolis: University of Minnesota Press.
Austin, J. L. (1962) *How to Do Things with Words*, New York: Oxford University Press.
Babcok-Abrahams, Barbara (1974) 'The Story in the Story: Metanarration in Folk Narrative'. Paper delivered at the VI Folk Narrative Congress, Helsinki, June 17.
Baker, Mona (2006) *Translation and Conflict: A Narrative Account*, Oxford: Routledge.
Baker, Mona (2008) 'Ethics of Renarration: Mona Baker Is Interviewed by Andrew Chesterman', *Cultus*, 1 (1): 10–33.
Baldwin, James (1985) *The Price of the Ticket*, New York: St. Martin's Press.
Ballard, Michel (ed.) (2001) *Oralité et Traduction*, Arras: Artois Presses Université.
Bardenstein, Carol B. (1999) 'Trees, Forests, and the Shaping of Palestinian and Israeli Collective Memory', in Mieke Bal, Jonathan Crew and Leo Spitzer (eds), *Acts of Memory: Cultural Recall in the Present*, Hanover, New Hampshire: University Press of New England, 148-70.
Barhoum, Ann (1990) 'Speak Bird, Speak, Again: Palestinian Arab Folktales by Ibrahim Muhawi and Sharif Kanaana', *Middle East Report*, Nos 164/165: 71.
Bascom, William (1955) 'Verbal Art', *Journal of American Folklore*, 68: 245–52.
Bateson, Gregory (1972) *Steps to an Ecology of Mind*, New York: Ballantine.
Bauman, Richard, and Joel Sherzer (eds) (1975) *Explorations in the Ethnography of Speaking*, Cambridge: Cambridge University Press.
Bellasco, Warren, and Philip Scranton (eds) (2002) *Food Nations: Selling Taste in Consumer Societies*, London: Routledge.
Ben-Amos, Dan, and Kenneth Golstein (eds) (1975) *Folklore: Communication and Performance*, The Hague: Mouton.
Benford, Robert, and David Snow (2000) 'Framing Processes and Social Movements: An Overview and Assessment', *Annual Review of Sociology*, 26: 611–39.
Ben-Yehuda, Nachman (1995) *The Masada Myth: Collective Memory and Mythmaking in Israel*, Madison and London: University of Wisconsin Press.
Ben Zvi, Tal (1999) 'Aval ani ve-rak ani asaper et ha-sipur sheli' [But I and only I Can Tell My Own Story], *Plastika*, 3: 75–81.
Bergson, Henri (1988) *Matter and Memory* [*Matière et mémoire*], trans. Nancy Margaret Paul and W Scott Palmer, New York: Zone Books.
Bettelheim, Bruno (1976) *The Uses of Enchantment: The Meaning and Importance of Fairy Tales*, New York: Knopf by Random House.
Bettelheim, Bruno (1981) 'Fairy Tales as a Way of Knowing' in Michael M Metzger and Katharina Mommsen (eds), *Fairy Tales as Ways of Knowing: Essays on Märchen in Psychology, Society and Literature*, Berne: Peter Lang Publishers, 11–20.

Blend, Benay (2001) '"I am an Act of Kneading": Food and the Making of Chicana Identity', in Sherrie A. Inness (ed.), *Cooking Lessons: The Politics of Gender and Food*, Lanham, MD: Rowman and Littlefield, 41–62.

Bolte, Johannes (1920) *Name und Merkmale des Märchens*, Helsinki: Suomalainen Tiedeakatemia.

Boyarin, Daniel, and Boyarin, Jonathan (1993) 'Diaspora: Generation and the Ground of Jewish Identity', *Critical Inquiry*, 19 (4): 693–725.

Brand, Hanita (2009) 'Palestinian Women and Collective Memory' in Meir Litvak (ed.), *Palestinian Collective Memory and National Identity*, Palgrave Macmillan: New York, 169–92.

Bresheeth, Haim (2007) 'The Continuity of Trauma and Struggle: Recent Cinematic Representations of the Nakba', in Ahmad H. Sa'di and Lila Abu-Lughod (eds), *Nakba: Palestine, 1948, and the Claims of Memory*, New York: Columbia University Press, 161–87.

Brown, Linda Keller, and Kay Mussell (eds) (1984) *Ethnic and Regional Foodways in the United States: The Performance of Regional Identity*, Knoxville: University of Tennessee Press.

Bruner, Jerome (2001) 'Self-Making and World-Making', in Jens Brockmier and Donal Carbaugh (eds), *Narrative and Identity: Studies in Autobiography, Self and Culture*, Amsterdam: John Benjamins Publishing Company, 25–38.

Budeiri, Musa (1997) 'The Palestinians: Tensions between Nationalist and Religious Identities', in Israel Gershoni and James Jankowski (eds), *Rethinking Arab Nationalism*, New York: Columbia University Press, 191–206.

Burke, Peter (1989) 'History as Social Memory', in Thomas Butler (ed.), *Memory: History, Culture and the Mind*, Oxford: Blackwell, 97–113.

Bushnaq, Inea (1990) 'Tales of Rural Life in *Speak Bird, Speak, Again*', *Journal of Palestine Studies*, 19 (3): 133–5.

Cadora, Pamela (1988) 'Palestinian Artists Visit American Galleries', *Al-Fajr* (Jerusalem), 6 March: 11.

Canaan, Taufik (1927) 'The Child in Palestinian Arab Superstition', *Journal of the Palestine Oriental Society*, VII: 159–86.

Carr, David (1986) *Time, Narrative and History*, Bloomington: Indiana University Press.

Carruthers, Mary (1990) *The Book of Memory: A Study of Memory in Medieval Culture*, Cambridge, Cambridge University Press.

Caruth, Cathy (ed.) (1995) *Trauma: Explorations in Memory*, Baltimore and London: Johns Hopkins University Press.

Caruth, Cathy (ed.) (1996) *Unclaimed Experience: Trauma, Narrative and History*, Baltimore and London: Johns Hopkins University Press.

Cavarero, Adriana (1997) *Relating Narratives: Storytelling and Selfhood*, trans. Paul A Kottman, London: Routledge.
Charmaz, Kathy (1994) 'Identity Dilemmas of Chronically Ill Men', *The Sociological Quarterly*, 35 (2): 269–88 (online at https://doi.org/10.1111/j.1533-8525.1994.tb00 410.x).
Christensen, Paul (2001) 'Mac and Gravy' in Sherrie A. Inness (ed.), *Pilaf, Pozole and Pad Thai*, Amherst: University Massachusetts Press, 17–39.
Coleridge, Samuel Taylor (1971) 'The Stateman's Manual', in Hazard Adams and Leroy Searle (eds), *Critical Theory since Plato*, New York: Harcourt Brace Jovanovich, 489–92.
Collins, Ronald, and David Skover (1992) 'Paratexts', *Sanford Law Review*, 44 (3): 509–52
Comito, Jacqueline (2001) 'Remembering Nana and Papu: The Poetics of Pasta, Pane and Peppers among One Iowan Calabrian Family', PhD, University of Iowa.
Conder, Claude Reignier (1879) *Tent Work in Palestine: A Record of Discovery and Adventure*, 2 Vols, London: Richard Bentley.
Confino, Alon (1997) 'Collective Memory and Cultural History: Problems of Methods', *The American Historical Review*, 102 (5): 1386–403.
Connelly, Bridget (1986) *Arab Folk Epic and Identity*, Berkeley, Los Angeles, CA, and London: University of California Press.
Connerton, Paul (1989) *How Societies Remember*, Cambridge: Cambridge University Press.
Cooper, Craig (ed.) (2007) *The Politics of Orality: Orality and Literacy in Ancient Greece*, Vol. 6, Leiden and Boston: Brill.
Crowfoot, Grace, and Louise, Baldensperger (1932) *From Cedar to Hyssop: A Study in the Folklore of Plants in Palestine*, London: Sheldon.
Davis, Fred (1979) *Yearning for Yesterday: A Sociology of Nostalgia*, New York: Free Press.
Davis, Rochelle (2007) 'Mapping the Past, Re-Creating the Homeland: Memories of Village Places in Pre-1948 Palestine', in Ahmad H Sa'di and Lila Abu-Lughod (eds), *Nakba: Palestine, 1948, and the Claims of Memory*, New York: Columbia University Press, 53–76.
Dégh, Linda (1981) 'The Magic Tale and its Magic', in Michael M. Metzger and Katharina Mommsen (eds), *Fairy Tales as Ways of Knowing: Essays on Märchen in Psychology, Society and Literature*, Berne: Peter Lang Publishers, 54–74.
Dickens, James, Sandor Harvey, and Ian Higgins (2002) *Thinking Arabic Translation: A Course in Translation Method*, London and New York: Routledge.
Dòmine, Marta Marín (2002) 'At First Sight: Paratextual Elements in the English Translations of La Plaça Del Diamant', paper published by Laurier University, https://periodicos.ufsc.br/index.php/traducao/article/view/6179.

Dorson, Richard (ed.) (1972) *Folklore and Folklife*, Chicago: The University of Chicago Press.
Doumani, Beshara (1992) 'Rediscovering Ottoman Palestine: Writing Palestinians into History', *Journal of Palestine Studies*, 21 (2): 5–28.
Drews, Robert (1998) 'Canaanites and Philistines' *Journal for the Study of Old Testament*, 23 (81): 39–61.
Druckman, James N., and ArthurLupia (2000) 'Preference Formation', *Annual Review of Political Science*, 3: 1–24.
Duggan, Joseph (ed.) (1975) *Oral Literature: Seven Essays*, Edinburgh: Scottish Academic Press.
Dundes, Alan (1969) 'The Devolutionary Premise in Folklore Theory', *Journal of the Folklore Institute*, No. 6: 5–19.
Dundes, Alan (1975) *Analytic Essays in Folklore*, The Hague: Moulton Publishers.
Dundes, Alan (1980) 'Texture, Text, and Context', in Alan Dundes (ed.), *Interpreting Folklore*, Bloomington: Indiana University Press, 20–32.
Dundes, Alan (1997) 'The Motif-Index and the Tale Type Index: A Critique', *Journal of Folklore Research*, 34 (3): 195–202.
Durkheim, Emile (1982) *The Rules of Sociological Method and Selected Texts on Sociology and Its Methods*, ed. Steven Lukes, trans. W. D. Halls, New York: Free Press.
El-Nimr, Sonia (1993) 'Oral History and Palestinian Collective Memory', *Oral History*, 21 (1): 54–6.
El-Shamy, Hasan (1999) *Tales Arab Women Tell*, Bloomington and Indianapolis: Indiana University Press.
El-Shamy, Hasan (1980) *Folktales of Egypt*, Chicago: The University of Chicago Press.
Erll, Astrid, and Ansgar Nunning (eds) (2008) *Cultural Memory Studies*, New York and Berlin: Walter de Gruyter.
Farr, James (1993) 'Framing Democratic Discussion', in George E. Marcus and Russell L. Hanson (eds), *Reconsidering the Democratic Public*, University Park: The Pennsylvania State University Press, 379–91.
Ferguson, Frances (1996) 'Romantic Memory', *Studies in Romanticism*, 35: 509–33.
Field, Sean (2006) 'Beyond "Healing": Trauma, Oral History and Regeneration', *Oral History*, 34 (1): 31–42.
Fine, Elizabeth (1984) *The Folklore Text*, Bloomington: University of Indiana Press.
Fine, Ellen (1988) ' The Absent Memory: The Act of Writing in Post-Holocaust French Literature', in Berel Lang (ed.), *Writing and the Holocaust*, New York: Holmes and Meier, 41–57.
Firro, Kais M. (2014) 'How Does Oral History Serve Palestinian History?', *Jadal*, No 20: 1–8.

Foley, John Miles (ed.) (1986) *Oral Tradition in Literature: Interpretation in Context*, Columbia: University of Missouri Press.

Forster, Kurt W. (1976) 'Aby Warburg's History of Art: Collective Memory and the Social Mediation of Images', *Daedalus*, 105 (1): 169–76.

Freud, Sigmund (1914) *The Psychopathology of Everyday Life*, trans. A. A. Brill, New York: Macmillan.

Freud, Sigmund, (1922) *Beyond the Pleasure Principle*, Trans C. J. M. Hubback. London, Vienna: International Psycho-Analytical.

Freud, Sigmund, (1925–91) 'A Note upon the "Mystic Writing-Pad"', in *On Metapsychology: The Theory of Psychoanalysis*, Vol. 11 of 'The Penguin Freud Library', ed. Angela Richards, trans. James Strachey, Harmondsworth: Penguin, 429–34.

Frisch, Deborah (1993) 'Reasons for Framing Effects', *Organizational Behavior and Human Decision Processes*, 54 (3): 399–429.

Gamson, William A. (1992) *Talking Politics*, New York: Cambridge University Press.

Gamson, William A., and Andre Modigliani (1987) 'The Changing Culture of Affirmative Actions', in Richard D. Braungart (ed.), *Research in Political Sociology*, Vol. 3, Greenwich, CT: JAI Press, 137–77.

Geertz, Clifford (1973) *The Interpretation of Cultures*, New York: Basic Books.

Genette, Gérard (1991) 'Introduction to the Paratext', *New Literary History*, 22 (2): 261–72.

Genette, Gérard (1997) *Paratexts: Threshold of Interpretation*, trans. Jane Lewin, foreword by Richard Macksey, Cambridge: Cambridge University Press.

Gerber, Haim (2004) 'The Limits of Constructedness: Memory and Nationalism in the Arab Middle East', *Nations and Nationalism* 10 (3): 256–8.

Gergen, Kenneth J., and Mary M. Gergen (1983) 'Narratives of the Self', in Theodore R. Sarbin and Karl E. Scheibe (eds), *Studies in Social Identity*, New York: Praeger Press, 254–73.

Gertz, Nurith, and George Khleifi (2006) *Landscape in Mist: Space and Memory in Palestinian Cinema*, Tel Aviv: Am Oved.

Giard, Luce (1998) 'Part II: Doing-cooking', in Michel de Certeau, Luce Giard and Pierre Mayol (eds), *The Practice of Everyday Life*, Vol. 2, *Living and Cooking*, trans. Timothy J Tomasik, Minneapolis: University Minneapolis Press, 149 ff.

Gillis, John R. (ed.) (1994) *Commemorations: The Politics of National Identity*, Princeton, NJ: Princeton University Press.

Gitlin, Todd (1980) *The Whole World Is Watching: Mass Media in the Making and Unmaking of the New Left*, Berkeley, CA: University of California Press.

Goffman, Erving (1959) *The Presentation of Self in Everyday Life*, Garden City, NY: Doubleday.

Goffman, Erving (1963) *Stigma: Notes on the Management of Spoiled Identity*, New York: Prentice Hall.

Goffman, Erving (1974) *Frame Analysis: An Essay on the Organization of Experience*, Boston: Northeastern University Press.

Gramsci, Antonio (1992) *Prison Notebooks*, Vol. 1, ed. Joseph A. Buttigieg, trans. Joseph A. Buttigieg and Antonio Callari, New York: Columbia University Press.

Granqvist, Hilma (1931, 1935) *Marriage Conditions in a Palestinian Village*: Vol. 1 & 2, Helsinki: Akademische Buchhandlung Helsingfors.

Granqvist, Hilma (1942) *Marriage Conditions among the Arabs*, 2 Vols, Helsinki: Akademische Buchhandlung Helsingfors.

Granqvist, Hilma (1947) *Birth and Childhood among the Arabs*, Helsinki: Akademische Buchhandlung Helsingfors.

Grodzinsky, Yosef (2001) 'Historic Commissions in the DP Camps: The Resilience of Jewish Identity', draft paper for the Remarque Institute Conference *Birth of a Refugee Nation: Displaced Persons in Postwar Europe 1945-1951*, April 19-21, 2001.

Gross, Toomas (2002) 'Anthropology of Collective Memory: Estonian National Awakening Revisited', *Trames*, 6 (4): 342-54.

Gürçağlar, Şehnaz Tahir (2002) 'What Texts Don't Tell: The Uses of Paratexts in Translation Research', in Theo Hermans (ed.), *Crosscultural Transgressions: Research Models in Translation Studies II: Historical and Ideological Issues*, Manchester: St. Jerome, 44-60.

Halbwachs, Maurice (1992) *On Collective Memory*, ed. and trans. Lewis A. Coser, Chicago and London: University of Chicago Press.

Hall, Stuart (1998) 'Notes on Deconstructing "the Popular"', in John Storey (ed.), *Cultural Theory and Popular Culture: A Reader*, Hemel Hempstead: Pearson/Prentice Hall, 442-53

Hall, Stuart, and Paddy Whannel (1998) 'The Young Audience', in John Storey (ed.), *Cultural Theory and Popular Culture: A Reader*, Athens: University of Georgia Press, 61-7.

Hammami, Rema (2004) 'Gender, Nakbe and Nation: Palestinian Women's Presence and Absence in the Narration of 1948 Memories', *Review of Women's Studies*, 2.

Hanauer, J. E. (1935) *Folklore of the Holy Land: Moslem, Christian and Jewish*, London: Sheldon.

Harmon, Gary L. (2006) 'On the Nature and Functions of Popular Culture', in Harold E. Hinds, Jr, Marilyn F. Motz and Angela M. S. Nelson (eds), *Popular Culture Theory and Methodology: A Basic Introduction*, Madison and London: The University of Wisconsin Press.

Harold Hinds, Jr, Marilyn F. Motz and Angela M. S. Nelson (eds) (2006) *Popular Culture, Theory and Methodology: A Basic Introduction*, Madison and London: The University of Wisconsin Press.

Hartland E. S. (1900) *Mythology and Folktales: Their Relation and Interpretation*, London: David Nutt.

Hirsch, Marianne (1996) 'Past Lives: Postmemories in Exile', *Poetics Today*, 17 (4): 659–86.

Hirsch, Marianne (1997) *Family Frames: Photography, Narrative and Postmemory*, Cambridge, MA: Harvard University Press.

Hirsch, Marianne (1999) 'Projected Memory: Holocaust Photographs in Personal and Public Fantasy' in Mieke Bal, Jonathan Crewe and Leo Spitzer (eds), *Acts of Memory: Cultural Recall in the Present*, Hanover: University Press of New England, 3–23.

Hirsch, Marianne (2008) 'The Generation of Postmemory', *Poetics Today*, 29 (1): 103–28.

Hirsch, Marianne, and Valerie Smith (eds) (2002) *Gender and Cultural Memory*, special issue of *Signs: Journal of Women in Culture and Society* 28 (1): 1–19.

Hobsbawm, Eric (1983) 'Introduction: Inventing Traditions', in Eric Hobsbawm and Terence Ranger (eds), *The Invention of Tradition*, Cambridge: Cambridge University Press, 1–14.

Holtzman, Jon (2006) 'Food and Memory', *Annual Review of Anthropology* 35: 361–78.

Honko, Lauri (1989) 'Variation and Textuality in Oral Narratives', Paper presented at the twelfth congress of ISFNR (International Society for Folk Narrative Research) in Göttingen, July 1998.

Hume, David (2002) *A Treatise of Human Nature*, ed. David Fate Norton and Mary J. Norton, introduction by David Fate Norton, Oxford: Oxford University Press.

Humphries, Isabelle, and Laleh Khalili (2007) 'Gender of Nakba Memory', in Ahmad H Sa'di and Lila Abu-Lughod (eds), *Nakba: Palestine, 1948, and the Claims of Memory*, New York: Columbia University Press, 207–28.

Iggers, George G. (1997) *Historiography in the Twentieth Century: From Scientific Objectivity to the Postmodern Challenge*, Hanover and London: Wesleyan University Press.

Iyengar, Shanto, and Kinder, Donald (1987) *News That Matters: Television and American Opinion*, Chicago: University of Chicago Press.

Jackson, Michael (2013) *The Politics of Storytelling*, Copenhagen: Museum Tusculanum Press.

Jacobs, Melville (1959) *The Content and Style of an Oral Literature: Clackamas Chinook Myths and Tales*, New York: Wenner-Gren Foundation for Anthropological Research.

Jakobson, Roman (1966) 'Grammatical Parallelism and Its Russian Facet', *Language*, 42: 398–429.

Jansen, William Hugh (1957) 'Classifying Performance in the Study of Verbal Folklore', in W. Edson Richmond (ed.), *Studies in Folklore*, Bloomington: Indiana University Press, 110–18.

Jayyusi, Lena (1984) *Categorization and the Moral Order*, London: Routledge.
Jayyusi, Lena (2007) 'Iterability, Cumulativity, and Presence: The Relational Figures of Palestinian Memory', in Ahmad H. Sa'di and Lila Abu-Lughod (eds), *Nakba: Palestine, 1948, and the Claims of Memory*, New York: Columbia University Press, 107–34.
Jennings, Lee B. (1981) 'The Role of Alcohol in Hoffman's Mythic Tales' in Michael M. Metzger and Katharina Mommsen (eds), *Fairy Tales as Ways of Knowing: Essays on Märchen in Psychology, Society and Literature*, Berne: Peter Lang Publishers, 182–94.
Kammen, Michael (1995) 'Review of *Frames of Remembrance: The Dynamics of Collective Memory*', *History & Theory*, 34 (3): 245–61.
Kanaana, Sharif (1994) *Folk Heritage of Palestine*, Tayibeh, Israel: Research Centre for Arab Heritage.
Kanaana, Sharif (2012) Interview, June 29.
Kanaana, Sharif (2017) 'Stories Told by and for Palestinian Children', *International Humanities Studies*, 4(1): 36–43.
Kapchan, Deborah (2003) 'Translating Folk Theories of Translation', in Paula G. Rubel and Abraham Rosman (eds), *Translating Cultures: Perspective on Translation and Anthropology*, Oxford and New York: Berg, 135–51.
Karmi, Ghada (1999) 'After the Nakba: An Experience of Exile in England', *Journal of Palestine Studies*, 28 (3): 52–63.
Kassem, Fatma (2011) *Palestinian Women: Narrative Histories and Gendered Memory*, London and New York: Zed Books.
Khalidi, Rashid (1982) 'The Role of the Press in the Early Arab Reaction to Zionism', *Peuples Méditerranéens*, No. 20: 105–24.
Khalidi, Rashid (1997) *Palestinian Identity: The Construction of Modern National Consciousness*, New York: Columbia University Press.
Khalidi, Rashid (1998) 'Deir Yassine: Autopsie d'un massacre', *Revue d'études palestiniennes*, 17 (69): 20–58.
Khalidi, Walid (ed.) (1992) *All That Remains: The Palestinian Villages Occupied and Depopulated Israel in 1948*, Washington, DC: Institute for Palestine Studies.
Kinder, Donald R., and Don Herzog (1993) 'Democratic Discussion', in George E. Marcus and Russell L. Hanson (eds), *Reconsidering the Democratic Public*, University Park: The Pennsylvania State University Press, 347–77.
Kirshner, L. A. (2005) 'Rethinking Desire: The Objet Petit A in Lacanian Theory', *Journal of the American Psychoanalytic Association*, 53 (1): 83–102.
Klandermans, B. (1992) 'The Social Construction of Protest and Multiorganizational Fields', in Aldon D. Morris and Carol McClurg Mueller (eds), *Frontiers in Social Movement Theory*, New Haven, CT: Yale University Press, 77–103.
Koş, Ayşenaz (2007) 'Analysis of the Paratexts of Simone de Beauvoir's Works in Turkish', Paper published by the Universitat Rovira i Virgili, Tarragona, http://www.intercultural.urv.cat/media/upload/domain_317/arxius/TP1/KosParatexts.pdf.

Kovala, Urpo (1996) 'Translations, Paratextual Mediation, and Ideological Closure', *Target*, 8 (1): 119–47.

Krappe, Alexander Haggerty (1930) *The Science of Folk-Lore*, London: Methuen.

Kreiswirth, Martin (2000) 'Merely Telling Stories? Narrative and Knowledge in the Human Sciences', *Poetics Today*, 21 (2): 293–318.

Kruk, Remke (2014) *The Warrior Women of Islam*, New York: I.B. Tauris.

Lacan, Jacques (2011) *Ecrits: A Selection*, trans. Alan Sheridan, London: Routledge.

LaCapra, Dominick (2001) *Writing History, Writing Trauma*, Baltimore and London: Johns Hopkins University Press.

Landsberg, Alison (2004) *Prosthetic Memory: The Transformation of American Remembrance in the Age of Mass Culture*, New York: University Press.

Le Goff, Jacques (1992) *History and Memory*, trans. Steven Rendal and Elizabeth Claman, New York: Columbia University Press.

Litvak, Meir (ed.) (2009) *Palestinian Collective Memory and National Identity*, New York: Palgrave Macmillan.

Lowenthal, David (1994) 'Identity, Heritage, and History', in John R. Gillis (ed.), *Commemorations: The Politics of National Identity*, Princeton, NJ: Princeton University Press, 41–60.

Lury, Celia (1998) *Prosthetic Culture: Photography, Memory, Identity*, London: Routledge.

Maclean, Marie (1991) 'Pretexts and Paratexts: The Art of the Peripheral', *New Literary History*, 22 (2): *Probings: Art, Criticism, Genre*, 273–9.

Magat, Ilan (2000) *Bira'm: A Mobilized Community of Memory*, 'Surveys of Arabs in Israel', No. 26, Giv'at Haviva, Israel: Institute of Peace Research.

Mannheim, Karl (1952) 'The Problem of Generations', in Paul Kecskemeti (ed.), Karl Mannheim, *Essays on the Sociology of Knowledge*, New York: Oxford University Press, 276–322.

Mancuso, J. C., and T. R. Sarbin (1983) 'The Self-Narrative in the Enactment of Roles' in Theodore R. Sarbin and Karl E. Scheibe (eds), *Studies in Social Identity*, New York: Praeger Press, 233–53.

McGlathery, J. M. (1981) 'E. T. A. Hoffmann and Liebesmärchen' in Michael M. Metzger and Katharina Mommsen (eds), *Fairy Tales as Ways of Knowing: Essays on Märchen in Psychology, Society and Literature*, Berne: Peter Lang Publishers, 168–81.

Merill, Christi (2009) *Riddles of Belonging: India in Translation and Other Tales of Possession*, New York: Fordham University Press.

Meyers, Miriam (2001) *A Bite off Mama's Plate: Mothers' and Daughters' Connections through Food*, New York: Bergin and Garvey.

Middleton, David, and Derek Edwards (1990) 'Conversational Remembering', in *Collective Remembering*, London: Sage, 23 ff.

Miller, Donald E., and Lorna Touryan Miller (1991) 'Memory and Identity across the Generations: A Case Study of Armenian Survivors and their Progeny', *Qualitative Sociology*, 14 (1): 13-38.

Milligan, Melinda J. (2003) 'Displacement and Identity Discontinuity: The Role of Nostalgia in Establishing New Identity Categories', *Symbolic Interaction*, 26 (3): 381-403.

Mink, Louis (1978) 'Narrative Form as a Cognitive Instrument' in Robert H. Canary and Henry Kozicki (eds), *The Writing of History: Literary Form and Historical Understanding*, Madison, WI: The University of Wisconsin Press, 129-49.

Muhawi, Ibrahim (1999a) 'On Translating Palestinian Folktales: Comparative Stylistics and Semiotics of Genre', in Yasir Suleiman (ed.), *Arabic Grammar and Linguistics*, Richmond, Surrey: Curzon Press, 222-45.

Muhawi, Ibrahim (1999b) 'The Arabic Folktale as Gendered Genre', paper presented at the Gender and Translation Conference, University of East Anglia, 17-19 December 1999.

Muhawi, Ibrahim (1999c) 'Storytelling in Palestine', in Margaret Read MacDonald (ed.), *Traditional Storytelling Today: An International Sourcebook*, Chicago: Fitzrory Dearborn Publishers, 344-8.

Muhawi, Ibrahim (2000) 'Performance and Translation in the Arabic Metalinguistic Joke', *The Translator*, 8: 341-66.

Muhawi, Ibrahim (2004) 'On Translating Oral Style in Palestinian Folktales', in Said Faiq (ed.), *Cultural Encounters in Translation from Arabic*, Clevedon, Buffalo and Toronto: Multilingual Matters, 75-90.

Muhawi, Ibrahim (2006) 'Towards a Folkloristic Theory of Translation', in Theo Hermans (ed.), *Translating Others*, Vol. 2, Manchester and Kinderhook, New York: St. Jerome, 365-79.

Muhawi, Ibrahim, and Sharif Kanaana (1997) *Il était plusieurs fois ... : contes populaires palestiniens*, Paris: Editions Arcantères/UNESCO.

Nasir, Amjad, (2002) in *Al Quds*, issue 4103, 26 July 2002: 20.

Nice, Pamela (2001) 'Juha, Donkeys and Thieves: Wit and Wisdom of Folk Tradition', *Al Jadid*, 7 (37): 57-8.

Nietzsche, Friedrich Wilhelm (1957) *The Use and Abuse of History*, 2nd rev. edn, trans. Adrian Collins, Indianapolis: Bobbs-Merrill Educational Publishers.

Nollendorfs, Cora Lee (1981) 'The Kiss of the Supernatural: Tieck's Treatment of a Familiar Legend' in Michael M. Metzger and Katharina Mommsen (eds), *Fairy Tales as Ways of Knowing: Essays on Märchen in Psychology, Society and Literature*, Berne: Peter Lang Publishers, 154-67.

Nora, Pierre (1989) 'Between History and Memory: Les Lieux de Memoire', *Representations*, No. 26: 7-25.

Novick, Peter (1988) *That Noble Dream: The 'Objectivity Question' and the American Historical Profession*, Cambridge: Cambridge University Press.

Olick, J. K. (2008) 'Collective Memory: A Memoir and Prospect', *Memory Studies*, 1 (1): 23–9.

Olick, Jeffrey K, and Joyce Robbins (1998) 'Social Memory Studies: From "Collective Memory" to the Historical Sociology of Mnemonic Practices', *Annual Review of Sociology*, 24: 105–40.

Olson, David R., and Nancy Torrance (eds) (1991) *Literacy and Orality*, Cambridge: Cambridge University Press.

Opland, Jeff (1983) *Xhosa Oral Poetry: Aspects of a Black South African Tradition*, Cambridge: Cambridge University Press.

Pan, Zhongdan, and Gerald M. Kosicki (1993) 'Framing Analysis: An Approach to News Discourse', *Political Communication* 10: 55–75.

Pappe, Ian (2006) *The Ethnic Cleansing of Palestine*, Oxford: One World Publishing.

Parmentier, Barbara (1984) 'Toward a Geography of Home: Palestinian Literature and the Sense of Place', MA thesis, University of Texas.

Patai, Raphael (1998) *Arab Folktales from Palestine and Israel*, Detroit: Wayne State University Press.

Personal Narrative Group (eds) (1989) *Interpreting Women's Lives: Feminist Theory and Personal Narrative*, Bloomington: Indiana University Press.

Peters, Issa (1991) 'Speak Bird, Speak, Again: Palestinian Arab Folktales by Ibrahim Muhawi & Sharif Kanaana', *Journal of Middle East Studies*, 23 (3): 440–1.

Poletta, Francesca (1998) '"It Was Like a Fever …" Narrative and Identity in Social Problems', *Social Problems*, 45 (2): 137–59.

Poletta, Francesca (2006) *It Was Like a Fever: Storytelling in Protest and Politics*, Chicago and London: The University of Chicago Press.

Portelli, Alessandro (1991) *The Death of Luigi Trastulli and Other Stories: Form and Meaning in Oral History*, New York: State University of New York Press.

Portelli, Alessandro (1997) *The Battle of Valle Giulia: Oral History and the Art of Dialogue*, Madison: University of Wisconsin Press.

Powles, Julia (2002) 'Like Baby Minnows We Came with the Current': Social Memory among Angolan Refugees in Mebeba Settlement, Zambia. Paper presented at the Annual Conference of the Association of Social Anthropologists of the UK and Commonwealth, Arusha, Tanzania.

Propp V. (1968) *Morphology of the Folktale*, Austin: University of Texas Press.

Renan, Ernest (1997) *Qu'est-ce qu'une nation?* Paris: Editions Mille et une nuits.

Reynolds, Dwight F. (1995) *Heroic Poetry, Poetic Heroes: The Ethnography of Performance*, Ithaca: Cornell University Press.

Ricoeur, Paul (1981) 'Narrative Time', in W. J. T. Mitchell (ed.), *On Narrative*, Chicago: University of Chicago Press.

Ricoeur, Paul (1984) *Time and Narrative*, Chicago: University of Chicago Press.
Ricoeur, Paul (1990) *Soi-Même comme un autre*, Paris: Seuil.
Ricoeur, Paul (1991) 'Life in Quest of Narrative', in David Wood (ed.), *On Paul Ricoeur: Narrative and Interpretation*, London: Routledge, 20–33.
Ricoeur, Paul (2004) *Memory, History, Forgetting*, trans. Kathleen Blamey and David Pellauer, Chicago: University of Chicago.
Rohrich, Lutz (1991) *Folktales and Reality*, trans. Peter Tokofsky, Bloomington and Indianapolis: Indiana University Press.
Rooth, Anna Birgitta (1976) *The Importance of Storytelling: A Study Based on Field Work in Northern Alaska*, Stockholm: University of Stockholm.
Rosenberg, Bruce A. (1991) *Folklore and Literature: Rival Siblings*, Knoxville: University of Tennessee Press.
Rosenwald, George C., and Richard L. Ochberg (eds) (1992), *Storied Lives: The Cultural Politics of Self-Understanding*, New Haven, CT: Yale University Press.
Rossington, Michael, and Anne Whitehead (2007) *Theories of Memory*, Edinburgh: Edinburgh University Press.
Said, Edward W. (1996) *Representations of the Intellectual: The 1993 Reith Lectures*, New York: Vintage Books.
Sa'di, Ahmad (2002) 'Catastrophe, Memory and Identity: Al-Nakba as a Component of Palestinian identity', *Israel Studies*, 7 (2): 175–98.
Sa'di, Ahmad H., and Lila Abu-Lughod (eds) (2007) *Nakba: Palestine, 1948, and the Claims of Memory*, New York: Columbia University Press.
Sanyal, Debarati (2010) 'Crabwalk History: Torture, Allegory and Memory in Sartre', in Michael Rothberg, Debarati Sanyal and Mixim Silverman (eds), *Noeuds de Mémoire: Multidirectional Memory in Postwar French and Francophone Culture*, 'Yale French Studies', New Haven, CT: Yale University Press, 118/119: 52–71.
Sayigh, Rosemary (1998) 'Palestinian Camp Women as Tellers of History', *Journal of Palestine Studies*, 27 (2): 42–58.
Sayigh, Rosemary (1999) 'National Identity and Myths of Ethnic Descent', in Anthony D. Smith (ed.), *Myths and Memories of the Nation*, Oxford: Oxford University Press, 57–95.
Sayigh, Rosemary (2007) *The Palestinians from Peasants to Revolutionaries*, London: Zed Books.
Schuman, Howard (2003) 'Keeping the Past Alive: Memories of Israeli Jews at the Turn of the Millennium', *Sociological Forum*, 18 (1): 103–36.
Schwartz, Barry (1990) 'The Reconstruction of Abraham Lincoln', in David Middleton and Derek Edwards (eds), *Collective Remembering*, Sage: Newbury Park.
Schwartz, Barry (1996) 'Introduction: The Expanding Past', *Qualitative Sociology*, 19 (3): 275–82.

Scott, James (1985) *Weapons of the Weak: Everyday Forms of Resistance*, New Haven, CT and London: Yale University Press.

Sedikides, Constantine, Tim Wildschut, Jamie Arndt and Clay Routledge (2008). 'Nostalgia: Past, Present, and Future', *Current Directions in Psychological Science*, 17 (5): 304–7.

Sedikides, Constantine, Tim Wildschut, Lowell Gaertner, Clay Routledge, and Jamie Arndt (2008) 'Nostalgia as Enabler of Self-continuity', in Fabio Sani (ed.), *Self-Continuity: Individual and Collective Perspectives*, New York: Psychology Press, 227–39.

Schmidt, Hans, and Paul `Kahle (1930) *Volkserzählungen aus Palästina*, 2 Vols, Göttingen: Vandenhoeck und Ruprecht.

Slyomovics, Susan (2007) 'The Rape of Qula, a Destroyed Palestinian Village', in Ahmad H Sa'di and Lila Abu-Lughod (eds), *Nakba: Palestine, 1948, and the Claims of Memory*, New York: Columbia University Press, 27–51.

Smith, Anthony D. (1986) *The Ethnic Origins of Nations*, Oxford: Blackwell.

Smith, Anthony D. (1999) 'National Identity and Myths of Ethnic Descent', in Anthony D. Smith, *Myths and Memories of the Nation*, Oxford: Oxford University Press, 57–95.

Smith, Edwin (1940) 'The Function of Folktales', *The Royal African Society*, 39 (154): 64–83.

Smith, Graham (2007) 'Beyond Individual/Collective Memory: Women's Transactive Memories of Food, Family and Conflict', *Oral History*, 35 (2): 77–90.

Sniderman, Paul M., and Sean M. Theriault (1999) 'The Dynamics of Political Argument and the Logic of Issue Framing', paper presented at the annual meeting of the Midwest Political Science Association, Chicago, April 15–17.

Snow, David (2007) 'Elaborating the Discursive Contexts of Framing: Discursive Fields and Spaces', *Studies in Symbolic Interaction*, 30: 3–28.

Snow, David A., and Robert D. Benford (1986) 'Frame Alignment Processes, Micromobilization, and Movement Participation, *American Sociological Review*, 51 (4): 464–81.

Snow, David A., and Robert D. Benford (1988) 'Ideology, Frame Resonance, and Participant Mobilization', *International Social Movements Research*, 1: 197–218.

Somers, Margaret R., and Gloria D. Gibson (1994) 'Reclaiming the Epistemological "Other": Narrative and the Social Constitution of Identity', in Craig Calhoun (ed.), *Social Theory and the Politics of Identity*, Cambridge, MA and Oxford: Blackwell, 37–99.

Sowayan, Saad A. (1992) *The Arabian Oral Historical Narrative: An Ethnographic and Linguistic Analysis*, Wiesbaden: Otto Harassowitz.

Spivak, Gayarti Chakravorty (2007) 'Nationalism and the Imagination', in C. Vijayasree, Meenakshi Mukherjee, Harish Trivedi and T. Vijay Kumar (eds),

Nation in Imagination: Essays on Nationalism, Sub-Nationalism and Narration, New Delhi: Orient Longman, 1–20.

Stein, Rebecca L. and Ted Swedenburg (eds) (2005) *Palestine, Israel, and the Politics of Popular Culture*, Durham, NC: Duke University Press.

Stephan, Stephan H. (1928) 'Animals in Palestinian Folklore', *Journal of the Palestine Oriental Society*, VIII: 65–112.

Stinson, John D. (1991) *Raphael Patai Papers, c1904–88*, New York: The New York Public Library,https://www.nypl.org/sites/default/files/archivalcollections/pdf/patai.pdf.

Stoller, Paul (1995) *Embodying Colonial Memories: Spirit Possession, Power, and the Hauka in West Africa*, New York: Routledge.

Suleiman, Susan Rubin (2006) 'Amnesia and Amnesty: Reflections on Forgetting and Forgiving', in Susan Rubin Suleiman (ed.), *Crises of Memory and the Second World War*, Cambridge, MA and London: Harvard University Press, 215–34.

Sutton, David E. (2001) *Remembrance of Repasts: An Anthropology of Food and Memory*, Oxford: Berg.

Sutton, David E. (2008) 'A Tale of Easter Ovens: Food and Collective Memory', *Social Research*, 75 (1): 157–80.

Swedenburg, Ted (1990) 'The Palestinian Peasant as National Signifier', *Anthropological Quarterly*, 63 (1): 18–30.

Tannen, Deborah (ed.) (1982) *Spoken and Written Language*, Norwood, NJ: Ablex.

Tannen, Deborah, and Cynthia Wallat (1993) 'Interactive Frames and Knowledge Schemas in Interaction: Examples from a Medical Examination/Interview', in Deborah Tannen (ed.), *Framing in Discourse*, New York: Oxford University Press, 57–76.

Tatar, Maria (1981) 'Folkloristic Phantasies: Grimms' Fairy Tales and Freud's Family Romance', in Michael M. Metzger and Katharina Mommsen (eds), *Fairy Tales as Ways of Knowing: Essays on Märchen in Psychology, Society and Literature*, Berne: Peter Lang Publishers, 75–98.

Tedlock, Dennis (1971) 'On the Translation of Style in Oral Narrative', *The Journal of American Folklore*, 84 (331): *Towards a New Perspectives in Folklore*: 114–33.

Tedlock, Dennis (1983) *The Spoken Word and the Work of Interpretation*, Philadelphia: University of Pennsylvania Press.

Vambe, Maurice T (ed.) (2001) *Orality and Cultural Identities in Zimbabwe*, Gweru, Zimbabwe: Mambo Press.

von der Leyen, Friedrich (1911) *Das Märchen: ein Versuch*, Leipzig: Quelle & Meyer (Arabic trans. Nabil Ibrahim, 1990).

Watts, Richard (2000) 'Translating Culture: Reading the Paratexts of Aimé Césaire's *Cahier d'un retour au pays natal*', *TTR: Traduction, Terminologie, Rédaction* 13 (2): 29–46

Webman, Esther (2009) 'The Evolution of a Founding Myth: The Nakba and Its Fluctuating Meaning', in Meir Litvak (ed.), *Palestinian Collective Memory and National Identity*, New York: Palgrave Macmillan, 27–45.

Weick, Karl E. (1995) *Sensemaking in Organizations*. Thousand Oaks, CA: Sage.

Weick, Karl E. (1999) 'Sensemaking as an Organizational Dimension of Global Change', in David L. Cooperrider and Jane E. Dutton (eds), *Organizational Dimensions of Global Change*, Thousand Oaks, CA: Sage, 39–56.

Weir, Shelagh (1989) *Palestinian Costume*, London: British Museum Publications.

White, Hayden (1978) *Tropics of Discourse: Essays in Cultural Criticism*, Baltimore: Johns Hopkins University Press.

White, Hayden (1987) *The Content of the Form: Narrative Discourse and Historical Representation*, Baltimore: Johns Hopkins University Press.

White, Hayden (1989) '"Figuring the Nature of the Times Deceased": Literary Theory and Historical Writing', in Ralph Cohen (ed.), *The Future of Literary Theory*, New York: Routledge, 19–43.

Wildschut, Tim, Constantine Sedikides, Jamie Arndt, and Clay Routledge. (2006) 'Nostalgia: Content, Triggers, Functions', *Journal of Personality and Social Psychology*, 91 (5): 975–93.

Winter, Jay, and Emmanuel Sivan (1999) 'Setting the Framework', in Jay Winter and Emmanuel Sivan (eds), *War and Remembrance in the Twentieth Century*, Cambridge: Cambridge University Press, 6–39.

Worthington, Ian (ed.) (1996) *Voice into Text: Orality and Literacy in Ancient Greece*, Leiden: Brill.

Yerushalmi, Yosef Hayim (1996) *Zakhor: Jewish History and Jewish Memory*, Seattle and London: University of Washington Press.

Yiftachel, Oren (2002) 'Territory as the Kernel of the Nation: Space, Time and Nationalism in Israel/Palestine', *Geopolitics*, 7 (2): 215–48.

Zemon Davis, Natalie, and Randolph Starn (1989) 'Introduction', *Representations*, 26, special issue: *Memory and Counter-Memory*: 1–6.

Zerubavel, Yael (1994) 'The Death of Memory and the Memory of Death: Masada and the Holocaust as Historical Metaphors', *Representations*, 45: 72–100.

Zerubavel, Yael (1995) *Recovered Roots: Collective Memory and the Making of Israeli National Tradition*, Chicago: University of Chicago Press.

Zipes, Jack (1983a) *Fairy Tales and the Art of Subversion: The Classical Genre for Children and the Process of Civilization*, New York: Wildman Press.

Zipes, Jack (1983b) *The Trials and Tribulations of Little Red Riding Hood: Versions of the Tale in Sociocultural Context*, South Hadley, MA: Bergin and Garvey.

Zipes, Jack (1988) *The Brothers Grimm: From Enchanted Forests to the Modern World*, New York: Routledge.

Zu'bi, Himmat (2014) 'The Importance of Women's Oral Testimonies in the Production of Palestinian History', *Jadal*, No. 20: 1–4.

Arabic texts

'Abdil Raḥmān 'Umar, Nimr (2000) *Al-malḥama al-sha'bya al-Falasṭīnīa (Manṣūr Bin Nāṣir)* [*Palestinian Popular Epic Poetry: Mansur Bin Naser*], Nablus: Publications of the National House for Translation, Printing, Publication and Distribution.

'Alqam, Nabīl (1993) *Madkhal lildirāsāt al-fulklūrya* [*An Entry in the Study of Folklore*], Al-Bīra: Reconstructing or Animating the Family Association.

Al-'Abnūdī, 'Abd al-RaḤmān (2002) *Al-sirā Al-hīlālīyya*, Cairo: Atlas Publishing House.

Al-Antīl, Fwzī (1965) *Al-fulklūr mā huwa?* [*Folklore: What Is It?*], Cairo: Al-Ma'ārif Publishing House.

Al-Asʿadī, Saʿūdo (2008) *Muqadima'n al-zajal al-Falasṭīnī* [*An Introduction On Palestinian Zajal*] www.palestineremembered.com/Safad/Qabba'a/Story11812.html [last accessed 7 August 2018].

Alʿ-shhab, Roshdī (2001) *Kān yā makān: ḥikāyāt sha'biya min madīnat al-Quds* [*Once Upon a Time: Folktales from Jerusalem*], 'Alūsh House: Birzeit Publishing House.

Al-Barghūthī, 'Abdil Laṭīf (1979) *Ḥikāyāt Jin Banī Zaīd* [*Jin Tales from Bani Zeid*], Beizeit: Birzeit University Press.

Al-Barghūthī, Abdil Laṭīf (1986) *Dīwān al-'atāba al-Falasṭīnī* [*Palestinian Ataba Poetry Collection*], Jerusalem: Institution of Bayādir Ṣuḥufya.

Al-Ghūl, Fāyiz' Alī (1966) *Al-dunyā ḥikāyāt* [*Life Is Stories*], Amman: The Association of Jordanian Publishing Workers.

Al-Ḥasan, Ghasān (1988) *Al-ḥikaya al-khuāfya'lā ḍifatay nahr al-'Urdun* [*The Legendary Tale on the Banks of the Jordan River*], Damascus: Galilee Publishing House.

Al-Jabūr Musṭafa, Ibrāhīm (2007) *Al-turāth al-sha'bī al-Falasṭīnī – hawya w'intimā'* [*Palestinian Popular Heritage: Identity and Belonging*], Ramallah: Jerusalem Open University.

Al-Jawāhīrī, Muḥamad (1972) 'Al-turāth al-sha'bī bayn al-fulklūr w'ilm al-'ijtimā' [Popular Heritage between Folklore and Social Sciences]', 3rd edn, 3rd series, *The Kuwaiti World of Thinking Magazine*: 90–120.

Al-Khalīdī, Walīd (1997) *kay lā nansā: al-ṭab'a al-'ūlā* [*So We Do not Forget*], Beirut: The Institute of Palestine Studies.

Al-Khalīlī, A῾lī (1977) *Al-turāth al-Falasṭīnī w al-ṭabaqāt* [*Palestinian Folklore and Social Classes*], Beirut: Dar Al-Adab.

Al-Khalīlī, A῾lī (1979) *Al-baṭal al-Falasṭīnī fī al-ḥikāya al-sha῾biya al-Falasṭīnīa* [*The Palestinian Hero in the Palestinian Folktale*], Jerusalem: The Institute of I῾bin Rushd.

Al-Sarīsī, ῾Umar (2004) *Al-ḥikāya al-sha῾biya fī al-mujtam῾al-Falasṭīnī* [*The Palestinian Folktale in Palestinian Society: Texts and Analysis*], Irbid, Jordan: Modern World Books.

Al-Sharīf, Mahir (2004) '*Al-dhakira al-shafhya al-Falasṭīnīa w al-hawya al-waṭanya fī ḍw῾ta῾adud al-manāfī w al-sāḥāt* [Palestinian Oral Memory and National Identity in the Light of Multiple Exiles and Fields]', *Ṣamid Economic Journal*, Series 26, n. 135.

Dakrūb, Muḥamad Husayn (1984) *Al-anthrubūbūlūjyā: al-dhakira w al-ma῾āsh* [*Anthropology: Memory and Living*], Beirut: Arab Institute for Development.

adād, Mun῾im (1986) *Al-turāth al-Falasṭīnī bayn al-ṭams w al-'ihyā'* [*Palestinian Heritage between Obliteration and Revival*], al-Ṭība: The Centre of Reviving Arab Heritage.

Ismaīl, A῾īz Al-dīn (1971) *Al-qaṣaṣ al-sha῾bī fī al-Sūdān* [*Storytelling in Sudan*], Cairo: General Egyptian Union for Writing and Publishing.

Kanāna, Sharīf (2000) *Dirāsāt fī al-turāth al-sha῾bī w al-hawya al-Falasṭīnīa / man nasīya qadīma tāh* [*Studies in Folk Heritage and Palestinian Identity: He Who Forgot His Past Is Lost*], Acre: Aswar Institution.

Kanā῾na, Sharīf, and Muhamed Ashtīh (1991) *Silsilat al-qurā al-Falasṭīnīaa l-mudamara* [*Series of Destroyed Palestinian Villages*], Birzeit University: Centre of Research and Documentation.

Khūrī, Ilyās (1990) *Dirā sāt naqdya: al-dhākira al-mafqūda* [*The Missing Memory: Critical Studies*], Beirut: The House of Literature.

Kwathrānī, Wajīh (2000) *Al-dhakira w al-tarīkh fī al-qarn al-'ishrīn al-ṭawīl: dirāsāt fī al-baḥs w al-baḥs al-tarīkhī* [*Memory and History in the Long Twentieth Century: Studies in Research and Historical Research*], Beirut: Al-Ṭalī῾a House for Printing and Publishing.

Muhawi, Ibrahim, and Sharif Kanaana (2010) *Qūl ya ṭayr: qiṣaṣ al-atfāl min al-turāth al-sha῾bī al-Falasṭīnī* [*Speak Bird, Speak Again: Children's Tales from the Palestinian Popular Heritage*], Beirut: The Institute for Palestine Studies.

Muna, Fayāḍ (2010) '*Qūl ya ṭayr, linastami῾ilā nabḍ al-turāth* [Speak Bird, Speak Again, Let Us Listen to the Beat of Heritage]' *Al-Ayam*, 15 (5283): 28 September: 34–50.

Roshdī, Aḥmad (1995) *Al-adab al-sha῾bī: al- juz'al-'wal* [*Popular Literature: Part I*], Cairo: Nahdda Egyptian Library.

Shaḥada, K., N. Maṣarwa, and Y. Mirūn (1997) *Fariṭ al-rumān: al-mar 'a al-Falasṭīnīa fī al-ḥikayāt al-sha 'biya* [Pomegranate Seeds: The Woman in the Palestinian Folktale], Menashe: Givat-Haviva.

Sirḥān, Nimr (1974) *Al-ḥikāya al-sha 'biya al-Falasṭīnīa* [*The Palestinian Folktale*], Beirut: the Arab Institute for Research and Publishing.

Slyomovics, Susan (1997) 'The Epic of the Bani Hilal Narrated by Awadallah Abd al-Jalil Ali,' in John William Johnson, Thomas A. Hale and Stephen Belcher (eds), *Oral Epics from Africa: Vibrant Voices from a Vast Continent*, Indianapolis: Indiana University Press, 240–51.

Yaḥya, 'Adil (1998) *Al-laji 'ūn al-Falasṭīnīūn 1948–1998 ta 'rīkh shafawī* [*Palestinian Refugees: 1948–1998 Oral Historisation*], Ramallah: Palestinian Institute for Cultural Exchange.

Websites

Al Jazeera Arabic (2007) *Interview with Elias Khoury* http://www.aljazeera.net/NR/exeres/F48116B0-F572-4052-A8F0-6A3FBCC85D5C.htm [last accessed 2 August 2018].

Ben-Yehuda, Nachman (2000) *The Masada Myth* http://www.bibleinterp.com/articles/masada.shtml [link no longer works: last accessed 24 October 2011].

The Fairy Tales of the Brothers Grimm, ed. Noel Daniel (2014) https://www.taschen.com/pages/en/search/brothers-grimm [last accessed 5 August 2018].

Ghassan, Kanafani' (2008) at http://www.kirjasto.sci.fi/kanaf.htm [link no longer works: last accessed 24 March 2012].

Institute of Palestine Studies, http://www.palestine-studies.org [last accessed 2 August 2018].

Jābir Sulaymān' http://www.palestine-studies.org/aboutus.aspx?href=mission [link no longer works: last accessed 1 March 2013].

Kanaana, Sharif (2006) 'Sharif Kanaana, Anthropologist and Folklorist', *This Week in Palestine*, 12 June, http://www.palestine-family.net/index.php?nav=3-83&cid=90&did=2273&pageflip=2 [last accessed 2 August 2018].

Kanaana, Sharif (2007) *Half a Century of Palestinian Folk Narratives*, http://www.thisweekinpalestine.com [last accessed 9 October 2008].

Kanaana, Sharif (2008) *Stories Told by and for Palestinian Children* on https://www.ihs-humanities.com/stories-told-by-and-for-palestinian-children [last accessed 4 November 2018].

Mahmud Darwish' (2008) http://www.kirjasto.sci.fi/darwish.htm [link no longer works: last accessed 24 March 2012].

Myers, Robin, and Shadi Rohana (2011) *Interview with Sharif Kanaana* http://electronicintifada.net/content/interview-sharif-kanaana-palestinian-folklore-and-identity/9825 [last accessed 2 August 2018].

Qattan Foundation, http://qattanfoundation.org/en [last accessed 2 August 2018].

Newspapers, Periodicals and Journals

Al Ahram Weekly
Al-ayām
Al Fajr (Jerusalem Weekly)
Al Karmel Quarterly
Al Quds
Al-turāth w Al-mujtam '[Heritage and Society]
Al-turāth Al-sh'bī [Folk Heritage]
Journal of Palestine Studies

Index

Aarne-Thompson system   63, 66, 204 n.25
Al-Abnoudi, Abd Al-Rahman   39
Abu-Lughod, Lila   79
active storytellers   81
aesthetic expression   80, 107
age   57, 77, 81
Al-'ajūz w al-bis. See 'The Old Woman and Her Cat'
Al-'anza al-'nayzīa. See 'The Little She-Goat'
Al-Aqsa Intifada (2000)   18
Al-baṭal al-Falasṭīnī fī al-ḥikāya al-sha 'biya al-Falasṭīnīa. See *Palestinian Hero in the Palestinian Folktale, The* (Al-Khalīlī)
Al-dīwān   5
Al-falāḥūn al-Falasṭīnīūn: min al-iqtilā 'ilā al-thawra. See *Palestinian Peasants: From Uprooting to Revolutionaries*
Al-ghālya w al-bālya. See 'Precious One and Worn-Out One'
Al-ghūla al-'ajūz. See 'The Old Woman Ghouleh'
Al-Ḥasan, Ghasān   29
Al-ḥaṭāb. See 'The Woodcutter'
Al-ḥikāya al-sha 'biya fī al-falasṭīnīa. See *Palestinian Folktale, The* (Sirḥān)
Al-ḥikāya al-sha 'biya fī al-mujtama ' al-Falasṭīnī. See *Palestinian Folktale in Palestinian Society: Texts and Analysis, The* (Al-Sarīsī)
Al-Jawāhīrī, Muḥamad   39
Al-khunfusa. See 'The Cricket'
Al-laji' ūn al-Falasṭīnīūn 1948-1998 ta' rīkh shafawī. See *Palestinian Refugees: 1948-1998 Oral Historisation*
allegoric tales   124–5, 128
All That Remains (Khalidi)   167
Al-samāk. See 'The Fisherman'
Al-shāb al-shujā'. See 'The Brave Lad'
Al-shāṭir Ḥasan. See 'Clever Hassan'
Al-sit tatar. See 'Lady Tatar'
Al-ṭayr al-akhḍar. See 'The Green Bird'
Al-turāth al-Falasṭīnī w al-ṭabaqāt. See *Palestinian Folklore and Social Classes* (Al-Khalīlī)
Al-turāth al-sha ' bī. See *Folk Heritage*
Al-turāth wa al-mujtama'. See *Heritage and Society*
Al- 'uṣfūra al-ṣaghīra. See 'The Little Bird'
American Palestine Educational Fund   54
A M Qattan Foundation   54, 204 n.21
Anderson, Benedict   24, 199 n.5, 209 n.4
anthropology   3, 62–3
Al-'Antīl, Fwzī '   46
Arab folk epic   39
Arab Folktales from Palestine and Israel (Patai)   212 n.7
Arabian Nights   53
Arabic language   24, 135
Arab Spring   1
Armenian diaspora   10
art   55, 107
Al-'As' adī, Sa'ūdo   78
aspiration   2, 11, 25, 30, 43, 77–8, 84, 87, 142
Assmann, Aleida   86
Assmann, Jan   9, 86, 118, 137, 139
authorial paratexts   202 n.14
authority   76–7, 82, 84–5, 93, 95, 102, 104, 106, 108, 121, 158
The Authors' Introduction to the Arabic Edition   49, 54, 60–3

Baldensperger, Louise   151, 160
Baldwin, James   7
Bani Zeid   33
Baqarat al-yatāmā. See 'The Orphan's Cow'
Bardenstein, Carol B.   150

Al-Barghūthī, 'Abdil Laṭīf 32–3
baydar 125, 209 n.3
Bayẓ faqāqīs. See 'Chick Eggs'
'Bear-Cub of the Kitchen' 208
beauty 44, 96, 100–1, 108, 116, 126, 128, 159–60
Bedouin folktales 37
beliefs 34, 40, 45, 55, 72, 83, 106, 115, 131, 134, 137, 139, 155, 158. See also religious beliefs
Bettelheim, Bruno 29
'Beyond the Pleasure Principle' 120
Bint al-tājir. See 'The Merchant's Daughter'
Birth and Childhood among the Arabs (Granqvist) 157
Birzeit 32, 33
Birzeit University 51, 167, 212 n.2
bishlīk 170'
Blend, Benay 154
bodily memory 149
Boyarin, Daniel 106
Boyarin, Jonathan 106
Brand, Hanita 75, 84
'The Brave Lad' 102, 108, 183
Bresheeth, Haim 18, 80
British Mandate 84–5
brother-sister relationship 88–9
Brother-Sister Syndrome 89, 207 n.13
Brown, Linda Keller 143
Bū al-labābīd. See 'Sackcloth'
Bushnaq, Inea 88

Canaan 201 n.9
Canaan, Taufik 160
Caruth, Cathy 15–16
'Chick Eggs' 152, 155, 156, 208 n.29
children 36–7, 43, 57, 72, 86–7, 93, 96, 98, 106–7, 109, 148, 151, 155, 160, 166, 169, 176
Children's and Household Tales. See Kinder- und Hausmärchen (Grimm Brothers')
Christensen, Paul 154
Christianity 46, 130, 138
'Clever Hassan' 104, 183–4
Coleridge, Samuel Taylor 124
collective identity 88, 102–3, 112, 119, 121–7, 129, 140

collective memory 1, 5, 36–8, 53, 64–5, 70, 71, 75, 77, 79, 84–5, 91, 94, 96, 116–17, 119–20, 122, 125, 127, 132, 139, 140, 144, 149, 150, 151–2, 153, 154, 155, 157, 163, 171, 174–6, 198 n.2, 199 n.3
Nakba (1948) 14–21
oral history 8–14
storytelling and language 21–5
trauma and nostalgia 14–21
collectivity 18–19, 22, 94, 115, 123, 125, 127, 128–9, 141, 146–7, 158
Comito, Jacqueline 143
commemoration 10–11, 17
commercial paratexts 202 n.14
communal identity and values 115, 122
communication 123, 127–8, 154
communicative memory 4, 8, 86–7, 91, 116, 118, 132, 134, 137, 142
'communities of memory' 13
'concretion of identity' 94
Conder, Claude Reignier 209 n.3
Connerton, Paul 142, 149
contextual approach 30
continuity 18–19, 69
'The Continuity of Trauma and Struggle' 18, 80
'Crabwalk History: Torture, Allegory, and Memory in Sartre' 124
'The Cricket' 75–6, 104, 106, 184
Crowfoot, Grace 151, 160
cuisine. See food
cultural identity 1, 3, 5, 8–10, 12–13, 20, 31–2, 34, 36, 39, 40, 43, 51, 53, 64, 69–71, 73, 74, 76, 77–8, 88, 90, 91, 98, 101, 106, 107, 111–12, 115–16, 122, 125, 128–30, 132–3, 136, 137, 139, 140–1, 150, 152, 154, 158, 161
cultural memory 2, 4–5, 12, 20, 64–5, 81, 85–7, 91–6, 103, 108, 111, 115, 117, 118, 132, 134, 137, 139, 142, 155
cultural resistance 2, 3, 5–6, 19, 27
culture 28–9, 33, 37, 39, 42, 46, 55, 56, 60–1, 61–2, 63, 67, 70, 83, 113, 170, 175. See also heritage; lifestyle; society; tradition
customs 34, 36, 67, 122, 157, 158. See also heritage; lifestyle; society; tradition

Dabit al-maṭbakh. See 'Bear-Cub of the Kitchen'
Darwish, Mahmoud   22, 150, 200 n.6
Davis, Fred   153
Davis, Rochelle   118, 121, 122
Dayr Yasīn massacre (1948)   18
desires   6, 17, 21, 27, 38, 41–3, 46, 60, 70, 96, 102, 108, 139, 141, 155, 157–8
diaspora   37, 60, 64, 106, 107, 143, 151, 153, 163, 171
Dickens, James   135
discourse   3, 5, 14, 20, 27, 29, 30, 69, 75, 109, 116, 157
disharmony   128–9
displacement   21, 119
Documenting the Destroyed Palestinian Villages (Kanaana)   13
double framing   52
Dundes, Alan   49–50, 52–3, 62, 169
'Dunglet'   68, 118, 128, 133, 147, 148, 190–2

education   39, 57, 87, 92, 96
Edwards, Derek   154
Einfache Formen. See Simple Forms (Jolles)
elite culture   50
embodied memories   149
emotions   42, 45–6, 66–7, 72, 87, 95, 108, 145, 149, 155, 172
endogamy   57, 92, 146
enjoyment   40–1, 53
epic tales   100
epitexts   202 n.14
ethnic identity   143–4
ethnography   52, 62, 65
European nationalism   24
experience   2, 6–9, 14–17, 19–20, 22, 33, 37–9, 38, 59, 67, 69, 75–6, 79–80, 84, 87, 94, 101, 106–7, 119–20, 123–5, 127, 132, 141, 144–5, 149, 154–5, 157, 165
extended family   92, 112

Fairy Tale, The (von der Leyen)   41
fallahi (village speech)   24
family   80, 82
  relationships   43, 57, 70–1, 86
  rules and desires   70
  structure   57, 77, 112

fantasy   83–4
Fariṭ al-rumān: al-mar 'a al-Falasṭīnīa fī al-ḥikayāt al-sha 'biya. See Pomegranate Seeds: The Woman in the Palestinian Folktale
fate   68, 129, 134, 136, 139
favouritism   93, 143, 146. *See also* gender favouritism; social favouritism
felt identity   19
femininity   90–1, 98, 157, 160
fertility   109, 111
fiction   28, 34, 56, 64, 83, 99, 129
fictive reality   28
first-cousin marriage   89, 92
First World War   15
'The Fisherman'   125, 126, 129
Folk Heritage   33
folk literature   32, 45, 63, 64, 163
folklore   23, 27–8, 34, 35, 94, 170
Folklore of the Holy Land (Hanauer)   32
folkloristic analysis   62–6
folklorists   31–2, 37, 40, 43, 45, 164, 172–3
folk narratives   31–9, 171
folk religion   58, 68, 127–39, 160
folktales function   39–47
  belief   46–7
  psychological   40–1
  social   41–6
Folktales of Egypt (El-Shamy)   63
Folk Telling in Sudan (Ismāʿīl)   40
folk tradition   24, 66, 99
food   58, 115–16, 122, 139
  and memory   140–53
  and women   153–61
Food, Culture and Society   140
Food and Foodways   140
Ford Foundation   54
formulaic language   128–9
'formula tales'   128–9
framing   47, 49, 65, 74, 92, 98, 173–6, 201 n.10
freedom   41, 46, 73, 96, 98, 101–2, 110
Freud, Sigmund   15, 120–1

'Gate of the wind'   119
Gaza War (2008/2009)   18
gender   57, 77, 83, 87
gender favouritism   44, 92

generational time 79
Genette, Gérard 48, 49, 201 nn.11, 13, 202 n.14
Gerber, Haim 24, 61
Ghoul 102, 130, 169
Al-Ghūl, Fāyiz 'Alī 42
Giard, Luce 149
'The Golden Pail' 65
'The Golden Rod' 67
'The Golden Rod in the Valley of Vermilion' 108–9, 110, 125, 184–5
Gramsci, Antonio 206 n.7
Granqvist, Hilma 43, 45, 82, 90, 101, 112, 157–8
'The Green Bird' 89, 90–1, 98–9, 176, 181–2
griefs 10, 79, 123
Grimm, Jacob 3, 50, 54, 203 n.17
Grimm, Wilhelm 3, 50, 54, 203 n.17
guilt 169
Gürçağlar, Şehnaz Tahir 49, 202–3 n.16
gustatory nostalgia 115, 152–3

'Hakawati' 211 n.2
Halbwachs, Maurice 9, 118, 199 n.3
'Half-a-Halfling' 92, 94, 111, 155, 182
Hammami, Rema 5
Hanauer, J. E. 32
harmony 39, 70, 88, 104, 109, 111, 112, 132, 144
Hassan, Nizar 80
hegemony 84, 206 n.7
heritage 12–13, 20–1, 27, 29, 30, 33–4, 37, 39, 63, 66, 69, 79, 91, 103, 107, 111, 128, 139, 165. *See also* culture; customs; lifestyle; society; tradition
Heritage and Society 33, 54
heroism 34, 92–3
ḥikāya 55
Ḥikāyāt Jin Banī Zaīd. *See Jinn Tales from Bani Zeid* (Al-Barghūthī)
Hirsch, Marianne 107, 124, 205 n.4
history 7–8, 16–18, 25, 33, 38, 42–3, 61, 69, 77, 79, 80–1, 91, 94, 113, 122, 154, 175, 198 n.2, 205 n.5, 206 n.6. *See also* oral history
Holocaust 10, 15–16, 107
Holtzman, Jon 146
homeland 113, 117–21

honour 5, 37, 45–6, 57, 101, 136
hope 12, 20–2, 37, 79, 120
humanitarian values 44, 94
humour 35, 41, 44, 96, 98, 106, 109, 152, 170
Hussein, Jabir Abu 39

Ibrahīm, Nabīla 41
identity 1, 3–5, 7–9, 14–15, 18–19, 23–5, 27, 29, 35–8, 39, 41, 59, 61, 71, 79, 85, 93, 94, 96, 100, 106, 108–9, 117, 120, 127, 149, 153, 165. *See also* collective identity; ethnic identity; national identity
Ilī tzawajat ibinhā. *See* 'The Woman Who Married Her Son'
illustrative paratexts 202 n.14
Im al-saba 'khamayr. *See* 'The Seven Leavenings'
'Im Awwad and the Ghouleh' 122
'Im Eshe' 109–10, 185–6
informative paratexts 202 n.14
Institute for Palestine Studies 54, 61, 203 n.20
intergenerational memory. *See* communicative memory
intimate and public memories 146–7
intra-village marriages 12
'Introduction of the Arabic Edition' 49, 54, 63–5
   afterword 64
   footnotes 65
Islam 46, 130, 133, 138
Ismā'īl, A'iz Al-dīn 40
Israel 10, 14, 52
Israeli folktales 175

Jackson, Michael 30
Jayyusi, Lena 22
'Jbene' 151, 155, 159
Jews 10
Jinn 33, 59
Jinn Tales from Bani Zeid (Al-Barghūthī) 32
Jolles, André 27
Judaism 46, 130
Juha (folk character) 200 n.5
'Jummez Bin Yazur, Chief of the Birds' 82, 88, 100–1, 108, 150, 155, 159, 183

Kahle, Paul 32
Kammen, Michael 14
Kanaana, Sharif 1, 3, 13, 23, 24, 31, 32, 34, 35, 43, 47, 49–62, 64, 67–8, 86, 89–90, 92, 94, 99, 106, 109, 112–13, 118, 120, 132, 142, 143, 146, 163, 164, 165, 166, 167–77, 203 n.18, 211 n.1
Kanafani, Ghassan 22, 200 n.6
Kān yā makān: ḥikāyāt sha'biya min madīnat al-Quds. See Once Upon a Time: Folktales from Jerusalem (Al-'shhab)
Kara, Yahaïl 33
Kassem, Fatma 5
Khalidi, Walid 167, 210 n.10
Al-Khalīlī, A lī 33, 34, 42
khurāfya 55
Kinder- und Hausmärchen (Grimm Brothers') 203 n.17
'The King of Al-Sukarīya' 45
kinship system 70
knowledge 3–4, 10, 29, 32, 37–8, 76, 94, 106, 121, 126, 143
Krappe, Alexander 46
Kruk, Remke 42, 100

Lacan, Jacques 208 n.1
LaCapra, Dominick 15–17
'Lady Tatar' 65, 122
Landsberg, Alison 80, 85, 206 nn.8–9
Langer, Lawrence L. 15
language 4, 8, 21–5, 29, 51, 55–6, 59, 61, 70–1, 73–4, 78, 96, 98, 109, 111, 115, 118, 124, 127–39, 153, 199 n.5
Lawlaba. See 'Lolabe'
Le Goff, Jacques 198 n.2
Les cadres sociaux de la mémoire (Halbwachs) 199 n.3
'lieux de mémoire' 117
lifestyle 36–7, 115–16, 117, 118, 126, 157. *See also* culture; customs; heritage; society; tradition
'The Little Bird' 95, 98, 101, 106
'The Little She-Goat' 68, 125
Litvak, Meir 14, 24
'Lolabe' 108
'The Louse' 68, 122, 124
love 37, 58, 89, 95, 145

madani (city speech) 24
'Mapping the Past, Re-Creating the Homeland' 118
marriage 43, 67, 70, 91, 98, 99, 101–13. *See also* intra-village marriages
Marriage Conditions in a Palestinian Village (Granqvist) 112
'Maruf the Shoemaker' 125
Maṣarwa, Nimr 33
memory 1, 3–4, 27, 30, 34, 36, 38, 40, 46, 69, 77–8, 87, 90–1, 106, 111, 115, 121, 123, 124, 127, 129, 133, 198 n.2. *See also* collective memory
  agents 153–61
  living 14
  and *Nakba* 5–6
  prospective 141–8
  sensuous 149–53
'The Merchant's Daughter' 125, 131
Meyers, Miriam 154
Middle East 1, 3, 11, 24, 83
Middleton, David 154
Miller, Donald E. 10
Miller, Lorna Touryan 10
Milligan, Melinda 19
Ministry of Culture 165
Ministry of Education 202 n.16
'Minjal' 121
Mirūn', Yoram 33
modernity 7
modernization 36, 44
Modern Standard Arabic (MSA) 64, 65, 169
The Monkeys of Dara'ma 131
mother-daughter narrative 71–7
motherhood 76
mother-son narratives 77–87
Muhawi, Ibrahim 1, 3, 23, 24, 31, 32, 34, 35, 43, 47, 49–64, 67–8, 86, 89, 92, 99, 109, 112–13, 118, 120, 132, 142, 143, 146, 163, 165, 167, 172, 174
Muqaṭa'it al-dayāt. See 'The Woman Whose Hands Were Cut Off'
Mussell, Kay 143
Myers, Robin 94
Myth of the Birth of the Hero (Rank) 31

Nakba (1948)   4, 8, 11, 32, 35–6, 38, 43–4, 69, 74, 79, 80–1, 94, 98, 121, 127, 155, 173
   and memory   5–6
   trauma and nostalgia   14–21
narration   16, 22–3, 41, 46, 55, 75–6, 96, 103, 109, 121, 166
narratives   22, 24, 28, 30, 69–70, 104–5, 127–9, 132, 142, 163, 166
   mother-daughter   71–7
   mother-son   77–87
   sibling   87–95
national identity   9–10, 11, 21, 27, 51, 77, 90, 96, 98, 116, 119, 127–9, 139, 144, 152–3, 161, 174–6, 199 n.5, 209–10 n.4
nationalism   14, 21, 24, 37, 127, 163, 209–10 n.4
nationhood   127
Nazi massacre   10
El-Nimr, Sonia   11, 12
1948 War   14–15
Nisa 'al-mukhayamāt al-falastīnīa: ruwāt al-tārīhk. See *Palestinian Camp Women as Tellers of History* (Sayigh)
Nora, Pierre   117
nostalgia   14–21, 29, 36–7, 46, 77, 115, 117, 119–21, 122, 125, 141, 142–3, 149, 157, 169. See also gustatory nostalgia
Nuṣ nṣīṣ. See 'Half-a-Halfling'

official religion   58, 68, 127, 130, 131, 133, 137, 139, 160
'The Old Woman and Her Cat'   68, 128, 147, 148, 187–8
'The Old Woman Ghouleh'   130
Olick, Jeffrey K.   7
Once Upon a Time: Folktales from Jerusalem (Al-'shhab)   34
On Collective Memory. See *Les cadres sociaux de la mémoire* (Halbwachs)
oral communication   9
oral culture   1, 84, 86, 103, 151
oral folktales   31
oral history   2, 4–5, 8–14, 32, 154
oral literature   1, 4, 10, 20, 21, 22, 24–5, 27, 35–7, 39, 78, 87, 90, 98, 107, 113, 140, 151, 152, 161, 163

oral testimonies   22
oral tradition   1, 50, 55, 75
oral vernaculars   24
'The Orphan's Cow'   88, 180–1

Palestinian Camp Women as Tellers of History (Sayigh)   13
Palestinian cinema   80
'The Palestinian Destroyed Villages'   167
Palestinian dialect   24, 32, 35, 51, 54, 61, 64–5, 74–5, 78, 115, 127–9, 134, 136, 161
Palestinian Folklore and Social Classes (Al-Khalīlī)   34
Palestinian Folktale, The (Sirḥān)   29, 33–4
Palestinian Folktale in Palestinian Society: Texts and Analysis, The (Al-Sarīsī)   33
Palestinian Hero in the Palestinian Folktale, The (Al-Khalīlī)   34
Palestinian Ministry of Education   165
Palestinian mothers   71
Palestinian National Theatre   211 n.2
Palestinian Peasants: From Uprooting to Revolutionaries (Sayigh)   13
Palestinian Refugees: 1948-1998 Oral Historisation   8
Palestinian women   67, 123, 174
   as heroines   95
   linguistic identity   75
   narratives   104–5, 109
   pregnant   156, 158
   roles   42–3, 56, 58, 87–8
   rural   84
   as storytellers   4–5, 13, 41, 69–71, 74, 79, 81–2, 85–6, 100–1, 116, 160, 163–4, 176–7
'Palestinian Women and Collective Memory'   84
paratext   201 nn.12–13, 202 n.14
Paratexts: Thresholds of Interpretation (Genette)   201 n.11
paratextual materials   48, 161
   pre-introduction   49–59
   within tales   59–65
passive storytellers   81

Patai, Raphael   32, 172, 212 n.7
patriarchal society   42, 96, 98, 109, 146
peasantry   12, 25, 43–4, 56, 58, 84, 116, 129, 148, 149
  and collective identity   121–7
  recreating homeland   117–21
'Peasantry and Collective Identity'   119
personal history   30
physical spaces   117
poetry   24, 27, 78, 122
polygamy   57, 92, 112
polygyny   86, 92, 111, 146
pomegranates   160
Pomegranate Seeds: The Woman in the Palestinian Folktale   33
'Pomegranate Seeds'   155, 159, 160
popular culture   1, 4, 20, 23, 27, 31, 50, 78, 84, 87, 98, 126, 131, 132, 143, 151
Portelli, Alessandro   9
post-memory   4, 21, 38, 53, 64, 79, 80, 91, 94, 107, 113, 120, 122, 143, 146, 163, 203 n.19, 205 n.4
post-*Nakba*   77, 79, 107
post-tales paratextual materials   65–8
Post-Traumatic Stress Disorder   15
Powles, Julia   149
'Precious One and Worn-Out One'   111, 118
prefaces to Qul Ya Tayer   60–5
pre-introduction paratextual materials   49–59
  acknowledgements   54
  foreword   49–54
  introduction   54–9
  key to references   54
  note on transliteration   54
pre-*Nakba*   1, 5, 21, 35–6, 38, 75, 77, 79, 102, 116, 117, 121, 150, 157
'Presentist' model   7
print capitalism   199 n.5
productive nostalgia   157
professions   44, 125–7
projected reality   28
prospective memory   115, 141–8, 157
prosthetic memory   21, 80, 84–5, 106, 107, 113, 206 nn.8–9
psychoanalytic approach   30–1
punishments   133, 137

Qattan, Abdel Mohsin   204 n.21
Qaẓīb al-zahab biwadī al-'qīq. See 'The Golden Rod in the Valley of Vermilion'
Qul Ya Tayer. See Speak, Bird, Speak Again (Muhawi and Kanaana)
Qur'an   24
Qurūd Dara'ma. See The Monkeys of Dara'ma

racial favouritism   44
Radcliffe-Brown, AR   40
Rank, Otto   31
reality *vs.* imagination   27–31
refugees   11–12, 15, 37, 94, 149
regeneration   6, 20, 21, 39, 69, 90–1, 99, 108, 115
religious beliefs   28, 45–7, 115, 136, 137
Remembrance of Repasts (Sutton)   140
Renan, Ernest   10
reputation   37, 57, 73–4, 101
resistance   22, 37, 44–5, 120. *See also* cultural resistance
rewards   133, 137
'The Rich Man and the Poor Man'   133, 156, 159, 196
Ricoeur, Paul   132
rituals   70, 99, 117, 129, 141–2, 145, 147
Rohana, Shadi   94
Rohrich, Lutz   28
romance   108
ruling system   44–5
rural dialect   32, 36, 56

Saarisalo, Aapeli   120
'Sackcloth'   108, 133, 144, 197
Sa'di, Ahmad H.   79
Ṣaleḥ, Ahmad Roshdī   37
Sanyal, Debarti   124
Al-Sarīsī, 'Umar   33, 34–41, 43–7, 99, 126–7, 131
Sayigh, Rosemary   12–13
Schmidt, Hans   32
Schuman, Howard   10
Scott, James   84
seasonal food   141
sensory memory   140
sensuous memory   115, 140, 149–53, 159–60

'The Seven Leavenings' 67, 109–10, 120, 185
sexual awakening 95–101
sexual desires 67, 83, 96, 101, 105
sexuality 57–8, 70, 90–1, 95, 108–9, 109–10, 111, 150, 155, 159–60
Shaḥada, Karmalā 33
'Shahin' 108, 144–5, 197
El-Shamy, Hasan 63, 89, 207 n.13
Al-Sharīf, Māhir 9
Al-'shhab, Roshdī 34
'Shoqak Boqak!' 82
'Shwesh, Shwesh!' 77, 83, 85, 86
sibling narratives 87–95
Simple Forms (Jolles) 27
Sīra 42
Sirat Bani Hilal 39
Sirḥān, Nimr 29, 33–4, 42
Smith, Antony 209–10 n.4
Smith, Graham 154
social favouritism 44
social identity 8, 53, 74, 87, 88, 95, 98
social interaction 115, 127, 141, 146
social practices 44, 92, 98, 122
social reality 34, 64, 68–9, 71, 86, 131, 133, 139
social structure 11, 41, 70, 76, 81, 88, 101
society 19, 31, 33, 37, 39–47, 55, 60, 63, 64, 80, 82, 84, 93, 111, 125, 132. *See also* culture; customs; heritage; lifestyle; tradition
solidarity 129, 158
Speak, Bird, Speak Again (Muhawi and Kanaana) 1, 3, 4, 6, 8, 24, 34–5, 43, 47–68, 69, 71, 76, 86, 90, 106, 109, 113, 116, 125, 128, 138, 140, 149, 159, 161, 163, 166, 168–70, 173–6, 204 nn.22, 24, 212 n.7
Spivak, Gayarti Chakravorty 96
Stoller, Paul 149
'Stories Told by and for Palestinian Children' 106, 211 n.1
storyteller 4–5, 28–30, 35–9, 41, 43, 45, 46, 54, 56, 73–5, 77, 78, 83, 88, 90–1, 96, 99, 103, 105, 106, 108, 153, 163, 164
storytelling 1, 9, 20–5, 29–30, 35, 36, 38–9, 42, 46, 70, 74–5, 79, 80, 84–5, 87, 91, 107, 124, 161, 164, 166, 170, 173

structural approach 30
structural trauma 16–17
suffering 9–10, 17, 18, 29, 152
Sulaymān, Jābir 60, 63–4, 204 n.22
'Sumac! You Son of a Whore, Sumac' 133, 149
supernatural beliefs 58–9
Sutton, David E. 140, 141, 149, 153
Swedenburg, Ted 121
symbolism 46, 124, 151, 157
synchronic approach 30

Tales Arab Women Tell (El-Shamy) 89
Taqdīm al-mū'lifīn lil ṭab'a al-'rabīa. *See* The Authors' Introduction to the Arabic Edition
Taqdīm al- ṭab'a al-'rabīa. *See* The Introduction of the Arabic Edition
Tawthīq al-qurā al-Falasṭīnīa al-mudamara. *See Documenting the Destroyed Palestinian Villages* (Kanaana)
Tent Work in Palestine (Conder) 209 n.3
testimonies 16
thematic approach 31
Thinking Arabic Translation (Dickens et al.) 135
time 77, 132, 134
Time and Narrative (Ricoeur) 132
trade 44
tradition 12, 14, 23–5, 29, 32, 35–9, 41–3, 56–7, 62–3, 66–7, 70, 76–7, 81–2, 93, 98–9, 102, 106, 116–17, 119, 123, 142–3, 146, 155, 160, 165–6, 170–1. *See also* culture; customs; folk tradition; heritage; lifestyle; oral tradition; society
'Traditionalist' model 7
transactive memory 116, 154–5, 159
trans-generational memory. *See* cultural memory
transliteration 54
trauma 8, 13, 14–21, 38, 69, 79, 85, 94, 107, 120–1, 205 n.4
Tukan, Fadwa 150
'Tunjur, Tunjur' 72–3, 86–7, 133, 155, 156

'Umar, Nimr AbdilRaḥmān   29
University of California   54
urban dialect   37, 56
urban society   36–7
Ustura (1998)   80

Vansina, Jan   8
village houses   118–19
village life   125–6, 140
virility   109–10
Volkserzählungen aus Palästina (Schmidt and Kahle)   32
von der Leyen, Friedrich   41

Warburg, Aby   118
Warrior Women of Islam, The (Kruk)   42, 100
wedding procession   99
Wegner, Daniel   154
Weir, Shelagh   12

wisdom   68, 75–6, 81, 84, 95, 102, 106, 108, 126, 133, 139, 158
'The Woman Who Fell into the Well'   134, 195
'The Woman Who Married Her Son'   77, 86, 158, 180
'The Woman Whose Hands Were Cut Off'   112, 119, 186
'The Woodcutter'   125
writing   21–2, 24
written literature   21, 25, 152
Wundt, Wilhelm Maximilian   200 n.4

Yaḥya, Adil   8
younger generations   76–7, 81, 85, 87, 89, 91, 92–4, 106

Zajal   78
Zerubavel, Yael   198 n.2
Zionist movement   11

www.ingramcontent.com/pod-product-compliance
Lightning Source LLC
Chambersburg PA
CBHW062137300426
44115CB00012BA/1952